"Caroline coached my son, Jason, and the coaching helped him to witness his own behaviours and see that some of them were inappropriate. The coaching also helped me to work with Jason between sessions and, when the coaching ended, to continue to expand his self-awareness and skills. Now he knows how to "Read the Room" and puts away his phone in favour of talking to a friend. He adjusts to a situation or lets people know he is sensitive to sounds. He has more authentic friends, sense of humour, tolerance, and patience. He is much more aware of himself, others, and social situations and he wants to create a good impression."

—Cydney H., Mother

"For years, I was told that my son was fine and that this behaviour was typical for boys. After my first meeting with Caroline, I was relieved that a professional really understood the diverse social challenges that children face. Sometimes these challenges don't go away as your child grows. My son worked with Caroline for over a year and in that time, he made incredible progress. Caroline was extremely approachable and helped to pull apart challenging social situations so he could begin to look at them from a different perspective with time, my son learned how to pause, observe, and reflect. He even got into a top private high school—before his interviews were a disaster, but after he worked on his social skills, my son was able to have more choices and he got into every school he applied to. Caroline Maguire is a hero in our family. *Why Will No One Play with Me?* will empower many families with the tools they need to make positive change."

—M.W., Mother

Praise for
Caroline Maguire
and
Why Will No One Pl

"My son and I often fought about the fact that he was rude to other people. He only wanted to play video games and wasn't interested in hanging out with others. Keith would not even engage in a discussion about his social skills. That is when we found the *Play Better Plan*. I learned to coach my son rather than telling him what to do. After a few weeks, he became willing to act polite even when he felt bored or frustrated. Our communication about his social struggles improved. *Why Will No One Play with Me?* helps me with continuous follow-through on what we've learned. It is a process that, given time, patience, and effort, will be worth it both for your child's social skills and for your parent-child relationship."

—Jennifer, Mother

"I was angry and frustrated before I went to see Caroline. I was getting calls from my son's school about him upsetting other kids. I thought I was doing something wrong—that I was a bad parent and that my son's behavioural problems reflected poorly on me. I did not know what to do. Then I learned how his brain worked and that there were ways I could help him. Now, because of the coaching programme, I have made real progress with Andy. We no longer fight, and he is doing better with other kids at school, and I am happy to say he hasn't had any incidents in the last month. We are still using the programme, and I have so much more confidence as a parent."

—Iris M., Mother

"The biggest gift the coaching programme gave all of us was in helping us recognise Gracie's strengths and uniqueness and accept that her ways of moving through the world are different than ours. She still gets herself into trouble from time to time, and she has to work to bring her best self to school each day. But she now has the tools to do that, and we are better able to support that effort. She has been working very hard, and she feels proud of her progress. She gets asked for playdates and activities, and is able to reciprocate invitations. What a difference! I wish there was more of Caroline to go around to all of the other mums, kids, and families who struggle with this same stuff."

—Gretchen L., Mother, Play Better Coaching Graduate

"When we started Caroline Maguire's coaching programme, we saw a huge improvement right away. The programme helped me communicate better with Jenny. I was able to help her look at those minor problems more objectively. Very quickly, Jenny learned to pause and problem-solve instead of overreacting. She learned strategies to cope with her emotions, and she learned to calm herself. Now, many years later, she is a successful college student with a strong group of friends. The coaching model helped Jenny develop life skills to manage emotions and get along with other people."   —Pam K., Mother

"I was leery of the *Play Better Plan*. I felt overwhelmed, sure there would be no way I could do this, much less get my kid to agree to it. At first he was resistant, but we learned how to have fun with it and laugh when we stumbled. Using coaching to talk about hard things with my son made the conversations less antagonistic—and it worked."   —Patrick M., Father

"This coaching programme changed our lives. Our child, Laura, was moody and unwilling to engage in most activities. In fact, she had her own 'policies' about joining groups. Caroline encouraged us to see Laura's gifts, and we used those gifts to encourage Laura to change. The coaching programme really shifted our whole communication pattern and helped Laura see how her inflexibility was affecting others. Laura became a joiner, working at a part-time job and participating in study groups. Now she is studying abroad and is an active member of her college community. As a family we are much happier."

—Jane B., Mother

Why Will No One Play With Me?

The Play Better Plan to Help Kids Make Friends and Thrive

Caroline Maguire

with Teresa Barker

1 3 5 7 9 10 8 6 4 2

Vermilion, an imprint of Ebury Publishing,
20 Vauxhall Bridge Road,
London SW1V 2SA

Vermilion is part of the Penguin Random House group of companies
whose addresses can be found at global.penguinrandomhouse.com

Penguin
Random House
UK

First published in the United States by Grand Central Publishing in 2019
First published in United Kingdom by Vermilion in 2019

www.penguin.co.uk

A CIP catalogue record for this book is available from the British Library

ISBN 9781785042232

Printed and bound in Great Britain by Clays Ltd, Elcograf S.p.A.

MIX
Paper from
responsible sources
FSC® C018179

Penguin Random House is committed to a sustainable future for our
business, our readers and our planet. This book is made from Forest
Stewardship Council® certified paper.

To my children, Lucy and Finn, and my husband, Craig, for supporting me and believing in me.

CONTENTS

PART III:
The *Play Better* Executive Function Social Skills Tracks

PART IV:
The *Play Better Plan:* To Playdates and Beyond

Why Will
No One
Play
with Me?

INTRODUCTION

I will never forget the first time a child asked me "the question." I was living the dream in my blossoming career as an academic and social skills coach for children. I had a full schedule and a waiting list, and I was working with clients at a world-renowned ADHD centre alongside some of the most respected leaders in the field. I gave parenting talks and professional workshops on how to help children pay attention and develop more effective study skills and self-regulation. It was thrilling to know that through this work, I was making a dramatic difference in the lives of hundreds of children and their families. Kids who had been overwhelmed by their struggle with schoolwork and behaviour issues were making remarkable progress.

Then one day, an eight-year-old boy's simple question revealed a secret suffering that haunted these children no matter how much their grades improved.

Jonah was a sweet but angry boy who struggled in school and flew into rages over homework. As we began to talk about his complicated school situation, I asked him, "If you could change anything, what would it be?" I thought he'd say something about his teacher or the ongoing battle over reading logs that featured nightly in his home. Instead, after a long, anxious pause, he replied: "Why will no one play with me?"

Why will no one play with me?

The hopelessness of that one question shook me to my core.

The things that were foremost concerns for Jonah's parents—his schooling, his homework, the reasons he was first brought to my office—were the furthest things from his own mind. Worse, they obscured the deeper problem he was wrestling with every day. Jonah wanted to know why he was left out. Why other kids ignored him or were mean to him. He wanted to fight less with his classmates. He was a desperately lonely child. He wanted to know how he could make friends, and if I could teach him.

Jonah was not a smiley kid, but when I told him there was a possibility that if he learned how to change his approach he could make more friends, he beamed. That smile! In that moment, I saw my first glimpse of what I would soon learn is a crippling, unmet need for millions of children—whether or not they have a diagnosis. And I discovered a way to help them. I had found my calling. I set out to make sure that no child would ever be left to struggle alone with that question. And no parent would have to struggle alone to figure out how to help. Thus, the *Play Better Plan* was born, and now this book.

I wish I could say Jonah is the only child who has asked me this heartbreaking question, but over the years, many, many more have asked the same, in one form or another. Some kids have asked me why they are invisible to others. Other kids wonder why people think they are weird or annoying or bossy. Some don't understand why they are the only kid in class not invited to a birthday party. Others have told me stories about how no one on their basketball team passes them the ball or how they are regularly ignored at break time. Others simply state that they don't have any friends. No one to play with. No one to share a laugh with, or a secret. And the parents of these children have echoed the same frustration, pain, sadness, and confusion, sometimes despair.

If you are reading this book, you may have heard something similar from your child or seen it yourself. Right now, you may even be acting as your child's best buddy and confidant because he doesn't have anyone else to hang out with. But as much as you love your child, you know that he is not meant to spend every Saturday night for the rest of his childhood with you. Of course, you see your child's flaws and foibles, but you also know his or her best self, the lovable one you wish everybody knew. But that's not the child the other kids see.

Maybe your reception class child is loud and can't sit still in school, and other kids in his class are put off by his volume and constant barging around. Maybe your nine-year-old child can't look other kids in the eye. Or your eight-year-old has a meltdown every time you ask her to leave a playdate, and the tantrums discourage other parents from inviting her over again. Or your ten-year-old says alienating things to other kids and they don't want to include her.

Watching your child struggle with loneliness is painful. You've probably tried talking to him about his behaviour, begged him to try harder or behave better in public. You may have tried bringing him to a new park or kids club, hoping he would find someone new to bond with, only to see the usual disappointing results. You may have tried talking to teachers and other parents about how your child has been excluded or perhaps bullied by others. But odds are, if you're reading this book, none of these efforts have led to lasting change. Unfortunately, this problem is not going to solve itself. Your child wants to get along, fit in, and make friends, but she doesn't know how.

Child development experts describe children who have a hard time understanding social cues and managing their behaviour as having *social skills deficits*, or weaknesses. These lagging skills basically mean the child's social radar and social response system aren't as robust as they need to be. That makes it hard for them to read social cues accurately or understand the unspoken rules of social relationships or play, or to adapt their behaviour in response to other kids or as a play situation changes. Without these skills, a child can no more be pressured or cajoled to become a better playmate than a child who'd never learned to swim could be pressured to swim across a lake. If they could, they would. But if they don't know how, then adding pressure only triggers more stress and that triggers the brain's fight-flight-or-freeze survival reflex—not helpful behaviours in a playgroup. Like all of us, your child needs to be able to cope with pressure and people to get along in the world.

This book, and the *Play Better* method itself, is based on the growing volume of scientific literature that addresses a full range of clinical and coaching interventions for children with executive function weaknesses. For that reason, the *Play Better Plan* can address a spectrum of issues and diagnoses that some children may have, including attention deficit hyperactivity disorder (ADHD), attention deficit disorder (ADD), nonverbal learning disabilities, dyslexia, learning disabilities, and autism. But to be clear, the *Play Better Plan* is designed for and works for *any* child who struggles socially. Whether a child is shy, has moved to a new community or changed school, or is anxious or discouraged by the way things have been, *Play Better* coaching and activities will help them learn new ways to connect with other kids and make friends.

I WAS "THAT CHILD"—LONELY, BULLIED, AND LEFT OUT

I know the problem only too well from my own childhood experience. When I was ten, I went to a private school. My class was small and happened to be filled with mostly athletic boys. Aside from myself, there were only two other girls in the class. These girls were mean—very mean—and unfortunately, I was often the target of their cruelty. They would constantly bait and humiliate me. Lunch-time dramas were a regular occurrence. "Caroline, come sit with us," they'd say sweetly. So I would join them, tickled pink. But as soon as I opened my lunch box and spread out all my food, they would get up and leave. During reading time, they'd ask me to read and then mimic my stumbling. One day, they even lured me into the school's basement toilets and locked me in. Because the wooden doors in the old 1940s brick schoolhouse were heavy and nearly soundproof, no one could hear my screams and tearful pleas for help. I was locked in the loo for over thirty minutes before the teacher realised I was missing.

My social radar was extremely sensitive and constantly on high alert, so much so that I was socially anxious. I was more attuned to grown-ups—they called me "an old soul" with some affection—but I just didn't know how to talk with other kids. I didn't understand these girls' motives and I would fall for their traps every time. Over the course of that year, my anxiety became debilitating. I grew fearful of going to the toilet, and I'd try to hold it until I got home. I stopped reading and speaking aloud in class whenever possible. I became self-conscious about body image, as most girls do at that age, but I avoided sports or other active social activities, which made me gain weight and grow only more self-conscious and miserable. My grades and my self-esteem plummeted, and I became lonely and very unhappy in my isolation.

My mother was attentive but at a complete loss as to how to help me. Talking with the teachers and administrators did not improve the situation. Much later in life, I was diagnosed with ADHD and dyslexia, but when I was in primary school, there was no name for what was holding me back. At that time, my parents and teachers were completely unaware of learning disabilities, ADD/ADHD, or social skills weaknesses.

As a child, my social skills difficulties and learning disabilities made my daily school life especially challenging. I remember thinking, "If I can't figure this out, I must be stupid." If it weren't for my mother's constant encouragement, I might have given up completely. Eventually, my family moved, and at my new school, a teacher saw my struggles and was able to teach me ways to cope with my disabilities and tune in to my peer group. Among other things, she taught me to pay attention to what the other kids talked about and to think about what I might have in common with them, how to calm down and sometimes not talk, and be more confident. Through her, I learned that the world was not going to come to me, and she showed me how to engage with that world of kids. I slowly made friends and regained confidence. Perhaps the most important lesson I learned was that I wasn't helpless to help myself—I just needed to learn how, and I needed someone to teach me.

This book teaches you how to offer those same lessons to the child in your life.

THE IMPORTANCE OF PLAY AND THE PLAY PARADOX

Social skills weaknesses are caused by a wide variety of factors, but the most common one—and the subject of this book—occurs when the part of the brain that manages the complex connections for social behaviour, the brain's network of *executive functions*, is unevenly developed. Executive function is the hub of skills such as attention, memory, organisation, planning, and other cognitive or critical-thinking skills, self-regulation, metacognition (the big-picture, bird's-eye view), and the ability to modify our behaviour in response to others to achieve a goal.

These are the basic skills every child needs to function well in the social world. In a nutshell, if a child's executive function social skills are weak, then he has a harder time understanding and managing social interactions. These problems show up in

- what children pay attention to in a social setting
- what they notice about their friends' needs and reactions
- how they respond to disappointment or manage other emotions
- how they think about friendship
- how they react to new or shifting social situations.

Play is the first and most natural environment for all learning. Social behaviour, by definition, is best learned in the company of others, where children can experience themselves in the context of spontaneous social activity and relationships, learn how their behaviour affects others, practise seeing things from another child's point of view, and learn how to get along with others. Children used to have more plentiful opportunities to learn these lessons naturally through the trial and error of old-fashioned unstructured play. In recent years, the loss of improvisational playtime has robbed all children of significant "practice time" for learning to get along and make friends. But the impact has been especially significant for those with executive function challenges that make it hard for them to adapt and find ways to socialise. In the world of invitation-only playdates, socially awkward or difficult children get left out and become only more out of step with their peers. As the gap widens, these children often become socially isolated. This play paradox—those with the greatest need getting the least opportunity—only complicates the challenge for those children and for their parents.

Many children with lagging social skills are highly intelligent or talented in other areas, such as athletics, mathematics, or music. Social competency simply is not one of them. Unfortunately, they pay a high cost in childhood, increasingly so in adolescence, and on into adult life, as people skills become essential in personal relationships and the workplace.

The good news is that social skills can be developed just like any other skill. Scientists have discovered that when children with social challenges engage in skill-building activities on a consistent basis, they can learn how to interact effectively with others in a social setting. And this means that, no matter how hopeless the situation may feel now, your child's friendship challenges are far from insurmountable. With your help, your child can build social awareness, improve executive function skills, and learn how to make and keep friends. This is the heart of social skills coaching and why it is so important for your child and for you.

WHAT COACHING IS AND WHY IT WORKS

Coaching is the process of teaching, guiding, showing, and practising skills with your child. It isn't helicopter parenting or micromanaging your child's behaviour or relationships. It's not about protecting them from the normal bumps and bruises that are a healthy part of growing up and taking charge of yourself. Quite the opposite: coaching helps prepare them with the basic skills they need to meet whatever comes their way, notably learning how to see their challenges clearly, strategising and setting goals, picking themselves up after a failure, and problem-solving so they can stay on their feet the next time.

Children learning to play football benefit from having a coach to explain the rules of the game, demonstrate and model the skills needed to play, practise the skills with them, observe them using those skills in action on the field, and give constructive feedback and encouragement after matches. If a football coach simply told a child, "Go score a goal," without showing how it's done, you wouldn't expect the child to play well. It's the child who must take the skills onto the playing field, take some spills and get a few bruises, but the coaching and skill-building prepare him to know the rules, hone the skills, and be the best he can be for the game.

Children with social skills weaknesses need help learning those basic skills so they can participate socially—so they aren't committing fouls constantly or getting sidelined season after season. On the social playing field, if your child is perpetually clueless and clumsy, she's going to get trounced. Telling a child to "behave" or "get along" on a playdate is just like sending that kid into the football match with no training. Skills are the crux of the matter, and coaching and practice develop the skills.

As your child's coach, you'll learn to ask, listen, and learn about your child's experience. You'll help your child understand the unspoken rules of social behaviour, how to watch for cues from other people, and how to adjust their behaviour as needed. You'll cheer small successes as the stepping stones to bigger ones. You'll work with your child to develop the game plan, the playbook, and the overarching goal: for your child to make friends more easily and "go along and get along" with others.

Here's what you *won't* do as your child's coach. You won't assume you know the reasons for your child's behaviour. You won't criticise, nag, or shame your child or impose your own goals; instead you will partner with him to help him develop his own. You won't pressure your child or rush the learning process. Most of all, you won't forget to show confidence in your child's capacity to learn and grow.

I often say that coaching is parenting with a playbook. In most instances, a child's social struggle is not for lack of a caring parent. Like many parents, you may have spent years advising, instructing, correcting, or cajoling your child to try harder to get along with other children, but nothing seems to stick. All of that shifts once you begin to use the simple, proven coaching techniques that make you a more effective listener, partner, and problem-solver with your child.

Like any of us, children share more when they feel heard and understood. They can let their guard down, engage more readily in the coaching process, commit to developing their social skills, and invest in their own success. The two-way coaching conversations you'll learn to have with your child will help her reflect on her behaviour and the impact it has on others and the way they treat her. Together, you'll identify the message her behaviour conveys and whether that message helps or hinders the way people understand and respond to her. Together, you'll use problem-solving steps to generate strategies your child can practise, then try out in playdates. New experiences of success build new self-confidence and ultimately give your child the awareness, motivation, confidence, and skills to be more socially active and at ease.

"IF THEY COULD, THEY WOULD": FIVE WORDS THAT CHANGE THE WAY YOU UNDERSTAND YOUR CHILD

A client from long ago told me that one of the most life-changing things I shared with her as I coached her daughter through some early learning and behavioural challenges was to remind herself: "If she could, she would."

In more than fifteen years as a family coach, this seemingly simple idea—*If they could, they would*—has unlocked solutions to some of the most stubborn problems children face. This simple distinction can transform your understanding of your child, change the story you may have had for years, and open a dramatically different field of play and growth for your child.

One of the grounding truths that modern psychology and child development research tells us is that, generally speaking, children do not willfully set about to self-sabotage, to fail at being a kid and disappoint their parents. Every child wants to succeed. Every child wants to "grow up" and develop the mastery to be a capable human being. To do that, they must learn to work with their own unique brain wiring—they must learn to figure out what's holding them back and then how to do something about it.

The idea that a child "would if he could" is important: When you frame the issue that way, you instantly reframe your perspective on the situation, on your child's behaviour, and on his potential for change and positive growth. Once your child begins to develop the executive function skills necessary for effective social interaction, every incremental success will motivate him to continue, and you'll see the results that wishful thinking could never have delivered.

Sure, *if they could, they would* asks you to take a little leap of faith. When your child seems oblivious to the feelings of others or to the way her behaviour affects how they treat her, it might seem logical to lecture longer and louder until she finally learns the lesson. But popular wisdom applies here. If the definition of insanity is doing the same thing over and over, expecting different results, then if lecturing and disciplining your child hasn't changed her behaviour by this time, where's the wisdom in continuing to do it over and over and imagine different results?

In many ways, this powerful philosophical shift is easier than you might think. You know your child better than anyone, and you know there is more to her than the behaviours that are holding her back socially. The big truth is that everyone is working on something. That's a powerful place to start, and a story line that opens a child up to change.

WHY *PLAY BETTER* AND WHY NOW?

Several years ago, parents and colleagues began urging me to share my *Play Better* method more broadly. Knowing how parents and kids alike are caught up in hurried lives, I set out to present the *Play Better Plan* in a book that you would find easy to read and fun to use with your child.

The *Play Better* lessons, materials, and activities come straight from my own practice, tailored for you, the parent-coach, and your child, to take advantage of everyday moments for practice and discussion. Activities are custom-designed to be fun and rewarding, with incentives to boost motivation. There, snags and missteps can be duly noted, discussed in postplay debriefing, and turned into learning opportunities, with attention to things that went right and to those that can be improved the next time around.

The *Play Better* Toolbox features engaging hands-on activities—questionnaires, activity sheets, and lessons—that you and your child will use to develop new skills.

Through coaching conversations and practice both at home and away, the *Play Better* method strengthens the executive function skills children must have to pick up on social cues, anticipate the impact of their behaviour in a situation, self-regulate and manage their emotions and responses in social settings, and connect with other children to make friends, play happily, and feel socially confident.

I've seen so many children move from feeling socially isolated, miserable, and misunderstood to feeling confident in their own capacity to connect with other kids and learn how to handle social situations that once overwhelmed them. I see parents shift from frustration or worry about their child to optimism they never thought possible. All of this *is* possible because you work together as your child learns these skills and practises problem-solving her way through new challenges. You'll learn so much about your child, and yourself, too. The effects of the coaching conversations reverberate in so many beautiful, unexpected ways through your relationships and your family life.

YES—YOU CAN DO THIS!

If this coaching gig sounds complicated or hard, I want to assure you: *you can do this*. Parents tell me that having the plan actually makes it easier to understand their child, talk with their child, and help their child find social strategies that work. And let's be honest, you've already been putting forth huge efforts to improve your child's social plight.

As a parent, you actually have an advantage over anyone else as a consulting coach. *You're there and you care.* You are always on the front lines with your child. It's those everyday "teachable moments" that make the *Play Better Plan* so successful.

I think of the mother who told me that the turning point for her six-year-old son came just a few weeks into the programme when he turned to her one day and acknowledged, for the first time ever, "I need to listen more." Or the ten-year-old who realised, "I have to talk to other people—they won't just come to me." For each child, these were steps in social awareness that they had never expressed before—that they never even had before. It wasn't that they'd never been *told* these things. It was that they had never reached these insights on their own. With this awareness came choices to do something a little different, perhaps practise listening when someone spoke or to try saying hello instead of always waiting for others to start a conversation. Every choice they made with this in mind opened new opportunities, new coaching conversations with their parents, and new experiences of success in simple social interactions with other children.

Every child is different, and the programme timeline will be different for each one. I've designed the *Play Better Plan* so you can adjust it to match your child's pace, whatever it may be. In the coaching process, some new skills may develop more quickly than others for your child. Generally, though, within a month of starting the plan, most children make noticeable progress in their social awareness.

HOW TO USE THIS BOOK

Why Will No One Play with Me? is presented in four parts.

Part I (Chapters 1–4) explains in simple terms the brain science and behavioural factors that cause kids to be left out, the science of behavioural change, how social skills coaching works, and how the *Play Better Plan* specifically, with you as your child's social skills coach, can launch a remarkable turnaround. These chapters help jump-start your understanding of the ideas that are woven throughout the *Play Better Plan* coaching plan, lessons, and activities. If you're in a hurry to get started, you can move ahead to Part II and return to Part I anytime you want to read more about the ideas.

Part II (Chapters 5–10) covers the hands-on, how-to *Play Better Plan* coaching principles that make the coach approach user-friendly for you *and* your child. I'll teach you the coaching strategies and skills to engage and guide your child and will give you the "game plan" you'll use to coach your child at home and in real-time social activities. Other features include:

- tips and scripts with simple questions, icebreaker comments, and coaching language to jump-start any conversation
- the *How Will You Know?* timeline tool, which shows you how to tell when your child has progressed in a skill area, how much, and when he or she is ready to advance to the next level
- questionnaires and other coaching materials, including lesson plans, activity worksheets, logs, and other how-to tools so that you and your child can easily complete tasks and chart your child's progress.

Coaching tools include the Executive Function Questionnaire, the Interactive Conversation Guide, and other guides and materials to help you identify your child's personal strengths and specific social skills challenges. Once you complete them for your child, these tools also help you prioritise behaviours to target for coaching, engage your child in the planning goals and strategies for practice, and respond effectively to new challenges or setbacks. You'll find a guide for using incentives and rewards to make the programme more fun for your child and that show how to follow through to continue to build and maintain results. You'll learn how to tell when your child is ready to shift from home practice to a playdate "mission," the goal of which is to use a specific skill that's been practised in a real-life play situation. Whatever else may go on in the playdate, every time your child uses the positive behaviour highlighted for the mission, that's a win: mission accomplished.

Part III (Chapters 11–19) includes the Executive Function Questionnaire Lesson Tracks and step-by-step skill-building activities. You'll use these lessons and activities to help your child plan, practise, and build new skills. Child-centred activities and lessons include the Social Spy, Mind Your PEAS and Cues, Never Let Them See You Sweat, Flexible Me, and other lessons designed and illustrated to appeal to kids.

Part IV (Chapters 20–24) moves from home practice to arranging playdates and using them as a source of continued coaching with your child through debriefing and strategising activities. Coaching guides include the Playdate Planner, Coaching from the Sidelines, the How'd It Go? debriefing guide, and Troubleshooting.

All *Play Better* lessons and activities include step-by-step instructions for you and your child, keyed to the skill development area that is your child's greatest need and highest priority and the suitable skill level.

READY, SET, PLAY!

As someone who was once "that child" who struggled socially, I know that pain intimately. As a mother now, I understand the predicament you're in when you have a child with social skills challenges. I have written *Why Will No One Play with Me?* to be a practical guide for lasting change and an evergreen companion for you as your child moves through the social challenges of different ages and stages. For those new to this subject and the *Play Better* coaching approach, I want to give you hope—realistic optimism. *Things can change*, and they will, once your child has the skills to make it happen.

PART I

What's the Story?

1

What's the Story?

We all have stories we tell to explain away problems that make us uncomfortable. It's only human—but it's not helpful!

Sam is a smart kid. In many ways, smarter than most eight-year-old kids, his classmates say. They'll give him that. But what they won't do is play, hang out with, or even choose to work with him on a group project. They just don't like him, and his smarty-pants attitude doesn't win anyone over.

Rory is the class clown, but he's more irritating than amusing. At ten, he's all about being funny, but he never knows when to stop. He'll drive a joke into the ground. He'll think something's funny even if nobody else does, and then he'll go on and on about it.

Sarah, eight years old, is the self-declared boss in any situation. She has to have her way and puts down anyone who disagrees. If someone else gets a compliment or gets a good mark, she turns the conversation to herself and boasts about things she has or things she's done.

Megan is the invisible girl in her year six class. She is shy and awkward, physically and socially. When she's allowed to, she prefers to skip lunch break and help her teacher in the classroom. When she has to go to lunch, she tries to find a place at the table between the two cliques, where she's less likely to be noticed and teased.

Danny is five years old and already a dinosaur aficionado. He plays by himself mostly, quick to roar like a *T. rex* if another child encroaches on his territory. His classmates have learned to leave him alone.

These children couldn't be more different. But in one striking way they are the same: their social behaviour gets in the way of developing a social life. They have a hard time making friends and keeping them. They seem clueless about how to fit in with other kids. At school, they don't reliably play well with others, and thus often don't end up playing with anyone at all. They don't get invited to playdates and birthday parties, or when they do, things frequently end badly. They have a tendency to behave in ways that others find odd, off-putting, or annoying. They are either too much (loud, active, pushy, or disruptive) or too little (anxious, avoidant, nervous, or awkward) to connect easily with peers. Whether intentionally excluded or just overlooked, they are the kids who get left out.

Something else these children have in common is that they each have their own "story." When kids aren't able to decode social cues and don't understand why no one will play with them or be friends, they create their own narrative, or story line, a shorthand rationalisation for why they behave the way they do and why others treat them the way they do. That's a human thing to do. It's a self-protection strategy for avoiding things that make us uncomfortable, whether those things are people, situations, ideas, or something about ourselves. A self-protecting story for the child who is left out often sounds like this:

I don't care if I have school friends.
People are just jerks.
I'm fine by myself.
All they care about is stupid stuff.
Smart kids don't have friends.
They're mean.
I don't have to be social if I don't feel like it.
You're the only one who thinks I have a problem!

Parents often tell me that their child's social behaviour is baffling. Their child complains about having no friends but then refuses all overtures. When asked if they want to play with someone, they say no. Or they say yes, but their behaviour shuts things down. One parent described bringing her child to a bouncy-castle birthday party, and while all the other children were running and playing, her child sat off to the side with a pocket gadget. The behaviours just don't make sense for a child who claims to want to have friends—or should want to have friends.

At the same time, parents are often reluctant to call this behaviour a "social problem," even when a child's behaviour is frequently annoying or off-putting—problematic—to other children. After all, none of us is aiming for a cardboard-cutout kid. You're not looking to raise a "pleaser" or a child who always goes along with the crowd, no matter what. You want to respect your child's individuality and encourage her to think for herself—that's important, too. So maybe you watch and wince but have told yourself it's just a quirky personality trait. In fact, that's one of the most common stories parents tell *themselves* about their child's social difficulty, in addition to the ones their child may put forth.

Here's the simple, working definition of a social problem that we'll use going forward so we can identify problematic social behaviour and help your child develop the skills to change the behaviour and learn how to be more comfortable, confident, and successful in a social setting: *Anything that keeps your child from engaging with a group, making friends and keeping them, getting along with peers, and navigating social situations as they arise is a social problem.*

However stubborn a problem behaviour may be, brain and behavioural sciences show that children can learn the essential skills they need to improve it and become their best selves—quirky or distinctive individuals *and* socially comfortable and connected. I'm going to show you precisely how to guide them to do that using the *Play Better Plan* coaching principles and practices in the chapters ahead, but first things first: your child's first step in that problem-solving process is your first step, too.

If your child is struggling socially, do you know why? What's the real story?

LONER OR LONELY HEART? THE STORIES WE TELL OURSELVES ABOUT OURSELVES SHAPE OUR BEHAVIOUR

Maybe the reasons your child is left out seem obvious. Perhaps he's the quirky kid whose interests just don't match up with those of kids his age. Or the one who is so obsessed with computer games that he rarely plays outside or gets together with other kids. The one who can't exit playdates or handle disappointment without a meltdown. One of those who, even at a young age, already has a reputation based on behaviour that sets him apart from other children: "crybaby," "troublemaker," "bully," "loner," "weirdo." Or they are socially awkward or anxious or so intense about their favourite things that they seem off in their own little world.

But even that doesn't completely explain it, you may think, because often it seems that they just don't try, or when they do, it's the same old story with a new unhappy ending.

Part of helping children learn new social skills is to figure out what's been getting in their way. What's holding them back while other children seem to learn more naturally what's expected and how to respond in social interactions? Brain science, behavioural research, and my own experience in the trenches with kids show that children's perception of themselves and others becomes a deeply imbedded inner narrative that can limit their understanding of how social behaviour works and how to connect with others in a positive way. This internal story of how they see their social world and themselves in it colours their view of every inter- action, every situation they anticipate or perhaps avoid. The power of that story grows as it becomes the filter for cognitive perception, or how the brain processes, interprets, and learns from experience. Through a negative or defensive lens, the brain is likely to interpret an experience negatively, which then has a ripple effect, heightening negative feelings, putting the damper on positive ones, and making positive social out- comes even less likely.

A negative filter colours not only social experience but social expec- tations as well.

If a child thinks, *When I'm cross about something, I can say what I want and other kids just have to deal with it*, then that story creates an assumption that it's okay to spout off when you're angry, with- out regard for your impact on others or for the consequences of your behaviour. Contrast that with a similar thought pattern—with a few important changes: *When I'm cross about something, I can think about what I do and say, and not just blow up.*

The stories also shape a child's understanding of her social role and can keep her from making friends and recognising the behaviour that she needs to change. "I stand there in the hall—other kids should invite me to go along with them," a nine-year-old girl explains to me. This belief of hers keeps her from approaching other people because she doesn't under- stand that she needs to step up sometimes, that other kids won't auto- matically invite her to join them just because she's standing there open to the idea. Her belief about the way things work is mistaken, but until she understands that, it will continue to shape her view of those social situations and her role in them. Even with an intellectual understanding of how things work and what behaviour is called for, she must develop the actual skills to do what's needed and the confidence that changes the filter, changes the self-talk, or inner voice, from *I can't* to *I can*.

A child may not even notice these little stories he tells himself about his social life. The coaching process enables a child to observe, reflect, come to insights about his situation, then draw from them to develop new strategies and new behaviours that eventually lead to new social success.

That's what it takes to make meaningful change, and that's what coaching helps them do.

PATRICK: LIGHTS, ACTION, SPOILER ALERT!

Twice a year—once in the summer, once in the winter—Patrick's large extended family gathered at a rented holiday home for a weekend of outdoor fun, shared meals, and the much-awaited movie night when the gaggle of young cousins got to pick the flick and plop into beanbag chairs for the evening feature. As a close family friend, I had the good fortune to be invited along for one of these when my work brought me to a community nearby just in time for dinner.

The seven kids, a mix of girls and boys ranging in ages from six to ten years old, gobbled down their dinner in about thirty seconds and raced downstairs to the television room where their parents had set up the beanbag chairs in front of the big flatscreen TV. Earlier, as a few of the parents were making dinner, they started talking about how seven-year-old Patrick always had a hard time in these situations, especially when two of the cousins, girls his age, would pressure him to go along with their movie choice. Inevitably, he'd feel forced, and then either get mad or cry. The others responded predictably, writing him off as a cry-baby or spoilsport ruining everyone's good time. This was his history, the miserable experience that coloured his expectations every time they got together. But it was also a shared history, so every time they got together, the cousins expected the worst from Patrick and he always delivered.

After several years of this unpleasant dynamic, with most of the attention on Patrick's behaviour and the unhappy effect on everyone else, his parents began to take a pre-emptive approach. They pulled him aside earlier in the afternoon to remind him that he needed to "be good about this movie thing." Patrick squirmed unhappily, and as dinnertime neared, his parents' reminders turned to warnings. "Remember," they said in an ominous tone. "Get along." That warning hadn't worked well in the past, and they really didn't expect it to this night. But it was all they knew how to do. Patrick looked only more uncomfortable and anxious. My curiosity overtook me—I wondered what this was all about. I had observed Patrick struggling to mix in before, struggling to meet the expectations of a group and failing, yet he clearly wanted to be with the other kids. I asked his parents if I could chat with Patrick and see what made choosing a movie hard.

Patrick and I chatted briefly, and after determining that he did want things to go better than they usually did, and he was willing to try, we agreed on a plan. He'd hang in there with the group and give it his best shot, but if he ran into snags, he could come to me and we'd figure it out together.

The first dustup struck when everybody in the group agreed they wanted to see a certain movie—everybody but Patrick. He wanted to see one that they'd all—including Patrick—seen a million times. Patrick and I stepped aside, to the quiet living room where no one had taken their seats yet. Here, no prying eyes could make him feel self-conscious.

"Patrick," I said, "what if we could make choosing a movie easier?" His face brightened; then he frowned, remembering that this had already not gone well.

"Not possible," he said.

"Sure it is," I said. "What is it you like about movies you've seen a million times?" I asked with genuine curiosity.

He thought for a moment. "I really like to know what's coming," he said.

"What does it feel like when you don't know what's coming?"

"I worry," he told me.

It turned out that the suspense of not knowing made Patrick uncomfortable. Even a Flintstones cartoon would affect him this way if he hadn't seen it before. Uncertainty made him anxious. And when he was anxious, he felt physically uncomfortable and uneasy. On top of that, he had to deal with the other children's negative reactions. He couldn't handle his own feelings, much less those of the other children, and under that pressure, he would become argumentative or disruptive over things that made no sense to the other children.

Patrick's face lit up when I said there might be something we could do. In this instance, we were able to go online and watch the trailers for the movie everyone else wanted. This instantly reduced Patrick's stress level. Now more at ease, he was able to get along and go along with the group's choice. For the rest of the evening, step-by-step, whenever Patrick hit a snag, he came to me and together we problem-solved his way to a solution that resolved matters to everyone's satisfaction. At the end of the evening, the cousins had been able to enjoy their movie night together and with Patrick.

Patrick finally got to experience being part of the cousin pack instead of the whining outsider. He'd also got to experience handling social stress and anxiety in a brand-new way. First, we'd pinpointed the source of his distress (anxiety over the unknown), then brainstormed possible ways he could reduce the stress around this movie choice (watch trailers online). We were able to do that through just a few minutes of simple back-and-forth conversation that had Patrick reflect on his distress and find a way to defuse it so he could watch a movie. This wasn't a quick fix for the host of underlying issues that made it difficult for Patrick in social situations. But it was a start on finding new ways for him and his parents to address his larger social problem step-by-step so he could problem-solve, experience some success, and begin to build on those small successes.

Patrick's behaviour had looked uncooperative, stubborn, and babyish to those around him. In truth, his behaviour had been an expression of escalating anxiety that he didn't know how to manage, as well as frustration and the lack of certain basic social skills you need for the give-and-take of social situations. That's a big learning curve for all kids, but it is especially steep for some. The complexity of seemingly simple social interactions can be overwhelming for a child who hasn't developed the brain-based skills to apply to basic goals of social and emotional behaviour: manage big feelings, see the big picture, understand his role and other children's expectations and feelings, and then adapt his behaviour to support his social intention.

The thing to remember is this: We don't always know what's bothering children, and we must not assume that we do. We need to consult them, ask them about their experience, listen without jumping to conclusions or telling them what to do. We need to make the point of it all to understand them first, then join them in exploring what they want and how we can help them change the way they are doing things.

CAN'T OR WON'T? BLAMING, SHAMING, AND OTHER OLD PARENTING STORIES GET US STUCK

As parents or teachers, we, too, may have our story about a child we find challenging. How many times have you heard a child's behaviour explained by others, or heard yourself sum it up with a shorthand description or label? *He never listens. She's stubborn and bossy. He's lazy. He's selfish. She's just an introvert—not everybody is a social butterfly.* That's the story we've chosen to assign to the child's behaviour.

There are certainly times when a child may be stubborn or selfish, but neuroscience and a growing body of behavioural literature hold that often it is a lack of skills—specifically the brain-based *executive function* skills—that drive the behaviour. Not willfulness or laziness. Not a lack of character. Executive function is the brain's hub of skills such as working memory, organisation, planning, self-regulation, emotional regulation, and the ability to modify our behaviour to reach a goal or respond to others. We'll take a closer look at the brain science in a moment, but when these skills lag, for whatever reason, the timeworn advice about pushing through, trying harder, and just making it happen do not apply. In fact, such blaming and shaming only make matters worse.

If your child's behaviour has you upset or concerned, you can spend a lot of time trying to figure out whether your child is behaving willfully—choosing to behave in problematic ways—or whether she honestly can't do any better and needs help. *Can't or won't?* The question itself is reasonable enough, but the problem with it is that it distracts you from getting help. Trying to diagnose *can't versus won't*, sifting through every playdate failure, every teacher's note reporting the day's infraction, only leaves you stuck in this debate with yourself. You're not really moving forwards. Neither is your child.

Moving forwards means recognising that your child's pattern of behaviour strongly suggests an element of *can't*—that there's more to it than willful disobedience, bad manners, or laziness. This doesn't mean you won't hold your child accountable for his behaviour. It means that you recognise that, whatever his strengths may be, they do not include an ability to read ordinary social cues and respond appropriately. Further, this is clearly an ongoing challenge and he needs help learning those skills. That's the starting point for understanding your child's challenge and the practical problem-solving skills he needs to figure out how to adapt, engage, learn, and thrive as a social being.

We would never expect a child to swim across a lake if she'd never learned how to swim. We wouldn't throw a kid into a tournament match on the football field if he'd never learned the basic skills to get the ball down the field, pass it, or shoot for a goal. Similarly, children with social skills weaknesses need direct instruction designed to develop the brain-based circuitry that helps them connect with other children.

When parents come to me with teens who need help, one of the most familiar laments they share is that they stayed in the endless *can't-or-won't* debate way too long. They feared "giving in," so instead buckled down on correction, consequences, and escalating punishments. As a result, their teen never received the targeted help with executive function social skills that was needed to develop those necessary skills at a younger age in the first place. The debate got in the way. Now, years later, their child is an adolescent or college age, the social behaviour problem is still there, and the stakes have only got higher. Can this coaching technique help an older child, or at some point is it too late to improve lagging executive function social skills? It is never too late to learn these skills. I have adapted the programme—aged-up the messaging, examples, and scenarios—for adult clients of all ages. In many cases, someone who has seen their career or personal relationships suffer due to their social behaviours is very motivated. But that doesn't mean that we should wait!

THE HIDDEN STORY: BRAIN-BASED EXECUTIVE FUNCTION SKILLS DRIVE SOCIAL BEHAVIOUR

Our tendency as parents is to jump right in to fix things we can see need fixing because that's what we do: a knot in a shoelace, a snag in scheduling, a broken toy. It's easy to develop the habit of assuming that the problem we see is what needs fixing. But behaviour you see is like the tip of an iceberg: The visible part of an iceberg is typically only about one-eighth of its mass, with the much greater mass below the waterline. It's that unseen portion that's the most formidable challenge to passing ships because there's no way to know just what's there. Below the surface

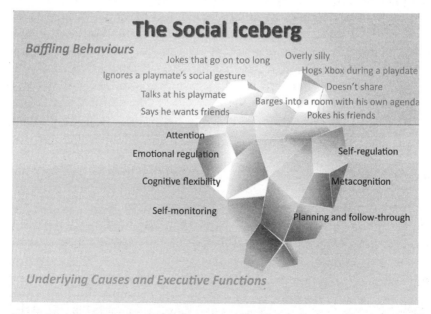

© 2018 Maguire. Adapted from Dendy, 2006; Delahooke, 2017.

Your child's observable behaviours—the ones you find baffling or frustrating—are like the visible tip of the iceberg. The reasons for that behaviour lie below the surface, in the way that your child is hardwired for certain strengths in brain-based skills, while some others are unevenly or less developed.

of a child's behaviour are the forces and factors that drive it. Coaching your child is going to take you to those deeper dimensions—the heart of your child's experience—and help you both develop the skills that foster change and growth.

Fran

Very soon after Fran joined the reception year, her teacher mentioned to her mother that Fran showed no interest in playing with other children. I observed in the class one day and noticed that Fran played contentedly by herself. Her body language suggested she was happy, but I also saw that when another child spoke to her, she did not respond. Children made overtures and she seemed to ignore them. She had arranged herself with toys in a small little circle and that was that.

Her solitary play didn't seem to bother anyone. The other children played among themselves. But the negative reports began to trail in. At school, she would have a meltdown over things that just didn't seem like big deals and didn't bother other children, like picking crayon colours to use on an activity sheet or taking turns with toys. Fran's lack of interest in other children started to worry her mother, as well as the idea that others would think Fran was just rude.

Fran's parents wondered: Would she outgrow this or did they need to do something? A formal medical evaluation might show no cause for concern. Or it might identify some specific issues that they could address now. They decided that if she needed help, better to find out sooner rather than later.

A professional evaluation found that Fran had a particular kind of speech-processing problem (receptive-expressive language disorder) that, for example, made conversations about preferences—for a toy, a crayon, a lunch choice—more complicated for her than for most children her age. If you asked Fran if she wanted a peanut butter sandwich, macaroni cheese, or a pizza slice for lunch, she might want the peanut butter sandwich, but she would *say* the last item on your spoken list. Given the pizza slice, she would fuss because she had chosen the sandwich—in her mind—but unfortunately, she'd asked for the pizza. This meant that other people frequently missed or misunderstood what she really meant to convey. When Fran appeared to ignore other children, she was in fact not able to fully process and respond accurately to what they were saying. That's frustrating for any five-year-old, but if it happens to you constantly, then you spend a lot more time frustrated and stressed than most kids do, and you are more likely to reach your limits and express that stress overload in meltdowns or argumentative behaviour.

Like so many children with brain-based social skills weaknesses, Fran's behaviours often seemed to suggest that she wasn't willing to play or try to get along with others, but that's not how she felt at all. She wasn't being willful or unfriendly. More often than not, she had to work harder to understand what people meant when they spoke to her, and then had to deal constantly with harsh or negative consequences. She was exhausted and confused.

"Not responding" can look very similar to "ignoring," which also can look very similar to being rude and not trying. These so-called topographic behaviours are the visible features of the landscape that we can see—the obvious, observable behaviours. But beneath the surface there is a range of reasons why your child might not be catching on or responding in expected ways.

Those brain-based mechanisms drive behaviours, and to change them, your child needs a specific kind of guidance and direct instruction to do what comes easily to many other kids. For many, even most, children with weaknesses in these brain-based social skills, strategic coaching, specialised instruction, and practice work where other approaches fail.

Going forwards, keep the iceberg model in mind as you think about your child's behaviour. Throughout this book we'll focus on different observable social behaviours and underlying brain-based reasons for them. For many, even most, children, executive function weaknesses are just that: weaknesses that respond well to strategic coaching, instruction, and practice. We'll explore executive function more fully in the next chapter, but just being aware of it is important to your understanding of your child's story and the story you may have been telling yourself about your child's behaviour.

WAIT-AND-SEE ISN'T THE ANSWER

Lag time is lost time

In many areas of childhood, wait-and-see often delivers what seem like little miracles. One day your toddler is toddling, the next he is running and jumping. Potty-training looms as a monumental challenge at first, and then one day it clicks and nappies are history. A child who can't ride her bike the first time around tries again in six months and can.

The challenge is different when it comes to social skills development. Children with social skills weaknesses face a play paradox they can't solve on their own. Play is the first learning environment for young children. In play with other children, they learn social behaviour and develop the brain-based networks and skills that affect all types of learning. These include problem-solving, negotiation, self-advocacy, emotional expression, "big picture" thinking, perspective-taking, and emotional regulation. But opportunities to play quickly shrink for kids who avoid social interaction or whose behaviour is out of sync or off-putting to their peers.

Friendships typically arise at school but are usually cemented outside school—at sleepovers, on trips to the park, or on other outings. Children bond over shared interests and activities, whether it is building forts in the sitting room or playing video games or creating funny skits for their friends or families. Children who are not invited on playdates are at a disadvantage because they don't have that opportunity to bond with friends or engage in ordinary developmental activities that promote social growth. They don't get as many chances to learn and practise social skills as other children do. And if a weary parent takes a pass on invitations because she'd prefer to avoid the uncomfortable outcome she's come to expect, that only further limits a child's opportunities for interaction and reinforces the role of odd-one-out.

Brain plasticity, or the brain's ability to change in response to experience, is at its greatest from birth to five years old, although it continues through childhood and adolescence. A growing body of findings underscores that early learning and development, especially the development of social and emotional skills, have a significant impact on a child's overall health and prosperity throughout life. As one study noted, loneliness and stress appear to be "the glue that binds poor social skills to health." This holds true for all children, but with even greater significance for the millions of children whose executive function skills lag behind those of peers and need targeted attention to bridge that gap. Most want to change the story they use to rationalise social isolation. They don't know how. *If they could, they would.*

START SIMPLY: LET YOUR LOVE AND CURIOSITY LEAD THE WAY

"What you pay attention to grows," a friend of mine likes to say. Your child has a story. You have a story. We need to pay attention to these stories so we can begin to recognise them and the way they get rooted and crowd out possibilities for new growth and change. They make it hard for us to change old patterns and perspectives.

Whatever the story, your child has been heavily invested in that story line and isn't going to change overnight. But change is inevitable as the coaching process opens up new experiences and confidence in the promise of change. For now, here's all you need to do: listen to your child. Listen for the story line you hear when he's lonely or angry or a playdate falls apart. Don't confront your child over it or challenge the story or your child's reasons for thinking that way. Just notice. In the coaching process ahead, these beliefs become openings for thoughtful reflection and conversation, goal-setting, and skill-building. They'll become the foundation for transformation.

I've seen clearly in my work with children that the self-limiting stories they believe about themselves, if left unchallenged and unchanged, grow stronger with every day's social failure. I've also seen that pep talks or stern advice fall short because they don't reach the roots of a child's problematic behaviour: the brain-based circuitry and skills that need to be strengthened to do their job. I consider kids among my most valuable teachers, and this connection between inner story, skills, and behavioural change is the lesson that their success teaches us again and again. As your child's coach, you will help her reframe her story, understand where the old one came from, and set about developing a new one, a story based on new skills and reasonable expectations for success.

For now, the first step is to recognise the power of this internal story, listen for it, and hear it for what it is. That's where the change begins.

What's Your Child's Story? Ten Ways to Find Out

This is a listening exercise.

1. Listen to the way your child describes social dustups or disappointments. What excuses, or self-protecting stories, does he give for his behaviour? For other people's behaviour? Just listen—don't jump in to correct him or argue. You can simply acknowledge what you're hearing: *It sounds like everybody had quite a wait for the assembly to start.* Or *It sounds like you were frustrated when Ginnie got to go first.*

2. Listen to the way your child describes herself in the role she believes she has in her peer group or in the family. Comments such as "I'm always the one who gets in trouble," "I'm just the funny girl," "I'm such a loser," "They're just stupid," show an underlying story, or narrative, she is telling herself. Look earlier in this chapter at the list of things kids often say, and see if any sound familiar to you. Then ask your child about those statements or little comments she makes. Some questions you can ask: "I hear you say that a lot—what do you mean by that?" "You say you were 'being good'—what does being good mean?"

3. If your child isn't a talker or has trouble reflecting and finding the words to express himself, you can help by modelling how to reflect. You can say "I notice..." and share an observation or an image, and ask if they agree or disagree with your perception. You can share an example from a "friend's child" or you can share something from your own past, telling it with detail. This helps open your child's own thought process.

4. Share from the descriptions of the children in the opening of this chapter—Sam, Rory, Sarah, Megan, and Danny—and the longer stories of Patrick and Fran, and ask your child if she knows any children like that at school or in other settings. Ask what she can tell you about them and what she thinks of them.

5. When does a belief about ourselves become a story? Bring this up as a curious subject someone brought up recently that got you thinking, and you wonder what your child thinks about it. What is a story we tell ourselves and how is it different from a fact? What kind of story can be helpful? What kind of story can hold us back? Be ready with child-friendly examples: *People once thought the world was flat. How did the change in their story affect what they thought was possible and they were willing to try?* Suggest some from your own experience: *I once believed that I would never _____, and then _____.*

6. Listen for comments that assume that nothing and no one can change. "I'll never be any good at this." "Nobody likes me." "Everybody hates me." Ask your child if she has ever changed her mind—about anything or anybody. Or changed her understanding of something (dinosaurs, football, or other favourite interests) when she learned more. Imagine a universe where nothing and nobody ever changed, where everything was frozen in time—what does nature tell us about change?

7. Identify a positive story or belief you wish your child could feel about his ability to improve his social situation, and ask your child to look at it with you. Examples might include: *Change is always possible; if you continue to meet people, you will make friends; we all have to work on our social approach and there is a big payoff for that.* Share them with your child and ask: *What would happen if you believed that? When I say (the positive belief), how do you feel about that?*

8. Ask about her assumptions. Does she tell you she'll "never be invited" or "it's not worth trying to see someone" or she wants "to keep trying on her own"? Explore her assumptions about social life and friendship.

Some responses include: "What makes you say that? How come? Tell me more about that."

9. In a gamelike way, make a statement and ask your child to fill in the blank. Present with something you feel he would say, such as "I can't change my friendships because..." or "I can't change because..." When he fills in the blank, repeat the finished statement back to your child—"So I hear you saying..." and ask, "How come? What makes you say this?"

10. Ask your child to draw a picture of what is hard about friendships. Then explore the drawing with her. Who are the people and what is she trying to show? What does she feel when she draws these scenes?

Your Turn
Listen for Your Story about Your Child

If you have watched your child's struggle from the sidelines or believe your child is beyond help, you may have come to believe a story about them or their situation. Often the stories we tell ourselves are more a reflection of our frustration or hopelessness than an accurate reflection of our child's potential for change and growth. Whatever the story, I'm asking you to shed that snakeskin right now. Understand that if you think of your child as just an annoying pain in the neck like his uncle and believe he'll never change, then that's going to hold you back and hold your child back. If you think smart kids don't have friends, think again—lots of smart kids do have friends. Yours can too. These questions can help you see unhelpful hidden stories:

- Do you frequently rationalise or make excuses for your child's social behaviour?
- Do you defend your child's behaviour as "just quirky" or "independent"?
- Do you frequently blame others for your child's behaviour?
- Do you expect others to accommodate your child's behaviour?
- Do you feel exasperated with your child's behaviour and feel she doesn't try hard enough?
- Do you hesitate to have your child professionally evaluated fearing others will label her?

- Do you feel your child is being manipulative?
- Do you blame your child's behaviour for tension with your parenting partner?

If you answered yes to any of these questions, that's a flag for you to take a closer look at a belief or story you have created that can hamper your ability to understand your child, see his challenge and the reasons for it clearly, and help him make meaningful changes in his behaviour.

Executive Function
The Brain's Ship Captain for Social Navigation

Imagine the brain as a busy harbour, ships coming and going, some docking and others manoeuvring their way out to sea, all under constantly changing conditions that can make for smooth sailing or stormy waters. Executive function is the "ship captain" that shapes your child's view of himself and others in the sea of social activity, organises the tools your child needs, and trains him in the skills and behaviours he needs to navigate social waters. The captain has a large crew and must coordinate all the activities on this big ship. Each member of the crew has a specific job: stand watch, read the map and chart a course, monitor defence systems, manage communications, maintain the engines, look out for other vessels, and play a role in the full range of day-to-day operations. If the captain is ineffective, then no matter how smart each of the crew members is, with a lack of skilled know-how at the helm, the ship can run aground.

It can be tempting to think that the answer to your child's lagging social skills is to change everything around her: the teacher, the school, the camp, the other kids. Or to give her a pass on behavioural challenges, hoping that she'll find her niche later as an adult. But unless you recognise what's really getting in your child's way—the internal, brain-based source of your child's difficulties—then these efforts to change the external landscape can have only limited effect.

Over the years, you have watched your child's social behaviour and wondered: *Why can't he just join in and get along with other kids?* Through the lens of executive function, you can see the "why." In the most general way, across all kinds of thought processes involved in learning and behaviour, executive function skills affect how your child:

- focuses attention
- organises information
- remembers and learns from past experiences
- integrates thought processes that shape perception and self-awareness
- self-regulates to manage physical, cognitive, and emotional stress
- regulates emotion to maintain equilibrium and avoid extremes
- adapts to new situations (cognitive flexibility)
- initiates and manages tasks
- sees the big picture (metacognition)
- visualises what they can do in a future situation (working memory)
- develops an inner voice (self-talk) to guide them (working memory)
- self-monitors and shows self-awareness
- reads conversational and emotional cues from other people, picking up on their thoughts, beliefs, and intentions and using that information to interpret what they say, make sense of their behaviour, and anticipate how they'll react to something. This is sometimes called *mind reading*.

All of these brain-based capacities and skills directly affect how your child behaves in social situations.

Advances in brain science in the past decade have provided new insights into executive function, its role as the link between the brain and behaviour, and its critical relationship to social skills weaknesses. Based on brain scans that show the brain in action as it performs certain tasks, we now know that the executive function command centre is part of the prefrontal cortex (PFC). Found in the frontal lobe of the brain, the PFC manages planning, organising, goal setting, and self-regulation. Executive function is a network of brain circuits devoted to these vital critical-thinking skills and coordinating them to connect smoothly with other systems in the brain and body.

In everyday behaviours, these executive functions show up as:

- what your child pays attention to
- what he notices about his friends' needs and reactions
- his ability to take the bird's-eye (metacognitive) view of his own behaviour and expectations

- how he responds to disappointment
- how he manages his emotions
- how he manages stressful demands, such as sharing or taking turns
- how he thinks about friendship and reciprocating in a relationship
- how he adapts or reacts to new or shifting social situations.

Weak executive functions translate into weak social skills. Specifically, they include a child's inability to:

- recognise that other people have feelings and those feelings may be different from your own
- predict or anticipate how other people are likely to feel, and read their emotional temperature
- interpret people's emotional cues accurately and respond in a socially accepted way
- recognise the basic content or information that someone is trying to tell you
- hear not only *what* someone says, but also *how* they say it; to accurately interpret tone, intention, and other unspoken cues
- recognise a listener's level of interest in a topic
- anticipate that your actions provoke reactions from other people
- recognise the unspoken rules and expectations that govern how people behave in a given situation, environment, or occasion
- respond appropriately to the other person's intended message.

Every child is a unique mix of executive function strengths and weaknesses, and every child's struggles will be different. Executive function isn't all-or-nothing; there are degrees of impairment, which is why your discerning eye as a parent is such an advantage as a coach. One child may be disorganised but have excellent emotional self-regulation, while another child may be completely organised but lack focus and adaptability. A child may be a precocious athlete, Lego builder, or creative writer, yet be clueless about how to read facial expressions, body language, or basic social cues from other kids. Some children do recognise the need to do so but need specific instruction and practice to learn how. Others are genuinely unaware that this is something they need to do, and that although they aren't doing it, they can learn how. Stress affects every child's executive functioning differently, too. A social situation that feels stressful to one child might not faze another, or might not affect them nearly as much.

You don't have to be a neuroscientist to observe your child's social behaviours through the executive function lens and identify patterns that are limiting your child's social opportunities. Are her social behaviours predictable and age-appropriate compared with those of her peers? Are the reasons she gives for being left out or avoiding social activities red flags? Here are a few of the most common ways these patterns show up in children's behaviours around interaction and play, and emotions and communication, along with some of the specific executive function skills involved. The key factors that flag a behaviour as cause for concern are frequency, intensity, and duration.

Is he a "space invader" who ploughs into other people's personal space?

Personal space includes not only physical space, but also conversational space and situational space. No one likes someone who is intrusive and disrupts others. A child must be able to slow down, read the social situation, and manage the internal impulses driving his physical and emotional behaviour. These are executive functions that drive self-regulation, attention, self-monitoring, and flexibility.

Is her humour or "goofy/silly" behaviour age appropriate or is it awkwardly out of sync with peers?

Does she miss the humour in things other people say and get stuck on the literal meaning? As they progress in their friendships, children need to be able to share jokes, funny moments, and the subtle inflections in tone that make a simple phrase humourous. Humour involves the executive functions for attention, self-regulation, self-monitoring, organisation, and metacognition.

Does he avoid or rarely participate in break time or group play?

Joining in involves being able to imagine a social scenario and see yourself taking that initiative—what I call *mind miming* for the way the brain enables us to "mimic" behaviour we can envision. Joining in also involves planning and follow-through, organisation, cognitive flexibility, and working memory.

Does she "monologue," or talk nonstop about only her own interests, oblivious to others who might want to talk about something else?

She needs to learn when to put the brakes on—when enough is enough and more is too much. Balancing personal interests with those of others involves listening and reading social cues, taking turns, and remembering that different people have different interests.

Can he carry on a reciprocal, two-way conversation?

Most of us don't think about what exactly makes a conversation reciprocal. But we manage early in life to pick up the back-and-forth process of advancing a conversation in everyday social behaviour. A child who hasn't picked that up naturally has to learn what reciprocal conversation is, understand its relevance to them personally, and then learn the skills for it. This involves attention and listening, self-regulation, and self-monitoring.

Is she sarcastic or characteristically negative in tone, unaware how her tone comes across as negative—dismissive or insulting—to others?

By the same token, is she unable to tell when others use sarcasm? Interpreting language involves attention, working memory, metacognition, self-monitoring, and organising/prioritising.

The Executive Function Questionnaire (EFQ) in Chapter 7 is designed to identify your child's executive function strengths and weaknesses, and prioritise them for attention as you work together to help your child set personal goals and a plan of action. For now, a walk-through of the executive function operations will familiarise you with the range of brain-based capacities that underlie social behaviour, so you'll be able to start recognising the outward signs—the tip of the iceberg—and these hidden drivers of your child's behaviour.

METACOGNITION IS SOCIALISATION: "THINKING ABOUT THINKING" BOOSTS KIDS' SOCIAL AND SELF-AWARENESS

Andy is eleven, a super-self-confident and sociable fellow who, despite those seemingly attractive qualities, is often left out or ditched by the kids at school. He has no idea why, and although he admits that it hurts to be treated this way time after time, he never changes his approach or response to the rebuffs. He does not read between the lines—or for that matter, even see the lines. He's oblivious to himself—to his own strengths and weaknesses. He is also oblivious to the way his behaviour affects other people and how they perceive him. Recently he tried out for a competitive gymnastics team. Most kids who tried out for this elite team had worked long and hard in weekly lessons, had been on a more junior team, and were recommended by a coach. Andy had taken gymnastics in preschool and that was it. So, his parents were baffled. Why would he try out? One reason is that he never anticipates the predictable outcome. Never.

Andy also thinks he is best friends with everyone. If someone shows him any interest, he doesn't notice that they are being just superficially friendly. He doesn't understand the unspoken rules, the change in dynamics within his group of schoolmates, and who his true friends are. He frequently invites himself along to activities, not really noticing the social nuances of the situation or whether or not he is invited. He ignores feedback from other kids, even when it's direct— "come on, dude, stop it." Or if they say sarcastically, "yeah, right," he doesn't hear that they are really taunting him. Recently he wanted to go to a baseball card signing at a sports shop and he kept asking kids he barely knows to go with him. When they told him they were busy or that they simply couldn't do it, he tried to help them problem-solve so they could come—ignoring their cues that they just were not into going with him.

We hear a lot about socialisation and especially how important it is for us as parents to socialise our children, from table manners to town sports, and of course to meet the timeless goal of early childhood achievement: to play well with others. What's often missing from that conversation is the role of metacognition. Metacognition is socialisation from the inside out—the capacity for social awareness and self-awareness that originates in the brain and shapes our every thought and behaviour.

Metacognition is most simply described as the ability to think about how we think, to take that bird's-eye view—the *meta*view—of our own cognition or thought processes. Metacognition is often talked about in the context of academic learning for its important role in critical thinking and holding big ideas in mind. But that capacity to see the big picture, and ourselves in it, has a profound effect on every aspect of our lives: It affects our perceptions of ourselves and others, our behaviour and our awareness of how it impacts others, our emotional responses and how we manage them, what we remember and how we learn from experience, and how flexible we are as thinkers and problem-solvers. Metacognition is another way to describe social awareness and self-awareness, which are, at the heart of it, the behavioural bedrock of socialisation.

Andy's lack of self-awareness and his inability to pick up on the unspoken rules in social situations or the explicit critical feedback from other kids is problematic. The fact that he has been this way since preschool, when his social world first expanded beyond family, means it's not a new thing that might be attributable to something going on around him. External factors like a new school, move, or new peer situation can make these lagging skills even more problematic, but essentially the gaps are there. Andy's chronic inability to see the big picture and to see himself and his role in it clearly is holding him back.

Experts once thought that metacognition was a late-developing skill, for most children not developing before eight to ten years of age. But more recent studies show that significant metacognitive development occurs much earlier. A snapshot of those findings:

- Metacognition grows significantly in the first six years of life, with the most dramatic changes occurring between the ages of three and four.
- Metacognition improves with both age *and* appropriate instruction. Significant empirical evidence indicates that children— including those with executive function weaknesses—can be taught how to reflect on their own thinking.
- Direct, explicit instruction has been shown to help children (1) think about their own thought processes, (2) practise self-regulation to stay on task and problem-solve toward goals, (3) collaborate with others, and (4) develop self-awareness about their perceptions and beliefs about themselves as learners.

THE EXECUTIVE FUNCTION ABCs OF SOCIAL AWARENESS

Because the complex networks of executive functions are so intertwined within the brain, a simpler way to understand them is to view them as the clusters of behaviours you see every day in your child and in other children. What follows are those core clusters of brain-based social skills and how weaknesses in executive functions affect your child's social behaviour and ability to be his best self among others. Here's the bird's-eye view—the metaview—that we'll unpack skill by skill and play by play in Part II.

Reading social cues

Social awareness is the bedrock skill your child needs to see the lie of the land and make her way successfully in any social setting. Social awareness has many elements, which I'll explore shortly, but all rely on effective *social communication skills*. From a one-on-one playdate to break time or the lunchroom, your child needs to be able to pick up on cues and communicate effectively with others in the social language of the realm. As different as the settings may be, all social settings share some common ground. Every social environment is like a little landscape. There are open spaces—times and physical spaces—where it's easy to go your own way, do your own thing. There are established paths of socially acceptable behaviour that make it easy to get from Point A to Point B, and unspoken rules of the road. *Make eye contact. Say hello.* Red flags that warn of potential social trouble zones: *She's in the middle of telling a story, so don't interrupt. They've already decided which movie to watch, so that's settled—not something to complain or argue about.*

When talking to children who struggle in this area, I find it helpful to encourage them to think like social weather forecasters. You have to watch the social "weather" and develop some forecasting skills. What's the emotional temperature of your friend or the group? How about your own? When a high-pressure front moves through (a disagreement or disappointment), how does your friend or your group tend to respond? How about you? And the terrain: Have things previously been a little rocky with these kids? Do other features in the landscape require special attention to navigate successfully? What happens when other people with their own ideas want to go in a different direction than you do?

Effective social communication skills involve listening, interpreting context and meaning, considering the interests and feelings of others, and expressing yourself in socially acceptable ways. Executive function skills are at the hub of communication skills because they coordinate the brainpower required to pay attention to multiple facets of a social situation, take a bird's-eye view of it and your role in it, organise information, and self-monitor. Your child must be able to read other people's cues—both verbal and nonverbal—then decode social rules and practise "if-then" thinking: If your classmate looks upset, then now is not the time to share your exciting news about a toy or a trip. You need to push pause on your impulse and wait for a better time. Each step in that process requires executive function skills such as attention, information, and sensory processing, as well as decoding, analysing, and acting on incoming information.

Social communication is, above all, adaptive communication. You can win the spelling bee, ace your English exams, and snag the lead role in the school musical, but if you're tone-deaf to the feelings of others or miss the real-life cues for social improv, then you won't get far making friends or being one. Forming friendships involves adjusting what we say and how we say it based on the feedback we get from the other person.

Setting social boundaries

No matter how many times Em's brother told her not to interrupt him when he was doing his homework, again and again and again she would dump her bin of Legos on the table where his social studies project was carefully laid out. Her year four teacher had a similar complaint about Em's behaviour in class, the way she disrupted other children as they worked, or intruded with her own agenda when others were already involved in play. She seemed oblivious to what others would consider ordinary social boundaries, or rules of behaviour that most people accept and expect of each other in a social setting.

Social boundaries are sometimes clearly communicated rules, sometimes not. In some homes, everyone removes their shoes when they enter the front door. In others, it's just expected that if your shoes are muddy, you'll drop them at the door. There may be a sign that tells you to do so, or it may be an unspoken house rule that family and friends simply understand and go along with. If you're a first-time visitor, you might not see a sign or know the rule, but you might notice the shoes by the door when you walked in, or you might notice other people slipping their shoes off and follow suit.

In this scenario, if your child arrived for a playdate, strolled right past the shoe drop, and tracked his muddy sneakers all over the carpet, he would likely be considered rude. His failure to pick up on the cues would likely result in other people having some negative feelings towards him. Meanwhile, he might be clueless about his social transgression and confused about the frosty treatment by others.

Social boundaries exist all around us, from physical spaces and the behaviour expected there, to conversations and relationships, and the unspoken rules that everyone just seems to know. They include comprehending the idea of personal space, understanding the degrees of friendship and intimacy, evaluating the many nuances and social rules in an environment, and internalising the appropriate behavioural responses. In other words, is your behaviour going to fit in comfortably for others or stand out in a negative way? A big part of socialisation in childhood is learning those generally accepted social boundaries, as well as learning how to pick up on the cues when you come into a new space or a new relationship.

If your child doesn't pick up on those cues, then his effort to be sociable can show up as too much: too close, too intimate, too pushy, too needy. He's basically tracking muddy shoes into the social sitting room.

Children with weak executive function social skills often lack *social recognition*, or the ability to decode social conventions. These skills are driven by the executive functions that include attention, self-regulation, self-awareness, and metacognition. Without them, a child may easily offend or annoy others, as in Em's case, oblivious to the cues or unaware that social boundaries exist and that signs are there if you know how to look for them.

Developing cognitive flexibility

It's break time, and Angela's year two classmates have declared the swing set a spaceship. They've hatched a story and rules in the time it took them to run out to play: The entryway to the spaceship is on the left, the command deck is the centre swing, and if you step off the swing set, you're lost to outer space. Angela wants to play but insists that they change the story and the rules. She continues to argue about the story line, when everybody else just goes along with it. She feels she's right and doesn't care what others think or feel about it. It doesn't even occur to her that it matters how other kids feel and that her behaviour annoys them.

We all know that sometimes it's important to go strictly by the rules. But if a child routinely seems to lack the flexibility to adjust to different situations calling for different expectations and behaviour, then it's an indication that the executive function for *cognitive flexibility* needs work. A child's rigid behaviour can start to eat away at friendships. Nobody likes it when you declare yourself boss every time, insist you are always right, or argue or insist on your own set of rules. Over time, people will choose not to play with you.

Cognitive flexibility involves the executive functions for attention and the ability to shift between tasks and to go from one mind-set to another—for instance, from the way you think about a sheet of maths problems to the way you think about playing with your friends on a swing set spaceship. To develop cognitive flexibility, kids must learn to take stock of a situation and their role in it, recognise the impact they have on others, and then adjust their behaviour to work well in the situation.

Cognitive flexibility affects your child's ability to manage transitions of all kinds. Transitions are woven into social life as well, requiring your child to recognise, for example, when a one-on-one time with a best friend must shift to a group setting where circumstances call for them both to pay more attention to others. Your child needs to be a flexible thinker to manage transitions of all kinds. Time pressure adds to the stress of transitions and demands on cognitive flexibility. The school day and after-school time for children today leaves little time for relaxed transitions. It may be time to put the puzzles or dress-ups away and move on to the next period or hop in the car to go to school or run errands, but a child who has a hard time with that is more likely to be crabby, tearful, or short-tempered. Some playdates, parties, or special events can present an additional challenge because children with poor adaptability may also not warm up to new people easily. They prefer a set routine and they find changing environments challenging. Visiting an unfamiliar house or meeting unfamiliar people can trigger anxiety, lighting a short fuse on behaviour.

Rigid thinking makes everything more challenging, but especially play and socialising, because there's naturally so much spontaneity involved and other people with their own ideas and preferences. If everyone at the sand table is pretending it's an ice cream shop and that sand is ice cream, then that's the deal. A child who is inflexible and insists that sand is just sand won't be part of the fun. The inflexible thinker needs to be taught to recognise that under some circumstances, other people see swing sets as spaceships and sand as ice cream. He'll need to understand that this is an example of situations in which he thinks differently from his peers, but that to play with them, he'll need to get comfortable with some magical thinking.

SELF-REGULATION: CHILDREN NEED TO KEEP "EYES ON THE PRIZE" TO MANAGE STRESS AND WORK TOWARDS A GOAL

"I'm always the one in trouble," Griff explained to me about his third-year classroom. He knew this, he said, because he was sent to the head's office so often. Sometimes he just couldn't sit still and he'd start to roam the classroom. When he was bored, he got jittery and would tap his pencil loudly and sigh theatrically. When he was tired, he became more reactive about people and situations that he didn't seem to notice as much when he was rested. When he was on edge, being in the noisy classroom or having to jostle through the crowded hallway to assembly could put him over the top. He might push another child, snap at the teacher, scatter the puzzle pieces from the table onto the floor. It was always worse when he was tired or hungry or stressed for any reason. And once his behaviour was on that hair trigger, all it took was a snicker from a classmate or frustration over a maths sheet, and he'd explode—sometimes in anger, sometimes in tears. Whatever good intentions he may have had for that class period or that playdate went out the window.

When Griff's unhappy teachers, classmates, and others describe him, it is almost always about his behaviour—disruptive, hyperactive, inattentive—and rarely about the qualities that those who know him love about him: inquisitive, enthusiastic, eager to please. One reason is that Griff has problems managing his feelings, thoughts, and behaviour so that he can do what he needs to do or even what he wants to do. Griff has problems with self-regulation.

Self-regulation is the way our brain and body work together to manage stress of all kinds and keep the brain functioning smoothly so that we can focus clearly, calmly, and thoughtfully on whatever we need to attend to. That's a big job.

A growing body of research supports the idea that what we often see as a child's *mis*behaviour is really *stress* behaviour. It's not a child's conscious decision to flout the rules or challenge expectations, but reflexive behaviour that's physiological in nature when they are overwhelmed by thoughts and emotions. Stress includes not only social and emotional stress, but also pressure from school work or other demands. In his book *Self-Reg: How to Help Your Child (and You) Break the Stress Cycle and Successfully Engage with Life*, Stuart Shanker describes self-regulation as the nervous system's way of responding to stress from several domains, or sources in the brain and body: social, emotional, physical, and cognitive. Stress in any of these domains (for our purposes, notably social, emotional, and cognitive) triggers the release of certain neurochemicals and hormones—adrenaline, cortisol, insulin, and others—that activate a system-wide alert so your heart, circulation, breathing, and muscles are primed for emergency action. Jitteriness, sweaty palms, racing heart, tight or queasy stomach, and muscle tension are physical cues that the stress response is shifting into hyper mode.

Another critical part of self-regulation is how well your brain can stay focused on a task or goal so that you can follow through to finish. In the grip of the full-on stress response, the brain shifts more immediate attention to an emergency response and less to deliberating, critical-thinking skills. The quicker you're able to bring executive functions back online, the better you're able to process what's happening clearly and calmly and restore your balance. The catch: someone with weak executive function has fewer "stop and think" skills to help them do that. And for the child who's a rigid thinker, that cognitive inflexibility becomes a huge stressor, along with the social challenge it presents.

The ability to hold a goal in mind, to understand and self-monitor your behaviour so you can tell when you're acting as you intended, or not, is essential. When you can direct your actions in a way that serves your goals, that's called *adaptive behaviour*. When your actions work against your goal, then you are stuck and static and your actions do not move you toward positive interactions. In a social context, a child first has to be aware that behaviour and goals are connected and that there are steps necessary to meet a social goal. Then they have a sense of what is expected, a sense of their future, and a clear idea of the choices they have socially. Part of self-regulation is the ability to weigh different options, calculate the risks and benefits, and identify how this action will affect their future self.

All of this taps into working memory—a collection of executive functions that operate together to enable you to draw from your store of memory and information, to hold it in front of you, look at it, manipulate it, and use it to guide your action in the moment. A child with poor working memory can't readily recall past experiences or connect them to the present circumstances. Griff's parents and teachers tell him what he should and should not do, but in the heat of the moment he does not pause and call up that feedback and act on it. Griff has to remember that he has a goal and that he wants to pause, but his emotions overwhelm him, and then he forgets. He can't hold the thought in his mind because he is flooded with emotion. And without that stop-and-think process, without the brakes to inhibit impulsive action and the working memory that draws from past experience to inform behaviour now, there's no clear path to even the simplest goal.

Self-regulation also comes into play when you need to change your behaviour to match a change in your role: At a social gathering, are you the host or are you a guest? Is the team at your house or are you at another team member's house? Is indoors an appropriate place for running or roughhousing, or do you need to wait until you get outside? Shifting to meet the demands of the situation requires self-regulation, and this is not something children do easily. They may have good intentions, but they must pay attention to their goal and manage their physical body and what they say and how they say it, all while keeping this intention at the front of their mind. Moreover, kids with poor executive function might not even recognise that the situation demands certain behaviour. *They have to know they have a goal.*

A fundamental aspect of self-regulation is following through on what you intend to do. Think about it: You intend to resist a doughnut, finish your taxes early, or demonstrate to your boss that you are a team player. But in high-stress mode, self-regulation is harder, and you may have trouble engineering your behaviour towards that goal. Your child is in the same boat. Despite your child's good intentions, if she is overwhelmed and unable to self-regulate, then she's less likely to be able to manage her behaviour.

Self-regulation isn't really about exercising more willpower. As your child develops the executive function skills that improve self-awareness and the ability for self-monitoring, self-calming, and adaptive thinking, his capacity to manage himself and control impulses grows; self-regulation improves. Then desirable behaviour isn't such a struggle; it isn't a test of willpower. It becomes the natural result of a calmer, more focused, and aware child who can take purposeful action to carry out his intentions—mentally, physically, and verbally.

EMOTIONAL REGULATION: BIG EMOTIONS TAKE A BIG TOLL

Shanti, eleven, tends to have a big reaction to even little problems. She can be snappy and irritable. She is anxious and agitated most of the day. She starts out happy enough, but soon she is consumed by thoughts of all the negative things that might happen and all the negative things people might be thinking about her. Her anxiety and emotions build through the school day, and although she works hard to tamp down her feelings, by 3:00 p.m. she is struggling to cope. She "holds on" until she reaches her house, but then it all hits like a big wave. Overwhelmed at that point, she isn't sure how to get her homework done. She isn't sure how to interact with her peers or teammates in after-school sports. She doesn't really reach out to other kids, and when she does try to make friends, she is so anxious that she comes across as uncomfortable and odd. She starts sentences and stops them abruptly, jumps into conversations, and sometimes ignores people because she is at a complete loss for what to say. Shanti spends most of her day teetering on the verge of a meltdown. It is exhausting and humiliating. She wants to behave differently, but in the grip of her emotional distress, she cannot.

Emotional regulation is how we use coping mechanisms to manage our emotions and behaviour—basically, it helps us keep our cool even when stress makes that difficult. Children with poor emotional regulation have poor coping mechanisms for emotional ups and downs. Repeated experiences of being overwhelmed this way make the stress response even more sensitive, what psychologists call "kindled" for reactivity, and the emotional flooding happens more quickly. Unprepared to understand or respond effectively in social interactions, a child like Shanti feels the pressure of social expectations and social missteps all the more, and that chronic stress load makes self-regulation all the harder. Unable to cope, she shuts down and pulls back from people and even shuns the idea of being around them.

As we talked one afternoon, Shanti described how it felt when she had to approach a group of kids, how nervous she felt, how her stomach clenched and her hands felt cold and clammy. She used the word *scary*. I explained how self-regulation and the stress response work, that it's an ancient system the brain devised to pull the alarm when we feel threatened and channel all energy and attention to protecting ourselves. Shanti was an artist and something of a visual learner, so I drew a sabre-toothed tiger stick figure to represent something scary, and she laughed as she nodded and said, "Yes, that's just what it feels like!"

The sabre-toothed tiger became a symbol for her. As we worked on specific executive function skills to improve the way she read and interpreted social cues, and to practise initiating a conversation or play-date, her self-awareness grew, too. She described how she could now visualise herself in those situations, taking the steps she understood she must: "But sometimes I have to face my sabre-toothed tiger and I can't—he's so real for me."

That new awareness and a way to talk about it was significant for Shanti and for her parents. Now she could express how big and exhausting it felt to initiate anything. From there, with coaching and practice, she worked on specific ways to break the big emotion of fear into separate pieces and she was able to begin engaging differently.

In the fight-flight-freeze of the stress response, big, dysregulating emotions may trigger any one of those behaviours, complicating social interaction. The "fight" response shows up in aggressive behaviour. The "flight" response may explain the child who retreats, in need of some distance to reflect, re-evaluate, and restrategise to re-engage. The child who is completely overwhelmed feels frozen, immobilised, shut down. Every child with social behaviour problems has his or her own version of the sabre-toothed tiger. Once children are able to understand what's happening, they're better equipped to learn to tame it.

How's Your Child's (Metacognitive) Bird's-Eye View?

You can ask your child questions to help him see the big picture and his role in it.

Choose a specific person (or situation) that's been difficult for your child, and explain that thinking about someone's past behaviour can help us figure out what to do right now. It can also help us predict their likely future behaviours. Offer an example from your own experience. Walk through the questions to have a dialogue about your child's view of the situation:

What do I know about this person's past behaviour or usual behaviour?
What are their interests?
How have they reacted to other similar situations in the past?
What social signals are they sending?
What choices do I have?
How do my choices come across as likable, appealing behaviours?
What reaction will my behaviour get in the future?
How can I consider this person's feelings—stand in her shoes, see her perspective—when making choices about how I speak or behave towards her?

Does My Child Need a Professional Evaluation?

Many things can cause behaviours that look like commonly diagnosed disorders, such as ADD or ADHD. Hyperactivity, for instance, can be caused by a wide range of factors. A child who appears inattentive or uncooperative may have trouble hearing. Sensory or food sensitivities, chronic stress, or emotional issues can make a child anxious, agitated, distractible, or listless. All of these can make it hard for them to feel sociable and engage with other children or do their school work.

If you sense that your child's social behaviours or symptoms affect multiple areas of her life—social, academic, home life, or after-school activities—then it's worth further diagnostic assessment with a medical professional to determine the severity of the symptoms and how they impair her ability to function fully. A clinical diagnosis can identify cognitive challenges that may be impairing your child's ability to progress in critical ways. These diagnoses may include ADD, ADHD, dyslexia, nonverbal learning disabilities, social communication disorder, pervasive developmental disorder not otherwise specified, learning disabilities, and autism spectrum disorder.

A professional evaluation is the first step in securing specific interventions at school, or other services.

How to tell if your child needs a diagnosis? If your child exhibits the following extreme behaviours consistently (every day), please consider taking her to a medical professional for evaluation:

- Explosive behaviour
- Complete social withdrawal
- Severe depression
- High levels of anxiety
- Constant hyperactivity
- Dangerous impulsivity
- Acute reading problems
- Faces repeated bullying and abuse

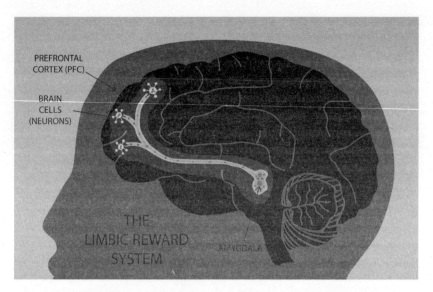

Executive function involves the neural networks for social behaviour, which can be triggered by the amygdala, which processes emotions. Full development of the prefrontal cortex (PFC) does not occur until the mid- to late twenties, but critical social, emotional, and educational development in childhood helps shape the way the cortex matures and manages the emotional reactivity of the limbic system. You want your child to have robust executive function skills for optimal development of brain-based social skills.

3

Parenting with a Playbook

You're a Natural, Coach

Nobody works harder or worries more about your child's social life than you do. At least that's true of the countless parents I've talked with and worked with over the years, parents who were concerned about their children's social awkwardness or difficulties in school and life and wanted to do something about it besides watch and worry. You may not have thought of yourself as coach material, especially not a social skills coach, but that's about to change. You're about to discover that you're a natural—in fact, you are the perfect coach for your child. Or will be soon. The basic principles and practices of social skills coaching may be new to you, but they're grounded in the same fundamental commitment you feel towards your child: You want him to have a good life, to find friends and be a friend. You want him to make a contribution and feel connected to the larger world outside himself.

You became your child's first social coach in your earliest exchanges—the loving gaze, the caring touch. You introduced the two-way "conversation" of body language, facial expressions, and emotional tone. You learned to decode his cries and sought to understand the source of his distress. You intuitively introduced the world of social cues through nurturing dialogue and the back-and-forth pattern of "serve-and-return" responses to your baby's coos and your toddler's first words. Perhaps your child's responses have been different in some ways than what you expected. But however different, you know your child's unique communication style better than anyone. That's a coaching advantage.

Studies across scientific disciplines have long established the primacy and power of parents in their child's social and emotional development.

Further, studies of children and adolescents show that at every age, parents' behaviour serves as a model for children's social skills development. What social behaviour do you model?

> Do you consistently pay attention to other people's feelings and treat them with respect?
>
> Do you engage in different kinds of conversation, from pleasant chitchat with a stranger to more substantive discussions with family, friends, and colleagues?
>
> Are you flexible, able to change plans or your approach to a situation when circumstances change?
>
> Do you venture outside your social comfort zone to meet new people or try new things?

Your child is watching and learning. By the same token:

> Do you snap at people when you feel impatient or frustrated?
>
> Do you live on your phone or laptop, often distracted by calls, texts, emails, or other digital activity?

As your child's original translator and interpreter of the world, you've been executive function personified—the ship captain's ship captain—managing those complex social tasks until your child develops the brain-based connections and skills to do it himself. Just as you showed your young child how to dress herself or tie her shoes, you are, by your own behaviour, saying, "Here, let me show you how."

Researchers at the Centre on the Developing Child at Harvard University identify three foundational principles for healthy child development:

1. Having a thoughtful, responsive relationship with your child.
2. Strengthening core life skills for social interaction, emotional health, and learning.
3. Reducing stress in all areas of life and learning.

The *Play Better Plan* is built upon those same principles. It's grounded in the power of the parent/child relationship. Think of it as parenting with a playbook: adding purposeful attention and problem-solving strategies to coach your child in social skills that are lagging. Your child learns that in this daunting arena of social learning, even on his worst days he can count on you, not only for comfort and encouragement, but also for meaningful coaching in the practical skills he needs.

Another advantage you have as coach: location, location, location. You're there. At pivotal points and unstructured stretches throughout your child's day, from drive times to bedtimes, from homework to housework, you can observe your child. You can plan coaching sessions for times when she is likely to have the attention and energy for them, take advantage of teachable moments that arise unexpectedly, and make adjustments as you go, play by play, through the day.

PAVE THE WAY FOR COACHING AND CONVERSATION

Before you start conversations with your child about tough stuff, it always helps to have prepped and paved the way. Take time to envision yourself talking with your child in a way that says you are loving and caring. What tone do you want to use? What relationship do you want to have in the future? It's not only that you want to pave the way for the coaching conversations. You want to create the experience of being a conversational family, a conversational partner, so your child knows: *In this family, we talk about things that matter to us. We care about each other and we're respectful, honest, and supportive in our conversation.*

You'll also want to be sure you practise what you preach. If you are a person who never socialises, then consider the message that sends to your child. If you tend to get really angry with your child when they push you too far, then your prep work is to practise pausing and calming your emotional reactivity. I know a mother whose route to our weekly appointment took her past a prison, and she always arrived at my office in tears. She explained that every time she looked at the prison, she felt overwhelmed because she feared that her son's learning disabilities would make him unemployable and friendless, and eventually he'd end up there. Her son could sense her dark expectations. Her prep work for herself was practising stress reduction and self-regulation. Learning to coach her son in these skills also helped her shift from those terrible fears and feelings of hopelessness to a more optimistic—and now realistic—view. Some parents tell me they have a lukewarm attitude about socialising. Said one, "I'm kind of guilty when it comes to the social stuff—I've always been kind of in-and-out, never really committed to group stuff—I never drink the Kool-Aid." If you're not social, then you'll need to work on that. You don't need to pledge allegiance to social groups, but it's up to you to live the example you want your child to learn. If you're routinely stressed out, as many parents are, your prep work is to practise stress reduction and self-regulation techniques.

SOCIALISATION BEGINS AT HOME

Your child may not have a social group of friends yet, but you have a family, and once your *Play Better* coaching and lessons begin, your child can practise new skills in the family setting.

That means eating together, putting the mobile phone away, having conversations. Create a vision for your family. Think about how you're going to shift your family system to make time to eat, work or study, play, and just hang out together. Dinner, movie nights, family walks, or weekly family rituals or community gatherings create shared experience and opportunities to chat and listen to one another.

This may be out of your comfort zone, and you may get pushback from some family members, but the results will be worth it for everyone. In my practice and among families that are home-coaching, the most successful families I've known have been those who embrace the idea that *everybody is working on something* and they all participate in this change process. Learning to talk about social matters, practising problem-solving to improve a situation, is what all this is about. Social behaviour isn't an isolated thing or a set of skills that apply only in certain situations.

In *The Big Disconnect: Protecting Childhood and Family Relationships in the Digital Age*, author and psychologist Catherine Steiner-Adair describes the family as an ecosystem that we can cultivate with intention to create the "sustainable family." She writes:

> The sustainable family is a family that has created a fabric of connectivity that is strong and many layered . . . It values family life above life online and has the wherewithal to understand that you cannot create a sustainable quality of family togetherness unless you make it a priority . . . That can seem a daunting task, but so much of it comes down to day-to-day choices we make in the moment with our children. That is not to suggest they are always easy choices to make or implement, but they are essential ones if we care about our children's futures.

Look at your family ecosystem, specifically the way your family time is structured to include shared "social" time together, as well as time for everyone's individual interests. These are the increasingly rare opportunities children have to be part of face-to-face, in-person conversations and pick up the nuances of language, tone, timing, facial expressions, the back-and-forth rhythm of conversation, and how all of those qualities affect the way we interpret what we hear, and how others experience us. If your child is withdrawing from the family, he isn't working on executive function social skills. He can't do it alone—or on a screen.

Social behaviour doesn't happen in a vacuum. Make socialisation something you *do* and *talk about* as a family: care, converse, work, and play together. Many of the *Play Better* activities you'll find in the pages ahead are fun for everyone.

YOUR CHILD IS WATCHING YOU

As you prepare to start this more purposeful coaching approach to your child's skill building, take stock of your own behaviours and mind-set, what they communicate to your child, and how you practise social skills in everyday interactions with your child, your family, your friends, and others.

You model the executive function social skills described in Chapter 2 when you

- show empathy (imagine someone else's experience and feelings)
- express genuine interest and curiosity in other people
- use a welcoming tone
- anticipate possible reactions of others to something you may do or say
- point out social cues in everyday settings like the checkout queue, a restaurant, a school, or a community event
- cope with disappointment (emotional regulation, reflection, interpreting unhappy moments as only temporary setbacks)
- talk about what is hard for you, what takes you out of your comfort zone
- resolve conflict without being aggressive, seek to repair frayed social relationships
- pitch in to help others or collaborate
- take mix-ups or mistakes in stride and refocus to try again (flexibility).

In your coaching, you'll engage with your child in a calm, thoughtful manner and organise time for coaching and playdates. You'll be the keeper of the plan and of the practice goals you'll develop together. In your back-and-forth conversation, you'll show what it means to take someone else's perspective, asking your child to share his point of view: "What was your experience?" "How did you feel about that?" "What are some different ways you might respond?" In this style of conversation, your child is naturally drawn into the practice of reflecting on her behaviour and emotional state, remembering an experience, and talking about it. You'll manage time, focus attention, point out successes, brainstorm new behavioural strategies, and maintain a positive outlook on your child's efforts.

As your child's coach, you'll come to see the world through your child's eyes and create the space and the conversation for her to come to her own insights about herself in relation to others. And then one day...she'll be able to do it herself.

The *Play Better* Simulation Practice

Stop-Action Cue and Review Helps Your Child Practise Self-Regulation

Instead of just scolding or correcting your child when behaviour goes awry, you can use my simple coaching technique called "simulation" to guide your child through a self-regulation exercise to read his own emotional state, recognise how it feels when big emotions are in runaway mode, and practise pausing to calm himself and choose how to manage his feelings effectively.

Other *Play Better* coaching techniques—discussing desirable behaviours, modelling, role-playing, and having your child practise them in coaching sessions—each teach in a different and important way. Simulation practice is unique in that you use it in everyday situations to help your child develop the executive function needed to interrupt spiraling emotional behaviour and practise self-regulation.

Remembering spoken instructions isn't a strong suit for a child with lagging executive function skills. But experience is remembered and retrieved quite differently in the brain. Practising an experience lays down a neural network that supports your child's ability to call it up and do it again. Simulation turns learning new executive function skills into an *active* experience in real time that involves the senses, movement and muscle memory, emotions and thought processes. That's what makes a lesson stick!

STEP 1: "HERE'S HOW IT WORKS"

Prepare your child for the simulation practice by recalling a recent time when you noticed that he became dysregulated or overwhelmed in a situation. Explain that simulation practice will be impromptu—when you see this happening again, you'll interrupt to do this practice together. You can say to your child: *We're going to work together on this because I understand that you want to improve this situation and use your strategies, but sometimes you forget them when you feel overwhelmed.* It's helpful to practise right then and there. Explain that in those situations, you're going to interrupt with a pre-agreed cue, have him pause to identify the feelings driving his behaviour, and coach him through other ways he could manage his emotional state in the moment. That's the deal.

STEP 2. PRACTISE SIMULATION IN EVERYDAY SITUATIONS

Pick your moments. It could be a squabble between siblings, signs of a meltdown coming over a TV choice or quitting a video game, or simply uncontrolled excitement that needs to be dialled down. The guided practice in which he experiences going from a dysregulated state to a calm one helps him learn what strategies work for him. No need to focus strictly on stressful situations to practise strategies. Silly or energetic play can become wild, uncontrolled behaviour that you can use to step in and guide a practice that involves the questions, reflection, and your child practising his strategies for calming and self-regulation and choosing a desired social behaviour to keep the play going—and fun.

STEP 3. CUE THE BREAK AND ASK OPEN QUESTIONS

Interrupt the hyper behaviour with a verbal cue.

You might say: *I notice that you're getting upset*...Or *You seem to be struggling with some big feelings*...Or *You seem to be having trouble calming down.*

Then make the connection between behaviour and emotions. You can say:

How do you feel?
What's going on in your body right now?
Describe what's happening for you right now.
What does this feel like?
How excited are you on a scale of 1 to 5?
What will happen if you keep on with (this activity) when you feel this way?
What do you think you can do differently?
How would that change the outcome?

STEP 4. BRAINSTORM STRATEGIES

Draw his attention to the connection between his feelings and his options for managing them in the moment. *What is something you could do right now to (calm yourself, bring those big feelings down to size)?* Brainstorm strategies. The experience of pausing, getting in touch with his emotional state, and calming so that he can resume play is the point of this exercise. Once your child is calm and your conversation concluded, play can resume. Review in your next coaching session.

"Game-ify" Everyday Fun to Exercise Executive Function Skills

You don't need an excuse to have fun with your child, but many simple games and family activities promote executive function social skills. They create an enjoyable experience that also prepares your child for the more focused coaching and lesson activities ahead. Guessing games like charades or "I spy with my little eye" or stop-and-start freeze-action games like "red light/green light" involve executive functions as a child watches or listens for cues, brainstorms ideas, takes turns, anticipates what's expected, and adapts to the unexpected, all in fun.

Because kids learn best by *doing*, the concept of simulation—activity that duplicates a real-life experience—is the basis for many of the *Play Better* lesson activities. For example, if your child has meltdowns over sharing, then in a simulation he would imagine himself in that situation and simulate how upset he gets—but then practise the new skill he'll use to stop, calm himself, and respond appropriately.

Get on the Same Page—with Enthusiasm and Support

As parents and family, it's important to show unanimous support for your child's effort and commitment to the *Play Better* coaching programme. If you are coaching solo, then enlist the support of close family and friends as an insider social group with whom your child can practise and complete other coaching activities. If any family members are unwilling to be actively supportive, then ask them to at least not stand in the way.

4

The Seven Things Everyone Needs to Be Able to Do to Be Socially Successful

You have to take the long view with kids and socialisation. It may be all you can do to focus on the challenges of one child, one day at a time. You have your hands full. So, please, let me.

I'm not concerned solely about whether our children survive the day without suffering social bruises or inflicting them. When we look at children and examine their executive function social skills development, we need the end-goal in mind. Our goal is that years from now these skills will have carried them through to make the most of their potential in their personal lives, their work, and their own sense of belonging in the world.

The mother of a brilliant ten-year-old boy was deeply worried because her son, Neil, had what she considered a serious attitude problem about school and making friends there. It showed up as disruptive behaviour during class that distracted other children and required the teacher's attention. His grades suffered, too, not because he didn't know the material but because he blew off assignments when he felt like it. Meanwhile, he had developed a negative attitude about school and homework, and he insisted that his lack of friends wasn't important; he said he didn't need them. That was his story.

Neil's parents were most frustrated about his grades—he had to have high grades to get into the school's more advanced-level classes, so he was shooting himself in the foot with his behaviour. His parents constantly appealed to teachers to give him a break, arguing that he was so far ahead of the other kids academically that he just couldn't relate to them. Then one day his mother read a *Forbes* magazine article that interviewed experts about the most important "people skills" everyone needs to succeed in the workplace. She looked down the list and she realised: "My son cannot do this." Seeing the description of these basic social skills and how the lack of them ultimately holds people back in their adult lives and careers jarred her out of rationalising any longer about her son's situation. As advanced as Neil might be in some subject areas, he was way behind the curve in these basic but essential social skills. A glimpse of the long view helped her focus on the concrete goal of helping Neil develop the people skills he'd need to take his great potential into the real world and, at the very least, hold down a job and function in his adult life in ten years' time.

Whatever your child's story, our job as parents is to prepare our children to survive and thrive in life. Social skills problems travel with children into adolescence, when they predictably worsen, and then into adulthood, where the lack of people skills not only isolates them socially, but also keeps them from getting or switching jobs, pursuing dreams, or speaking to their boss or attaining promotions. Now is the time to start. Like tying their shoes or learning to read, eventually they'll forget what it took to learn it—the skills become second nature.

BEHAVIOURS EVERYONE NEEDS TO BE SOCIALLY SUCCESSFUL

- **Manage emotions rather than let them manage you.** The ability to realise when you are experiencing "big emotions" and adapt, rather than expecting everyone to change for you. You need to be able to respond to disappointment and have coping techniques to respond to flooding emotions without becoming overwhelmed.

- **Read the room.** What's the prevailing vibe or emotional tone of those present? Is there an activity or conversation under way? Is it structured, with expectations about your role and how to participate? Or is it less structured, allowing for a more casual and spontaneous way for you to join in? What do you need to do to adjust your energy level, tone, or expectations to match the setting? What would others expect of you in this setting?

- **Meet people halfway.** This could mean introducing yourself, starting a conversation, or answering a question when you're asked. Even just a smile and friendly acknowledgement can be enough to signal to another person that you're sociable and open for business. Sometimes halfway means physically stepping forwards to be social rather than hanging back on the edges, or just staying home.

- **Understand social cues and unspoken rules and be ready to change your behaviour in response to them.** This involves reading people's facial expressions and body language, and being aware of your own. Verbal cues might seem easier, but they require that you pay attention to what others are saying, which can be challenging if you routinely tune out others and prefer to stay tuned in to your own thoughts.

- **Learn to walk in someone else's shoes, or see things through their eyes.** To understand someone else's perspective means to understand, to some degree, their motives and reactions. This includes their reactions to you. You need to understand that every behaviour and every action you take makes an impression on other people, and they operate and react to you with those thoughts in mind.

- **Be flexible and adaptive.** Don't be the Rule Police. Accept that you are not always right. Understand that part of your social role is to compromise, and recognise that at times it's appropriate to place friendship or the larger group ahead of being right. Don't be argumentative. This includes knowing when to drop the debate and accept no for an answer.

- **Know your audience and adapt your communication to be appropriate.** For a five-year-old this means filtering what is public and private information and learning not to insult teachers and friends by saying thoughtless things that hurt feelings or ruffle feathers, like "Your dress makes you look fat," or "My mum says you are lazy." A ten-year-old needs to be able to anticipate or predict what friends want to hear about, what they find interesting, and what they would like to talk about. You may also need to adapt your tone, stories, and other information you choose to share, depending on the age and interests of those around you.

Chances are that your child faces some challenges in at least a few of these essential social skills—that's why you're here. In the chapters ahead, we'll get down to the coaching conversations, skill-building lessons, and practice and problem-solving strategies that are going to give your child the skills and confidence to change his behaviour. How we approach that task, and how we teach our kids to do so, is based on the science of behavioural change and the steps that have a track record of success in helping people make the changes they desire.

A MEMORY OF ONE SUCCESS CAN BE YOUR CHILD'S TOUCHSTONE FOR CONFIDENCE TO TRY

When a child is attempting to change behaviour in an area of weakness, he needs to remember that things *can* work out. There are experiences that can make you aware of your greatness or potential. These can be galvanising.

We're always trying to get kids to move forward, but one of the hardest parts is for them to believe that change can actually happen. So, one thing we talk about a lot is "knowing." If a child has a strength and can remember a time they did something amazing—and every child has one of those—then we can revisit that memory with them and bring it alive for them. What resides *in* memory now becomes accessible for them to draw *from* memory. In a social setting, this ability to remember and apply lessons learned to new situations is an executive function skill that helps them in many other ways. This is how they'll remember when their behaviour has worked well for them and when it didn't. They'll use it to remember how a particular child responded to them or a situation, and to think about that the next time they are around that child.

A memory of success—any success—acts in the brain as a shortcut to confidence. As parents, we typically praise our child's accomplishment, but as a coach, the point is to help them connect with the feeling of confidence and the excitement they felt when they experienced the success. As a coach, we remind them, "You have had this experience of success," and we can say, "Tell me about that time, and what it felt like and how you did this." In recognising this past experience and talking about it, the memory becomes a "knowing" about themselves; it helps them see that, based on their own experience, things *can* work out for them, especially around their strengths. We can ask them to take that leap forwards as they meet new challenges in coaching. Not a leap of blind faith but a leap based on their own knowing.

WITH PRACTICE AND "MINI-WINS," SOCIAL SKILLS BECOME HABITS OF BEING

When we talk about the social behaviours that everyone needs to have, we're referring to more than isolated performances of a skill. We're talking about habits of being. In *The Power of Habit: Why We Do What We Do in Life and Business*, author Charles Duhigg suggests that a habit takes 18 to 254 days or an average of 66 days to develop. So the *Play Better* exercise,

Reading the Room, isn't just an activity. With repetition, reading the room can become a habit.

Science tells us that the longer we hold on to perceptions and habits of thought, the more deeply imbedded they become. The brain's circuitry—the networks of neurons and the paths they create—becomes stronger with use and weaker with less use. The brain actively prunes away the lesser used connections in favour of the more heavily used ones. In this way, your child's story about his behaviour becomes the self-talk, the inner voice that encourages or discourages him. Studies also show that in the brain, negative self-perception intensifies our reaction to negative thoughts and experiences and weakens the impact of positive ones. That's how self-talk becomes a self-fulfilling prophecy: *I just don't fit in. I'm too stupid. I don't…I'm not…I'll never.* It becomes harder and harder to dig out of that self-talk rut and the behaviours that only dig the rut deeper.

For that reason, the sooner we address these stories that hold children back, the less entrenched those narratives are and the sooner we can help our kids change the story and the self-talk. Step-by-step, with incremental successes—mini-wins—your child builds the skills and strengthens the brain's circuitry for positive social behaviour.

PART II

The *Play Better Plan*

The Coach's Playbook:

Coaching Guides, Questionnaires, and Tools

5

The Eight Elements of Highly Effective Social Skills Coaching

EFFECTIVE COACHING IS A WAY OF BEING WITH AND COMMUNICATING WITH YOUR CHILD

The core principles of effective parent coaching for social skills are based on proven strategies and techniques that support positive behavioural change. You don't have to be some superparent with all the answers. You don't have to fix your child or fix everybody else to accommodate your child. Set aside every discouraging assumption you've ever had about your child and remind yourself: *If they could, they would.* If they had the executive function skills to connect with others and make friends, then they would. The way your child's brain is wired makes it harder for her to connect socially with other children. Your coaching and the *Play Better* playbook is about to change that.

Effective coaching is more than an attitude or a superficial style. It is a way of being and communicating with your child—a positive predictability and problem-solving approach in the way you listen and respond to your child. Positive predictability means that you reliably respond in ways that encourage, illuminate, engage, and empower your child, cultivating his innate capacity to change and grow. "How would you like things to be different?" "How would you rather be in that situation?" "What would you like friendship to look like?" You want to give your child the roadmap for change by asking where she wants to go, rather than simply telling her to change or even telling her what she needs to do to change. A problem-solving approach means leading your child through the process to help her develop problem-solving skills—not trying to solve the problem *for* her.

Your child needs direct experience in the step-by-step brain-based processes that develop social awareness, self-awareness, self-regulation, and positive social behaviours. Your coaching, using the following simple techniques and the *Play Better* lessons, coaching tools, and skill-building activities, creates those learning experiences for your child.

THE COACH APPROACH

Reflective listening, open inquiry, and praise and prompting

Three basic communication techniques are the foundation for all of the *Play Better* coaching principles, practices, and activities ahead. The parent/child relationship is a powerful channel for communication, and these techniques build on that natural connection. For that reason, they are simpler than you might think. They enhance your communication with your child *any*time, so go ahead and start using them. The more your child becomes accustomed to this quality of conversation with you in everyday ways, the more you are prepping and paving the way for the coaching conversations and lessons ahead.

Reflective listening

In reflective listening, you first listen to what your child tells you, then restate or summarise—reflect back to your child—what you've heard, showing that you understand what's been said. If you haven't understood, then your child can say so and clarify so that you're both on the same page as you continue your conversation. Reflective listening helps you understand and empathise with your child. It helps her feel understood and validated. That's especially important for children who struggle socially: they typically spend a lot of time feeling misunderstood and misjudged, never getting a chance to explain themselves.

Because you paraphrase his comments and reflect his ideas back to him, you also allow your child to hear himself more objectively, which can lead to insights that he might miss in the rush of an ordinary conversation. For example, he might declare that he believes that "people should invite me to play—I shouldn't have to approach them." When you "reflect" this statement back to him—"What I hear you saying is that you won't approach anyone; they must come to you"—you accomplish two things. First, you invite him to clarify or correct what he intended to communicate when he said that. Also, by inviting him to review your interpretation of his statement, he hears it fresh himself, through you and not solely in the echo chamber of his own mind. The simple act of hearing his ideas expressed back to him, then thinking about how he was heard and how that compares with what he intended to communicate, are all executive function tasks that your response has now prompted him to do. Over time, your practice of reflective listening will enable him to develop his thought processes and insight about his social behaviour.

Open-ended questions

The second basic coaching communication technique is to ask non-judgemental open-ended questions—questions that begin with *how, what, when, and where.* These questions invite conversation instead of yes/no responses, which are conversation dead ends. Open-ended questions tap into a child's curiosity and her eagerness to offer information that you value. "How did the other kids act when Martin did that?" "What do you think made Kate get angry?" What you're really asking is for your child to think about what she observed in a social setting. You're asking her to bring the memory forwards, think about it in retrospect, and glean social and emotional clues now that she wasn't necessarily tuned in to at the time. When children are asked these types of questions, they learn to self-evaluate, comparing their own ideas about their behaviour and the social world against their parents' ideas and expectations. The combination of open questions and reflective listening promotes a wide range of executive function skills required for social problem-solving. *(To adapt open-ended questions for children with autism spectrum disorder, see the sidebar on this later in this chapter.)*

The question you want to answer in your own mind is this: *How come?* How come the other children don't want to play with my child? How come my child is melting down or blowing up in this situation? Look at the difference between the question, *Lucy, why did you do that?* which puts the child on the spot to explain herself, and the more effective *How come?* questions designed to help you both better understand: *What happened? What do you believe about why it happened? How do you feel when someone behaves that way towards you?* That's how you get the accurate information you need to understand why this is happening to your child, and focus your coaching more effectively.

If your child says, "I don't know" or "I don't remember," you can ask these questions:

- What do you think your (teacher, friend, or other) would say?
- Can you tell me what you know about this?

- What is one thing, no matter how small, that you can remember?
- If you had a golden ticket like Charlie in the Chocolate Factory, and you could say anything on this topic, what would you say?

When a child feels put on the spot with questions, they sometimes freeze up. Give them time and circle back.

Use humour. *Let's make a deal: Tell me four words you do not want me to say today. If I promise not to say those four words, then you promise not to say "I don't know."* Give them crazy options and get them laughing and they'll protest: "No, it's not *that*—it's *this*!"

Praise and prompting

Praise and prompting are how you acknowledge your child's effort and progress. For a child who is struggling, praise is a clear and encouraging message that he is making progress. Celebrate every win, stop looking for complete transformations all at once, and instead say, "Wow, I saw you try, and that is progress." Maybe your child stopped himself from responding impatiently or angrily to someone. Maybe he offered to share a toy. Your praise is for taking that positive step forwards. A child who is oblivious to his role in a social setting first has to develop the awareness that he *has* a role before he can make the connection between awareness, intention, and action. Rather than constantly look for your child to get everything right, acknowledge and cheer signs of change and effort. Awareness, intention, or any demonstrable action *is significant* progress.

Prompts are signals or cues to remind children of a positive behaviour they want to practise. In coach mode, you'll use prompts or cues discreetly to draw their attention to their behaviour. You might have agreed that a certain cue means, "What do you think your friend wants to play?" Like a high five or thumbs-up, this shorthand messaging can help children make a quick mental connection between their action and the intention they've been focused on in their coaching lesson. It is also a way to prompt them to pause and pay attention to their emotions, body, and environment.

COACHING IN ACTION/LISTEN IN

PARENT: Hey, buddy, I notice your friend left. What's going on?
NED: He left because no one likes me and he was just boring anyway.
PARENT: Hmm, what if you walked me through the playdate? What did you two do?

NED: I played a video game.

PARENT: Interesting. What about your friend?

NED: He watched.

PARENT: I am wondering what your friend felt when he did not play and he just watched?

NED: Oh, he likes it.

PARENT: Hmm, but what if *you* just watched and didn't get to play? What would that feel like?

NED: I would be fine.

PARENT: Hmm, I am wondering, what is your job as a host and a friend? What does it look like to play with someone?

NED: Oh, I guess I kind of just played and didn't think about him.

Ned just acknowledged that he doesn't think about his friend's feelings. Ordinarily, that would be a disappointing thing to hear. But Ned wasn't divulging anything his mother didn't know already. What was new, and represented important progress, is that he had come to this realisation about his behaviour himself. It was his insight, not his mother's corrective mantra.

THE EIGHT PRINCIPLES OF HIGHLY EFFECTIVE COACHING

These are the eight guiding principles that will make you the very best, most effective social skills coach you can be for your child. They become your frame of mind and help keep you grounded in coach mode, mindful of your purpose and your role as a coach as you engage with your child in the conversations and activities ahead. Whenever a trying moment threatens to derail you, let these principles help you get back on track.

1. Ask, don't tell
2. Listen and learn
3. Keep your cool
4. Hold the metacognitive mirror up
5. Honour your child's *aha*
6. Prep first, then pave the way
7. Meet them where they are
8. Be a cheerleader

Principle 1: Ask, don't tell

Ask questions with genuine, respectful curiosity to find out what's going on for your child. You want to understand what is happening and understand it through her eyes and her experience. We miss so much when we assume that we know someone's reasons for their actions or beliefs, their fears or hopes. Anytime your child baulks at doing something you've suggested, who's to say whether it's because she's afraid of the unknown, she's remembering a past experience that makes her cautious, or she'd just rather do something else? You don't know until you hear her reasons.

Peel the onion. Peel away the layers to find out more about the problem, what's really going on.

Principle 2: Listen and learn

Welcome what your child has to say. Be calm, listen, and make him comfortable. Hold the moment open in a neutral way. When you feel the urge to do or say something to *fix a situation* or *correct* your child, push pause on that impulse: self-regulate! Take a deep breath. Relax your shoulders. Let go of the need to do more than invite, listen, acknowledge, and accept.

As parents, we're limited by the fact that we don't know what goes on at school or whenever we're not around, and what's getting in the way for our child socially. You need intel and your child has it. Ground yourself in the coaching moment:

> I'm in learning mode.
> I'm curious.
> The purpose of this conversation is to figure out what my child thinks—not what I think.

Principle 3: Keep your cool

Coaching calls for a little detachment so you can be the calm partner your child needs for problem-solving. This is about your child—not about you. It's important to keep your cool even if what you hear makes you angry or frustrated. Remember that you're not looking for a single answer and you're not looking to be right. You want to create an emotionally safe, supportive environment based on mutual respect, trust, and appreciation. Your child likely already spends a lot of time feeling unheard or misunderstood. He needs to be assured that you're there *to talk about things in a calm way and that you believe in him.* Kids are thrilled, or at least relieved, to be able to tell their side of the story to us.

Think of yourself as a detective, not a judge. You want to gather information and try to see your child's social situation from her perspective. Your calm coaching response will allow you a little emotional distance, which goes a long way to finding a helpful middle ground to problem-solve with your child. No need to fuss or fume. No need to lecture or bring up the past. No need to get agitated if she doesn't respond to a question right away or get irritated if her response frustrates you. Breathe in, breathe out. Compose yourself.

Principle 4: Hold the metacognitive mirror up

We can't always see ourselves through others' eyes and understand how our behaviour is affecting other people and influencing the way they treat us. Metacognition and the other brain-based executive functions that enable us to see ourselves as part of a bigger picture serve as a kind of mirror that lets us see our behaviour and its impact with some objectivity. When children lack that metacognitive mirror, we can hold it up for them until they learn how to do it themselves. In coach mode, we can ask, "Okay, what do you wish you had done?" We ask about next time and the playmate's feelings: "How would you feel? I notice that sometimes you forget about your playmate's feelings—you said you didn't think your playmate cared, but think about how you just said you would feel. Given that, how important is it to remember to think about a friend's feelings?"

When you ask your child to describe his own or someone else's behaviour, or to reflect on how someone made him feel, or to imagine how his behaviour made someone else feel, you're holding the mirror up for him. When you hold the mirror and engage your child in the kind of conversational inquiry we've outlined above—*ask, don't tell* and *listen and learn*—you actively coach him through the steps of metacognition and those brain-based skills of reflection and perspective-taking. This is how an exercise becomes experience, how coaching for executive function social skills becomes the experience itself in the brain, and builds those skills.

Principle 5: Honour your child's *aha*

An *aha* is simply a moment of self-discovery. We've all had epiphanies in our lives and you know from experience that no one can have an *aha* for you. It's an inside job.

In coaching, your child's *aha* will arise from realisations in the process of growing awareness, reflection, goal-setting, and problem-solving. At the start of your coaching lessons, your child's *aha* may disappoint you because it isn't what you'd hoped for. He may come to the *aha* that "I don't listen" or the realisation that "I'm not working that hard at this friendship stuff because I don't think there's any point." Recognise that every *aha* is progress. If we shut them down with a quick correction or lecture about how they *should* be, then we've shut down the conversation, their process of reflection, and the opening for the next *aha*.

Even the smallest *aha* is a bold expression of the brain's executive function bringing a child's picture into focus in her own mind. Executive function connects the dots, and every *aha* is a dot in the picture. Whether your child is five years old or fifteen, she's going to have these realisations when she's ready, developmentally and emotionally. Coaching isn't about ordering up the *aha* or telling your child what it should be. Coaching creates the space and time for her to discover this insight herself, which is the most powerful source of learning a child can have.

Principle 6: Prep first, then pave the way

We often talk about "paving the way" for a sensitive or difficult conversation. But even before we pave the way, we prep the ground. You may be coaching only one child through the *Play Better* lessons, but everyone in your household is on their own learning curve—*everyone is working on something*—and you can establish house rules and family routines that include together time, habits of conversation and routine social interaction, and problem-solving and thinking about how our words and actions affect other people. This starts with one another. Lay the groundwork for problem-solving and changing habits of behaviour by modelling for your child that it's okay to need help and ask for it. Share stories from work and elsewhere about how people do what they can for themselves, but sometimes they need to ask for help—it's normal! Let your child know what a go-to person is and that you would love to be her "go-to" person for social situations and friends and all things.

Principle 7: Meet them where they are

If your goals or expectations are always more than your child is ready to tackle, you're going to spend a lot of time making plans that fall through and feeling frustrated (or worse) with your child for failing to measure up. Your child's experience will be one of not only failing in her social task but failing you, too. Better that you recognise your child's capabilities at the present time and work with what's real. That helps you both focus on goals and plans that are realistic. That's where the wins come.

Also, if your child is immature or shy or an extravert or an introvert, that is who they are. We are all just becoming our best selves. As parents and as coaches, we aren't trying to change an introvert into someone they are not. We're trying to help them be able to make choices, have choices, and go after whatever fulfills them, from preschool to careers, from friendships to family relationships. If they are immature *for their age*, then our goal is to show them what age-appropriate reactions and expectations are, and help them get there.

Principle 8: Be a cheerleader

When you celebrate positive steps, small wins, or your child's *aha*, that's how you keep the momentum going. Some parents worry that this is false praise. It isn't. Small successes are progress and deserve a high five. They are essential steps to reach the larger goals.

Your newborn didn't arrive with the motor skills to run a marathon. You didn't see your toddler take her first steps and shrug because she wasn't on the track team yet. You cheered. You encouraged. Now, for your child, the executive function social skills challenges are the marathon. Mark the milestones. You're saying to your child, in effect: "You put yourself on the field, you caught the ball, you tried harder at something that's hard for you. Those are three things to celebrate."

Positive reinforcement isn't empty praise. What you pay attention to grows, and when you highlight a desired behaviour with positive recognition, the brain makes a mental note of it—literally. It reinforces the neural connections to do it again.

How to Trade the Language of "Tell-Tell-Tell" for "Listen and Learn"

How many times have you said, "How many times have I told you...?"

To make the shift from the "tell-tell-tell" mind-set to the more effective coaching practice of "listen and learn," start by trading phrases.

- Instead of *try harder*, you can say: "What's getting in your way? What would you like to do differently? What are you expected to do as a friend?"
- Instead of "Be more friendly," you can say: "What do you think being friendly and likable looks like? What are you doing that is friendly?"
- Instead of "Stop being difficult," you can say: "What's going on for you right now?"

- Instead of "Your attitude about this is so negative," you can say: "What is the story you are telling yourself?" Or "I hear you being kind of negative. What is going on for you?"
- Instead of "Get control of yourself," you can say: "You're the boss of your behaviour—how can you take charge of (your body, your words) right now?"
- Instead of "You have to approach other children," you can say: "What could you do to help you join a group of children playing? What would it be like to approach other kids instead of playing alone?" or "What do you like about playing alone?"

BUT... WHAT IF MY CHILD DOESN'T JUST "OPEN UP" AND SHARE WHAT'S GOING ON?

Ask around. Get information from other sources. Chapter 9 will show you how to bring up hard topics and share information with your child, incidents you have learned about from school counsellors and teachers, from your own volunteering at school, from other siblings, and from family or friends. Don't hesitate to reach out to find the information you need to know.

If Your Child Has Autism or Difficulty with Open-Ended Questions

Children (and adults) with autism spectrum disorder can do this programme, but they will struggle with open-ended questions. Questions need to be more situation-specific because children with autism struggle to imagine wide-open situations and to pinpoint an answer. The lessons are wonderful to develop perspective-taking, self-regulation, and the other executive functions. Questions just need to be adjusted. So instead of "What can you do to fit in?" you would say, "Let's pick some specific things you can do to fit in." I find that the *What do you notice about...* questions work well. And "How does Mummy act when she is busy? What do you guess Mummy feels when she is busy?" are ways to develop essential mind-sets to understand the social world. Note: Adding any visual cues and pictures to lessons and discussions will help a child with autism develop an understanding of the lesson.

YOU'VE GOT THIS!

These are the guiding principles of coaching, especially coaching children. In the chapters ahead, you'll see how to use them with your child, from the kitchen table to drive times, from playground to playdates to parties and beyond. The more you use them, the easier they become. That's what makes them habit-forming—in the best way!

6

The Processing Style Questionnaire

Assessing Your Child's Strengths, Interests, and Processing Style

Strengths, interests, and processing style make learning "stick."

Most of us would rather do things we're good at or enjoy. Children are no different. Your child will be much more invested in tackling social skills challenges if some part of it involves something she already feels good about. Her strengths are natural links for developing skill-building strategies and practices.

Doing something fun or interesting makes the brain brighten up—*activate*—eager and open and ready for action. That's the first step in bringing executive functions online. One child may brighten at the prospect of building structures or solving puzzles. Another might prefer playing make-believe or football. Your child may not think of these interests as strengths—they're just stuff he likes to do. But that's the point. To borrow from *Mary Poppins*, your child's strengths and interests are the spoonful of sugar that helps the medicine go down. Especially if your child has had a tough time socially, it helps to feel a bit of confidence or enthusiasm heading into the challenge of changing their behaviour and learning new skills.

The science and theory of behavioural change says that if you want to shift your mind-set and be more open to learning new things, being in your house of strengths really helps. It's like an open door and a welcome mat to what's new; it helps learning stick. You can't stay in that house *all* the time. You need to step out and make your way in the world. But when you can carry some confidence in your pocket, you're better prepared to meet new challenges and opportunities.

STRENGTHS-BASED LESSONS AND COACHING BOOST CONFIDENCE, COMPETENCE, AND DEEP LEARNING

Drawing on the abilities and skills we have helps any of us problem-solve through new challenges. With every incremental step towards her goals, your child's confidence and competence grow. Self-awareness deepens. Think of it as a bank account. Her assets are always there to draw upon, and every new gain goes into the bank and expands her resources for new ventures.

Kids who struggle socially often feel stuck and tend to be a bit shut down. They don't see their own strengths, or what I call their Inner Titan. They often see themselves as "losers" or "not good at anything." When their social efforts fail and they are constantly confused or unsure why, that only makes them feel worse about themselves. In the coaching conversations ahead, with the insights you gain from the Processing Style Questionnaire (PSQ), you'll be able to hold the mirror up—point out your child's strengths when he can't see them. When a child can remember and reflect on an experience of success, that sense of competence in one area can boost his sense of confidence in others. This can be especially helpful when your child hits a snag or setback and needs an extra boost to re-engage in lessons and practice.

Strengths make learning stick. As the cognitive psychologist Peter Brown and his co-authors explain in *Make It Stick: The Science of Learning*, new research tells us that the brain-based skills that determine how memory is encoded, consolidated, and later retrieved make for deep learning. Every step in the *Play Better Plan* is designed to reinforce those brain-based mechanisms for memory, along with other brain-based skills, to make the lessons stick.

YOUR CHILD'S PROCESSING STYLE IS A HIDDEN STRENGTH

You may have heard the term *processing style* used to mean a "learning style." In the *Play Better Plan*, I use *processing style* simply to mean the way the brain most readily processes information and experience. Think of it as a strength. Learning often takes us outside our comfort zone—that's the point! Behavioural change is especially challenging, and children with lagging executive function social skills are routinely outside their comfort zone. Your child's processing style becomes a brain-based strength for learning new social skills.

Scientists and theorists have many explanations for the ways that our brain perceives experience and how we learn from it. The *Play Better* coaching approach and the PSQ that follows represent my own take on four particular models in the field: Howard Gardner's multiple intelligences; Peter Brown and his colleagues' deep work on learning that sticks; Lea Waters's work on strengths-based learning; and Carol Dweck's defining work on developing a "growth mind-set."

The six processing styles I use are based on Howard Gardner's theory of multiple intelligences and other theories that dovetail with Gardner's:

1. Auditory (music, sound)
2. Kinesthetic (hands-on and physical movement)
3. Verbal (spoken)
4. Conceptual (ideas)
5. Visual (sight)
6. Tactile (touch)

Processing styles aren't rigid learning paths; they're accessible pathways that can help children get where they want or need to be. Each processing style has a range of ways it can be useful in tailoring lessons and activities to be a good fit for your child. For instance, a child with strong tactile and visual processing might love Lego or dollhouse play, but socially might also enjoy an art class or knitting or sewing group or playing dress-up, because those activities have strong see-it/do-it components.

Think about your child's processing style as you approach coaching sessions and the specific social skills lessons. Children with strong verbal processing abilities may be eager partners in the conversational part of coaching sessions with you. Conceptual learners likely want to understand the why and the bigger picture that makes social skills important and how a particular lesson is important to them. Some children want to sit quietly with you to engage in a two-way conversation; others open up more easily if you take a walk or shoot hoops. Whatever a child's preference, their processing style is a natural strength for learning new skills because it's already a comfort zone.

In the chapters ahead, we'll go more deeply into the step-by-step lessons that develop attention, self-awareness and awareness of others, metacognition, and other skills needed for social engagement. However, to start, the PSQ identifies ways you can coach your child and tailor lesson activities for learning that sticks.

THE PROCESSING STYLE QUESTIONNAIRE

The PSQ is designed to show patterns in the way your child most read-ily processes information and experience. Does she need to know the "why" behind something to remember it? Does she remember what she hears? Does she enjoy word play and rhyming? Base your answers on watching her in action: What engages her attention? How does she figure out new things? When you finish the questionnaire and tally the scores, the pattern of responses shows your child's dominant process-ing style and strategies for optimal learning.

Processing Style Questionnaire

Think about the six processing styles when you complete the questionnaire below, and either engage your child in the process or consider his prefer-ences when you answer.

Directions: Read the statements below and decide if they apply to your child. Put a number in the space provided, to the right of each statement/ question. Total the score for each section. A score of 17 or more indicates that that is a dominant processing style. The highest score is your dominant processing style. Many people have more than one processing style—note the other three highest scores.

Rating
1—Seldom/Never   2—Sometimes   3—Often

Auditory

Needs to hear instructions or what is being said	
Prefers to get information by listening	
Remembers what is heard	
Uses jingles and rhymes to remember things	
Associates certain big life events with music or what was said	
Speaks information out loud to clarify and remember it	
Total	

Rating
1—Seldom/Never   2—Sometimes   3—Often

Conceptual

Needs to get a big-picture understanding with all the pieces clear	
Needs to know the why behind something to remember it	
Is able to remember information when it is in the form of an analogy or example	
Understands the patterns and relationships of facts	
Teaches other people things and then the topic becomes clearer	
Likes to know the fine points of meanings	
Total	

Kinaesthetic

Needs to move in order to focus and understand	
Needs to move in order to learn and remember	
Prefers hands-on learning such as playing with objects to learn	
Assembles parts without reading directions	
Requires physical activity to learn better	
Starts a project before reading directions	
Total	

Visual

Needs to see it to know it	
Has difficulty with spoken directions	
Doodles and draws pictures and symbols to help learn information	
Thinks with pictures instead of words	
Needs to write things down or see it written down to remember	
Visualises information to remember it and remembers what is seen	
Total	

Rating
1—Seldom/Never   2—Sometimes   3—Often

Verbal

Needs to talk to work out thoughts and feelings	
Remembers when you sing things or make up little rhymes	
Talks through the steps out loud for any activity or project	
Remembers when you use a mnemonic device or script or create a song	
Talks things out to understand them	
Speaks directions out loud	
Total	

Tactile

Needs to touch or feel an object to learn. Needs to touch with hands to learn	
Needs to see someone else do an activity or have a live model before following directions	
Has trouble giving verbal explanations or directions	
Likes to solve problems through trial-and-error approach	
Likes to work on puzzles to learn or play games	
Thinks about the texture and flavours of something they are learning	
Total	

Results

Highest Score—Dominant Processing Style	
Next Highest Score	
Next Highest Score	
Next Highest Score	
Congratulations! Your Dominant Processing Style is:	

THE STRENGTHS/INTERESTS MATCHMAKER

The Strengths/Interests Matchmaker gives you specific ideas for play activities and environments that are likely to be a good fit for your child, based on the patterns you see in the PSQ and on areas of skills weakness or low-interest.

Strengths/Interests Matchmaker

Directions: Using this chart, match your child's strengths, skills, and interests within larger categories. The Strengths/Interests Matchmaker questionnaire will help you see patterns and categories of strengths and interests that are your child's natural assets. Consider the following as you determine if something is a strength:

- What are things that hold your child's attention the longest?
- If your child could do anything for a day, what would he do?
- What causes your child to express joy and happiness?
- What does he seek out?
- What does his natural curiosity bend towards?
- What does he like to do after school?

Strength (+)	Weakness (−)	
Artistic/Creative		
		Likes to paint
		Works hands-on with clay and sculpting, photography
		Loves creating, crafting/hobbies, using his/her hands
		Takes random household objects to make art
		Draws cartoons
		Writes anime books
		Cooks
		Makes potions from dirt and sticks in the garden
		Creates sandcastles
Designing/Inventing		
		Loves to make things
		Sews
		Writes software
		Designs games
		Creates Lego villages
		Uses discarded junk to create new things, such as robots

Strength (+)	Weakness (−)	
Musical/Theatrical		
		Likes to make up plays
		Writes poems and songs
		Loves to perform
		Has a natural propensity to sing, dance
		Creates skits with her toys, creating characters
		Elaborates on plotlines
		Imitates the scenes of a musical and knows every line
		Creates costumes and sets
		Enjoys dress-up
		Plays musical games
Building/Assembling		
		Loves to build
		Manipulates objects
		Always works with tools
		Crafts and creates
		Builds trains or plays with wooden blocks
		Makes models
		Glues creations together
		Makes forts
Scientific/Mathematical		
		Sees and understands patterns in nature
		Sees and understands patterns in numbers
		Loves to investigate
		Craves knowledge about how things work
		Conducts small-scale experiments
		Enjoys an ant farm
		Explores plants and animals
		Craves more knowledge about scientists and how things work

Strength (+)	Weakness (−)	
Achieving/Entrepreneurial		
		Likes to start new clubs
		Often chosen by peers to lead
		Others defer to her/him
		Thinks of solutions and then takes action
		Organises people towards a goal, bake sale, orchestra
		Plans a specific outing
Teaching/Learning		
		Curious and eager to learn new information and to share it with others
		Helpful and cares for others
		Likes to demonstrate and show things
		Teaches younger children new things
		Helps classmates understand the class project
		Good with siblings, modelling how-to and caring for them
		Athletic, and mechanical/physical
		Highly physical with excellent motor skills
		Always interested in games and sports
		Treats furniture as if it's just one big jungle gym
		Finds new sports and athletic challenges fun
		Turns every piece of paper and paper clip into a game
Results: Strengths (+) _____		Weaknesses (−) _____

YOU'VE GOT THIS!

Strengths and processing styles help you see ways to make learning—even social learning—fun. Children engage in the activity more enthusiastically, learn the lesson more deeply, retrieve and apply it to a new situation when the lesson is also fun. You'll also overcome potential objections and resistance. The results are exciting for children *and* for parents!

No Half-Empties: Every Child Is a Glass Half Full

It's easy to lose sight of your child's strengths when you're preoccupied with their weaknesses. When parents come to me with concerns about their child, it's often about disappointing marks or behaviour. They're surprised to discover that one of the first things we do is shift focus to identify their child's strengths, interests, and brain-based processing style. These are your child's inner assets and they make social learning more engaging—and successful.

7

The Executive Function Questionnaire
Assessing Your Child's Executive Function Social Skills

When you clearly see the social skills that your child needs to build, you can coach for the goal.

You would never set out on a cross-country road trip or a long hike without a map and coordinates or a navigational system. The Executive Function Questionnaire (EFQ) is your GPS. It's going to flag the problem areas, identify which ones need the most attention, and show you how they fit into the overall map of where you want to go, or in this case, where you need to coach your child so he can get there.

Once you look closely at what is getting in the way for your child, you can better understand it and how you can tailor the *Play Better* coaching conversations, lessons, and activities to pinpoint the behaviours and skills that need the most work, most urgently. What you focus on flourishes, and when you focus your coaching and your child's skill-building practice in those areas that need the most attention, you are going to see results.

The first step is to identify the most significant lagging executive function social skills and related behaviours for change. Then you can prioritise the specific new behaviours—the desirable alternative behaviours—and needed skills you'll focus on in coaching. I define a desirable behaviour as something that follows social guidelines, is positive social behaviour, and—specific to the coaching objective—is the behaviour you are looking for your child to demonstrate.

HOW IT WORKS

The EFQ scores identify which behaviours should be top priority as you start the *Play Better* programme. These are behaviours that are:

- causing social friction
- keeping your child from developing reciprocal relationships
- keeping your child from being adaptive with other children and adults
- something your child cannot demonstrate in different environments, including structured and unstructured social activity.

You'll also use the scores to identify the lesson track that's the best fit for your child, meeting them where they are in their social skills development, so that the challenge is optimal—not harder than it should be but with sufficient challenge that your child has to stretch just enough.

How do you decide whether to mark a behaviour "rarely," "sometimes," or "often"? Here's a guide:

5 = *Almost never demonstrates the skill.* Maybe he has done it once, but he cannot produce the skill on demand, or as needed.

4 = *Rarely demonstrates the skill.* Your child has demonstrated the skill—not often, but you have seen it.

3 = *Sometimes demonstrates the skill.* In certain circumstances your child can demonstrate the skill, but not consistently.

2 = *Often demonstrates the skill.* She cannot do it 100 per cent of the time, but she can do it most of the time.

1 = *Almost always demonstrates the skill.* Your child consistently demonstrates the skill in unstructured and structured play and with any child.

You'll want to take into account whether the social setting—structured or unstructured—makes a difference in whether your child demonstrates a particular behaviour. This goes for desirable behaviours or problem behaviours alike. For example, if your child demonstrates a desirable behaviour often, but only in a particular type of setting, then she needs to work on generalising that behaviour to include other social settings as well. Knowing this helps you plan practice sessions and playdates that offer the opportunity to work on the behaviour in the setting where it presents the challenge. Once you have your child's score, the simple chart in the EFQ will show you which focused EFQ Lesson Track is the best match once your child has completed the Starter Track for Everyone!

AS YOU START

- **Take your time.** Don't rush through the EFQ. This information will guide your choices through the rest of the programme. It's okay to take a few days on this!
- **Observe and reflect.** You could sit down and just do this, but I encourage you to first observe your child at play and in social situations for a few days and use that information to inform your answers to the questions. No need to go overboard on that observation either, thinking that you need to analyse your child's every move or word. Just observe your child at play with a bit of detachment—coach mode.
- **Ask others to share what they've observed.** Ask teachers and coaches for their observations. Involve your partner and family members who can share their experience of this child. Siblings may see this as an opportunity to launch a gripe session, but your point isn't to try to resolve those differences right now. Make it clear that your interest is solely to get a clear picture of their experience.
- **Draw from your own experience.** You've watched your child for years. Draw from that, too. If your child is unusually tired or stressed the week you want to get started or want to update the EFQ, or you've had some big shift in your family, then observe at a different time.
- **Remember to stay in coach mode.** Coach mode is important even before you begin actively coaching your child. In this observation step, as a parent you may be wishing to see your child's behaviour in the best light, overcompensating for behaviour that is actually a problematic pattern. As a coach, remember to practise detachment and see as objectively as possible: *He pretty much never…She pretty much always…More often than not…*

Executive Function Questionnaire

Directions: Use the questions and score guide below to rate your child's skills based on her social interactions. Consider situations where you have observed your child's social struggles and ask yourself how consistently your child demonstrates the positive social behaviours below. (*Consistent* means *almost always*—your child demonstrates these friendship behaviours generally, and in any situation.)

Write the score for each skill in the blank provided (see sample below). Then add the scores together for an overall score for that social skills category. Write that score in the box marked TOTAL. Do this for each of the eight categories.

Finally, list the top five highest-scoring categories in the space provided at the end of the questionnaire. These identify the skills most lacking, the ones your child needs to work on. Use these to create a prioritised list for coaching attention (e.g., if one skill is a 45 and another is a 40, make the 45 your first priority, followed by the 40, then the 35 scores).

Each skill category corresponds with an Executive Function Lesson Track listed below the score section. Your child's highest-score category will lead you to the matching EFQ Lesson Track.

After your child has completed the lesson track for the highest-score category and each skill is reliably demonstrated, you can return to the prioritised list and continue with the next lesson track for the next highest score skill. A skill is considered "mastered" when your child is proficient at it, meaning he is able to demonstrate the skill at least twice without prompting or cues during a playdate for three playdates in a row. Refer to the *How Will You Know?* and the *Bridge to Betterment* tools to help you determine if your child has mastered a skill and is ready to move on to the next skill category and EFQ Lesson Track.

Rating
5—Almost Never 4—Rarely 3—Sometimes
2—Often 1—Almost Always

Cooperation, Participation, and Problem-Solving

Initiates play or social outings with her peers outside the home (in an age-appropriate way)	
Interprets the nonverbal signals, social cues, or desires of peers and adapts his behaviour based on those cues so play continues	

Rating
5—Almost Never   4—Rarely   3—Sometimes 2—Often   1—Almost Always

Cooperation, Participation, and Problem-Solving (continued)

Engages with other children at a social event (e.g., a holiday, BBQ, birthday party, playdate)	
Stands back and takes a bird's-eye view of her own situation and will problem-solve (in an age-appropriate way)	
Adapts to changes in rules, play, and shifts in the group's play so play continues	
Actively negotiates a compromise with a friend so play continues	
Engages in spontaneous play in unstructured environments with his peers	
Takes turns and shares in a typical, age-appropriate way	
Understands expected friendship rules and behaviours to join a group and engage in cooperative play	
Skill Score	

Friendship Communication

Makes eye contact with peers and adults	
Builds on conversation topics and adds to the conversation	
Talks about a conversation topic presented by the group even if it does not interest her or she is unsure of the topic	
Monitors the interest level of his playmate by interpreting nonverbal and verbal signals	
Actively listens to peers and adults and carries on a reciprocal, two-way conversation	
Understands degrees of social intimacy and adjusts the information she shares to meet the level of intimacy	
Demonstrates that he is paying attention to adults, teachers, coaches, and playmates by maintaining eye contact	
Remembers details about a friend and calls up that information at the right time	
Shows interest in others, and asks them about their lives, interests, emotions	
Skill Score	

Rating
5—Almost Never 4—Rarely 3—Sometimes 2—Often 1—Almost Always

Reading the Room

Understands basic social signals and unspoken rules in any environment and adjusts her behaviour based on those cues	
Decodes the mood or nuanced expectations in a situation and adapts his behaviour to those signals	
Recognises the feelings of others, and adjusts her behaviour to those feelings	
Understands how to adapt behaviour to meet the social norms of different environments, situations, and people	
Infers meaning from tone of voice, body language, gestures, and facial expressions	
Uses information and details about peers and adults in a situation to influence how he behaves and his choices in an age-appropriate way	
Remembers and evaluates prior social missteps and behaves differently	
Picks up on the intentions and motives of another person and adjusts his behaviour	
Observes what happens to others in social interactions and changes her behaviour based on that information	
Skill Score	

Emotional Regulation

Self-calms when upset or disappointed (in line with age-appropriate expectations)	
Copes with emotions when something feels unfair	
Demonstrates an expected level of emotional reaction, given the event, concern, or situation	
Accepts no for an answer	
Takes responsibility for his mistakes	
Copes with sensory stimuli (sound or noise, touch, smells, visual, etc.) and manages emotions	
Manages anxiety and interprets social cues even when anxious	

Rating
5—Almost Never   4—Rarely   3—Sometimes 2—Often   1—Almost Always

Emotional Regulation (continued)

Manages feelings of upset or overwhelm and engages in play despite those emotions	
Handles emotions when given feedback or criticism from adults or peers in an age-appropriate way	
Skill Score	

Taking Another Person's Point of View

Steps into someone else's shoes and understands their perspective	
Reads between the lines to understand the subtext of messages and adjusts behaviour to meet the unspoken messages of peers and adults	
Shows an understanding of another person's feelings and makes appropriate comments and adjusts behaviour as a result	
Anticipates that one's actions provoke reactions from other people	
Picks up on someone's intentions and inferred messages and motives	
Takes a bird's-eye view of the situation and alters behaviour based on this self-awareness	
Considers someone else's perspective and can shift focus and conversation in response	
Evaluates the impact of behaviour on others and their feelings as a result of his actions	
Recognises when her actions or topic of discussion are alienating others	
Skill Score	

Shifting Communication to Meet Needs of Audience

Manages his tone so he does not hurt the feelings of his playmates and so his actions match his intentions	
Can be polite and show interest in a socially appropriate way even if she's not enthusiastic	
Adapts his stories and communication to meet the expectations of his peers or other audience	

Rating
5—Almost Never   4—Rarely   3—Sometimes 2—Often   1—Almost Always

Shifting Communication to Meet Needs of Audience (continued)

Adjusts her tone of voice to meet the demands of the situation (i.e., lower voice or speak more gently)	
Shifts off a topic or interest to meet group expectations	
Tempers his truth-telling and is not overly blunt	
Creates an appealing tone and does not engage in zingers and sarcastic remarks	
Predicts a person's actions, motives, and reactions based on their history	
Decodes sarcasm and humour	
Skill Score	

Flexibility/Adaptability

Compromises with peers	
Takes turns with peers	
Adjusts and adapts to a situation when the group desires change	
Understands when rules need to be bent sometimes to meet the needs of playmates	
Engages in positive, flexible thinking and does not catastrophise	
Understands that rules are not absolute and that they are situationally based	
Recognises that he is not always right	
Makes the mental switch when a plan, rule, or the demands of the situation change	
Lets go of blame, grudges, or hurt feelings with peers	
Skill Score	

Self-Regulation

Copes with winning and losing	
Lets someone else go first and takes turns	
Identifies when she is too silly or excitable and adjusts behaviour	
Walks away from a fight	

Rating
5—Almost Never   4—Rarely   3—Sometimes 2—Often   1—Almost Always

Self-Regulation (continued)

Tells age-appropriate jokes and is able to self-regulate energy and emotions rather than become overly excited	
Refrains from blurting out, interrupting, and spontaneously making noises or comments	
Recognises when he is losing control of his behaviour and can calm himself	
Self-regulates desires to meet social guidelines and group norms	
Resists impulsive actions or responses with peers	
Skill Score	

Total Skill Scores

In your notebook list the skills with the highest scores. These are the high-priority skills your child needs to develop. The EFQ Lesson Tracks are introduced in the next chapter.

Sticker Shock
Don't Let the Numbers Scare You. Be Calm and Carry On.

Something about scores and tallies and assigning ratings to our child's behaviour can push our emotional buttons as parents. Especially when a high score shows where our child needs help. One parent described "sticker shock" at her child's high EFQ score—it was the first time she'd seen an objective measure of the behaviours and skills that were seriously lagging for her.

The scores aren't a judgement of your child. They're just a tool. You needed to see her strengths and challenges clearly. Now you'll use the EFQ to evaluate your child's progress as she continues in coaching. Her scores will change over time as her skills begin to develop. Advancement in one skill often brings improvement in others. The point is to get an accurate picture of your child now—or at any given time—so you can tailor your coaching priorities, lessons, and tool tracks to match your child's executive function needs and development.

The EFQ score may suggest your child has two or three behaviours that are the most problematic, or it could show more than that. Whatever the numbers show, prioritise the behaviours and skills for attention as you make choices in the *Play Better* coaching lessons and activities ahead. Plan to tackle one executive function priority skill before moving on to the next. After each new skill is reliably demonstrated, you can return to your prioritised list and focus attention on the next goal that the score highlighted.

Remember, the EFQ score is simply a way to create a game plan to work with behaviours that you've seen and been concerned about for some time. As you move on to the *Play Better* tools and lesson plans in the next chapter, you get to focus forwards, see how the programme supports you and your child through the coaching experience, and discover your sense of optimism as you prepare to introduce your child to the plan.

YOU'VE GOT THIS!

You are about to take a life-changing journey with your child so he'll be able to make friends and have a life full of possibilities. This EFQ is an early step in this journey, but it's how you'll pinpoint the executive functions that are most challenging for your child. Then you're on your way. What you learn here will change the way you understand and interact with your child for the better, forever. You are giving him a gift, the gift of having the social skills he needs to go anywhere and do anything.

8

The EFQ Lesson Tracks at a Glance

Bridge to Betterment and How Will You Know?

Fun, child-friendly lessons and activities help your child learn brain-based social skills step-by-step through coaching conversation and experience.

At the heart of it, social skills are like bridges between people. They give you a safe, sturdy, reliable way to connect. Children who struggle socially have to build their bridges. If you want to build a bridge, you need some basic materials, a set of lessons, and directions to show you how to do it. Now that you've identified which problem behaviours your child will be targeting for change first, it's time to familiarise yourself with the "construction materials" that you and your child will use to build those bridges.

The full EFQ lesson plans, including discussion and activity guides, visual aids, and other interactive materials, appear in Part III. The tools also include guides just for you as coach—tips, strategies, and sample coaching dialogue—to support you as you work with your child. The brief descriptions of the EFQ tracks that follow show you where your child's EFQ score matches up and which EFQ Lesson Track you'll use once your child finishes the *Play Better* Starter Track for Everyone! Everyone begins with the Starter Track because the skills they develop are the core social skills that everyone needs and are the basis for moving forward in all of the more specialised EFQ Lesson Tracks.

Following the EFQ Lesson Tracks list are two tools for tracking your child's progress:

1. The *Bridge to Betterment* is a child-friendly chart that shows your child's progress along the bridge, or learning curve.
2. *How Will You Know?* The easy evaluation tool helps you tell when your child is ready to advance from one skill challenge level to the next.

With the start of the coaching programme, these tools, activities, and lessons will lead you and your child step-by-step through the problem-solving process of discussion, reflection, goal-setting, practice, and advancing as your child's emerging social skills grow. Each of the EFQ Lesson Tracks in Part III are self-contained and include a series of sequenced lessons and activities that walk you through each step of the skill-building process for your in-home coaching sessions.

Children learn from *doing*. Hands-on experience engages your child *in* the lesson. Practice makes the learning stick. Because children whose executive function skills lag will benefit from more direct instruction and parent coaching in those areas, the *Play Better* tools and EFQ Lesson Tracks provide the structure and content needed to set reasonable goals and move through coaching conversations and activities step-by-step to reach those goals.

Now that you have your child's EFQ scores, scroll through the eight EFQ Lesson Tracks that follow to find the one that corresponds with your child's score. The EFQ score will be your simple guide to finding the match. From that point on, just follow the prescriptive yellow brick road through the lessons and coaching conversations laid out in Part III. For each track, you'll find the full complement of specific tools that make the lessons fun and engaging for your child.

All of the executive function social skills are important, and over time you and your child may decide that working on a different skill and using a different lesson track would be beneficial. That's fine! But start with the area of greatest need, because once your child begins to develop and strengthen her executive function skills in that area, she'll be better prepared to tackle the others.

Because repetition builds the skills, each time your child practises, the same lesson takes them further. The lessons are designed to level up the challenge in terms of what they ask of the child, wherever your child is in his skill building. The *How Will You Know?* tool shows you how to tell when your child is ready to advance to the next level.

INTRODUCTION TO THE *PLAY BETTER* LESSON TRACKS

The Starter Track for Everyone!

Yes, everyone starts here.

I've known countless children who started the *Play Better Plan* barely able to make eye contact who went on to become well-adjusted, socially comfortable young people because they worked hard and made meaningful progress in the fundamental executive function social skills that had been sorely lacking before. I developed the Starter Track for Everyone! because however different children are in so many ways, they all benefit from developing or strengthening these brain-based social skills: reading the room and picking up on spoken and unspoken rules about social behaviour and expectations; managing emotions and developing a more flexible, adaptive way of responding in social situations; and learning how to make conversation and make friends. Once kids develop even a modest proficiency in these basic social skills areas, they're ready to advance to the more specific areas of challenge that you'll tackle in EFQ Lesson Tracks.

The Starter Track for Everyone! includes some of the lessons and activities that kids have told me are their favourites and that parents tell me they all enjoy so much that the language and ideas remain part of the family conversations long after the child has advanced to more challenging tracks. Social Spy, complete with a spy notebook and fun activity sheet, shows your child how to gather social clues—seeing how children interact, observing social rules, noticing social cues, and comparing their own behaviours to that of their peers. Children love it. Like This, Not That helps your child learn to consider how a person, place, or situation is similar to a past experience; how it is different from the past; and how that is relevant right now. Those are just two of the many lessons that kids love and everyone starts with.

When your child has successfully completed Starter Track for Everyone! she'll have a head start on the EFQ Lesson Track tailored to help her with her most pressing area of lagging executive function social skills.

See Chapter 11 for the Starter Track for Everyone!

FIND YOURS: THE EIGHT EFQ LESSON TRACKS AT-A-GLANCE PREVIEW

Each of the eight EFQ Lesson Tracks represents a distinct cluster of executive function social skills, and they correspond to the EFQ categories used to identify your child's most challenging social skills. Each EFQ Lesson

Track contains directions on how to set up the lesson, role-play options, tips, and coaching questions you can use to help your child think about the skill and lesson goals. Specific how-to instructions help your child get the most from an activity. These include pointers about their tone, body language, or other details in the way they'll carry out the exercise.

The lessons also provide methods to help your child generalise learning—adapt new skills to a range of settings. For example, after your child has completed the Learning to Walk in Someone Else's Shoes tool, you'll continue to ask in other lessons, "How do you think that makes your playmate feel?" As you work with your child, advancing through the various lessons, continue to use the *Bridge to Betterment* and *How Will You Know?* (see each tool's respective section) for signs that your child is progressing.

Flexible Me: Flexibility and adaptability

Some rules exist as guidelines, others are hard and fast, and your child needs to be able to discern the difference or his behaviour will seem extreme. Flexible Me helps your child learn to tolerate social and emotional discomfort, let go of the need to be the Rule Police, and adjust his behaviour based on feedback that he receives from others. Some behaviours that will be addressed include obsessing over the rules and wanting everyone else to be governed by their interpretation of them; not letting go of the need to be right; being quick to point out errors that others make; or challenging the "rightness" of every choice or decision. Exercises help your child learn what being flexible looks and sounds like, and helps her recognise what Rule Police behaviour looks like and feels like to her peers.

Sticky Brain helps him identify how his thinking gets stuck, and he'll learn how My Way or the Highway behaviour works against him.

The Flexible Me Lesson Track begins in Chapter 12.

Mind Your PEAS and Cues: Reading the room

Everyone needs to be able to read the room and interpret the unspoken rules. This is how you develop so-called situational awareness, picking up on what's going on around you—the people, the setting, your role in it, and what it means. Your child will learn how to pick up on and interpret social signals and how to consciously consider other people's perspectives and expectations as she steps into a group. This lesson track helps your child learn how to overcome physical hesitation to mix in, how to step forwards and truly engage with the group; develop the capacity to interpret the mood, intentions, and motives of other people; and remember what interests them and how they've responded to certain types of interaction before, and other nuances, to better gauge how they might react now. To simply understand that you even *need* to read the room is not something some kids get.

The Mind Your PEAS and Cues Lesson Track begins in Chapter 13.

Who Is Your Audience? Shifting communication to meet the needs of the audience

Your child learns to adapt his communication to different people, learning to filter information. Not everyone wants or needs to know everything on his mind. He learns about the concept of context so he can adapt his message to reflect the situation and anticipate the motives and reactions of people in different situations. Finally, lessons in this track help your child hear tone, sarcasm, and zingers so she learns to hear her tone with other people and adjust it as needed.

The Who Is Your Audience? Lesson Track begins in Chapter 14.

Build on That: Friendship communication

A fun block tower–building activity and others help your child learn the skills for "building" a conversation: how to initiate a conversation, keep it going, shift from one topic to another (even when it's not his choice of topic) to go with the flow of reciprocal conversation, and not interrupt his partner in conversation. Understanding levels of social and emotional disclosure and intimacy is important in friendship: What do you share with someone you're really close with and what do you share with someone who is just an acquaintance? Remembering details about a friend is important, too; if you don't, then people think you are rude.

The Build on That Lesson Track begins in Chapter 15.

Friendship Is a Two-Way Street: Cooperation, participation, and problem-solving

Some children do not know how to mix in, and that shows itself in a range of behaviours, from being habitually timid and shy, to being one who barges in. This lesson track helps shape a success-ful approach to friendship, including how to physically approach a group and join group activities. Activities help your child create reciprocal relationships and meet people halfway, respond to people's friendly gestures or overtures, and prioritise cooperating with friends over her own desires. Your child develops skills for cooperation, for identifying times she can more actively meet people halfway, and for understanding the stages of friendships and how they progress from saying hello to eventually finding things in common.

The Friendship Is a Two-Way Street Lesson Track begins in Chapter 16.

Learning to Walk in Someone Else's Shoes: Taking another person's point of view

Your child learns to take someone else's perspective in a situation, demonstrate a greater sense of empathy, and understand and predict the motives and expectations of other people. Learning to take someone else's point of view—perspective taking—is often treated as if it's a simple courtesy. When you look at the chain of behaviours involved in this executive function, the complexity of the task is impressive. First, you have to be able to anticipate someone else's thoughts, actions, motives, and messages and how they're likely to respond to something. Then, as a social skill, you need to be able to shift your own responses in anticipation of all that.

The Learning to Walk in Someone Else's Shoes Lesson Track begins in Chapter 17.

Once Was Enough: Self-regulation

Self-regulation has been described variously as the ability to pause and gather your thoughts, the ability to manage feelings and be calm, and the ability to do both so you can adapt behaviour to match what's needed for a task or situation. Self-regulation is a challenge for most kids—they're all working on it. That's what childhood is for. But if this category is a high score on your child's EFQ, it's because a combination of factors indicate that self-regulation presents a *significant* social challenge for your child. Once Was Enough is about paying attention to your body signals and realising when levels of physical, emotional, or sensory energy or stress— what I call *activation*—get to be too much.

This cluster of social skills weaknesses shows up in a child's inability to self-regulate to match group expectations, cope with winning and losing, refrain from being too silly or excitable, or avoid getting stuck in the goofy-silly mode, unable to adjust his behaviour and move on. It also shows up in aggressive behaviours when a child is unable to walk away from a fight or manage anger effectively in other circumstances. A child whose temper is on a hair trigger needs coaching that breaks down the process of self-regulation into manageable steps that can interrupt the "fight" in the fight-flight-or-freeze response. The lessons help your child learn how to read his stress levels and recognise when stress-related activation is leading to dysregulation (loss of self-regulation). Then he'll learn steps for regaining calm and self-regulating through the ups and downs of play.

The Once Was Enough Lesson Track begins in Chapter 18.

Never Let Them See You Sweat: Emotional regulation

Emotional regulation is an essential building block in social behaviour. In this lesson track, your child learns to more fully understand emotions and how they trigger her stress response; she then learns how those emotional states affect her and others. She'll learn to recognise when she is experiencing those emotions and moving from a calm emotional state to a reactive one—and what to do about it.

The Never Let Them See You Sweat Lesson Track begins in Chapter 19.

THE *PLAY BETTER BRIDGE TO BETTERMENT*

The *Bridge to Betterment* helps you identify where your child's skills, mind-set, and behaviours are in the "bridging" process of change. I'll guide you in choosing the lessons and activity skill levels that match your child's readiness for building out—challenging himself to the next level in a particular skill he has chosen to work on in coaching. The *Bridge* makes your child's progress more visible and fun to track. It's also instructive, showing how the steps in behavioural change occur in a progression—a chain of behaviours—from the first step in awareness through concerted efforts to change, to potential setbacks and eventual change, then steps to maintain the change.

Along that chain, some behavioural changes are subtle and can be difficult to see in progress, but there are signs. The noted psychologist and behavioural change theorist James Prochaska and colleagues identified five stages of readiness for change that are helpful to keep in mind as you listen to your child's story for signs of his readiness to invest in addressing his social challenges. The stages are:

- Not ready (pre-contemplation): No intention to take action in the foreseeable future and possibly unaware that their behaviour is problematic
- Getting ready (contemplation): Beginning awareness that their behaviour is problematic, and starts to look at pros and cons of their continued actions
- Ready (preparation): Awareness and intention to take action in the immediate future, may begin taking small steps toward behaviour change

- Action: Takes specific steps, action to modify their problem behaviour or acquire new, healthy behaviours
- Maintenance: Able to sustain the new, healthy behaviour for at least six months and works to prevent relapse.

By understanding the predictable stages of behavioural change, you're better able to take your child's actual readiness for change into account in your coaching and discuss readiness in those conversations.

For instance, as we saw in Patrick's story, it's a huge leap for a child to adapt to the expectation to meet group consensus over the choice of a movie—a leap from one end of the bridge to the other. Your child can't make that leap in a day or by hearing you lecture her on it. First, she must become aware that it is a problem when consensus is needed and someone refuses to consider compromise. Then she'll be able to understand why her refusal to consider other options is a problem in a social group. Next, she'll begin to notice when she is doing this—she'll hear herself, catch herself arguing unceasingly for her movie choice. And eventually, with practice, she'll be able to consciously choose a more collaborative response, the desirable behaviour, in such social situations. These are the steps you'll chart on the *Bridge*—and your child will be able to see her progress. You can use the *Bridge* to chart this process for developing all executive functions.

The *Bridge to Betterment*

STEP 1. Dawning awareness. A child at this very first stage lacks awareness, does not realise he has a problem, and likely does not have self-talk or the ability to take a bird's-eye view of a situation or have the executive function skills necessary to create cooperative play and adaptive friendships. He may not even intend to change; his story may be to blame everyone else, saying that "everyone is mean" or that "no one cared."

STEP 2. Notices social guidelines and unspoken rules. Understands that everyone has a social role. While the child doesn't yet understand her own role and how the world works, she is clear that if she wants to have friends, she needs to do more. But she may still say or show through her behaviour that she believes "people should come to me" or "people should do what I want to do."

STEP 3. Notices his behaviour as same or different from peers. The child understands the ways in which his behaviour fits into the social norms and when it doesn't, and he can observe other people's behaviour and reflect on it. At the core, he's beginning to show awareness that his problems are "things that are getting in my way."

STEP 4. Shows self-awareness and awareness of others. Your child is clearly aware of her problem behaviour. *Here's the problem—here's what I'm doing.* For example, she might say: "I guess I'm like a ghost—I don't join in."

STEP 5. Catches himself and is aware enough to say, "Oh, I'm doing it." You give him a gentle reminder or his playmate says something and they adapt based on that feedback. In the past, they would have just rolled right past that moment, unaware of the need to make their own course correction.

STEP 6. Adapts some of the time. This is how different environments and different playmates become relevant. Some children might start adapting behaviour around adults or in the actual session with you or with certain younger playmates. But they don't do it 100 per cent of the time, just sometimes in certain environments and under certain conditions. They're not yet consistent.

STEP 7. Initiates social connections. They are able to approach someone. Make chitchat. Ask someone to play. This is a big step.

Sometimes kids will rehearse in home coaching but have trouble actually doing it spontaneously in a playdate setting.

STEP 8. Anticipates or predicts the behaviours of others. They show that they can read people—read the audience—and think of what another person would like or not like. A friend likes stickers a lot and Lego not so much? With this relevant information in mind, your child picks the sticker book for the friend's birthday present. This is the ability to understand a person's social database—information that helps us understand them—and predict how our messages will be received.

STEP 9. Adapts behaviour. In varied social situations across multiple settings, they can adapt their behaviour and change with the social demands and expectations. A boy who habitually blurts into conversations now realises that he ticks people off. He might say to you, "I want to stop, but I don't know what to do." You can say, "That's okay. I don't expect you to stop all at once. It's a big step to know what you need to do it and try." If even in one conversation he is able to stop himself from blurting, that would be adaptive behaviour. The measure of the growth is to be able to do so two to three times in different settings.

STEP 10. Maintains the behaviour. Your child is able to continue that particular behaviour and continue adapting and correcting herself. Slips may still happen, but if your child is in a play setting and can recognise when she is slipping into that old behaviour, she can say to herself, "This is out of control" and correct for the better behaviour. She doesn't have to become a different person—this is a child becoming the better version of herself. She can see when she's doing something wrong, self-correct, and it works.

How will you know?

Even long-standing experts in behavioural science have skirted the question of how long a parent should coach a child who needs executive function social skills coaching. The reason is that every child is different and responds to coaching at his or her own pace. While it is predictable that children improve with the *Play Better Plan*, their timing varies. Some show marked progress in weeks, others in months. There is no precise answer. But I've taken what parents tell me about their children's signs of progress using the *Play Better Plan* and created this coaching tool—*How Will You Know?*—to gauge "levels of mastery" of skills so you can more easily recognise progress and see your child's positive trajectory.

Here's an example using the EFQ Lesson Track for self-regulation:

Level 1: Children might notice signs that their emotional reaction is escalating and they are becoming upset, and they may begin to notice that when they breathe mindfully or pause, they feel better. They might do this only when prompted, but they notice.

Level 2: They think sooner about their behaviour or catch themselves as their behaviour begins to slip. They become aware of the impact of emotions on behaviour—which may include observing it in someone else. Your child might point out when *you* appear to be happy, angry, sad, or tired!

Level of Tools for This Stage	Stage of Change in the *Bridge to Betterment*	Behaviours You Might See	Things You May Hear
Level 1 Tools	Dawning awareness	Self-talk is largely absent, or he does not tune in to self-talk	"I don't have a problem. It's everyone else."
		Does not understand social guidelines or unspoken social rules	"People are mean."
		Does not pay attention to social signals and cues	"It was just this one time that this was a problem."
		May not create cooperative, reciprocal play with his peers	"Oh, it's okay—no one cared. It was only my brother."
		Is unaware of the little stories he tells himself	"I should not have done it, but it's okay. Only a few people saw."
		Appears to be unaware of his behaviour and the effect on others and that peers react to him based on his past behaviour	
	Notices social guidelines and unspoken rules and understands that he has a social role	Might intend to change, but he is not aware of *what* he needs to change about his social approach	"I want to talk to her, but I am not sure how."
			"I just get so annoyed! I put my hand up in her face to hush her—which wasn't nice."
	Notices his own behaviour and how it is the same or different from his peers	Starts to intend to complete a mission	Your child looks at you and says, "I don't know what you mean. I need to understand." This is a sign that he wants to understand the problem.

	Shows self-awareness and awareness of others	Begins to notice and have some self-awareness of his social role	"I know I need to talk to people at lunch, but I don't know what to say."
		Begins to try to choose alternative behaviours and strategies	"What happens is I go, and then I am in my own brain and then I get into trouble."
		Works through some stories, mind-sets, lies, that keep him from moving forwards	"I need to be interested in other people."
		Can *notice* and point out desired social behaviours	
		Catches himself some of the time and is aware even for a few minutes of his mission	
	Catches self and is aware enough to say, "Oh, I'm doing it."	Tunes in to self-talk some of the time	"I know what I want to do, but I cannot make my body go that way."
		Starts to speak aloud or recognises his self-talk	"I interrupt too much."
			"I talk too long, and I don't care about anyone else's agenda."
			"I was kinda lost in my own world, so I did not talk."
			"This is hard for me"; "I need to listen more."
	Adapts some of the time	Begins to notice social expectations and predict the behaviour of others *some of the time*	"Oops, I'll wait until you're done talking."
Level 2 Tools	Initiates social connections	Begins to use alternative behaviours and strategies	Child at Thomas the Tank Engine table notices another child and says, "Hey, he likes Thomas the Tank Engine, too."
		Some of the time and in some settings participates with groups of kids	A child makes a gesture at the water table to play, too, and your child smiles back.
		Begins to have cooperation, reciprocal play, or conversation in structured environments	"I played Gaga ball today (for the first time) and it was great!"
		Takes a bird's-eye view of the social situation	"I did not talk to them, but I was talking to them in my mind."
		Understands that she needs to meet friends halfway and adapt to their play plan	
	Anticipates and predicts the behaviour of others	Working on her social missions and is aware of what gets in the way	"Other kids listen to music and watch YouTube. I don't, but it's no big deal, so I can do it just to hang out."
		Acts on unspoken rules and reading the room	"I don't think Laura will want to play that; she is more of an outdoor girl."
		Notices signals and signs of social expectations	
		Understands the motives, emotions, and intentions of peers	

Level of Tools for This Stage	Stage of Change in the *Bridge to Betterment*	Behaviours You Might See	Things You May Hear
	Adapts behaviour	Makes choices to ensure play continues	"I let her ride my bike—she did not have one."
		Uses self-talk	Starts to get upset and then takes a deep breath, unprompted, and says, "I need a break."
		Walks in other people's shoes, thinks from their point of view	
		Even when she gets off track, she adapts her behaviour	Child is losing a game and says, "It's okay; it's only a game."
		Implements strategies to self-regulate and to manage emotions	
	Maintains the behaviour	Scans a situation and understands the demands of that social situation	"One of my friends plays soccer, and even though I don't like it, I played."
		Engages in social problem-solving	

YOU'VE GOT THIS!

Now you're ready to move forward, share this with your child, finalise the plan together—and start!

Introducing the *Play Better Plan* to Your Child

The Interactive Conversation Guide

Difficult subjects can make for difficult conversations, but they don't have to. How do you broach the subject of your child's social challenges? You now understand that this is a problem. What do you do if your child is in denial about having a problem? How do you win her cooperation for the coaching plan without making her feel worse? How do you start the conversation? The Interactive Conversation Guide: How to Engage Your Child helps you have a productive, interactive conversation with your child about social challenges and helps you introduce the social skills coaching programme in a positive way.

Coaching conversations and practice are the linchpins of the *Play Better Plan* because they draw your child into authentic interactive experiences that develop the executive function social skills that have been offline or lagging until now. Starting with this conversation, you are not lecturing or talking *to* your child, but rather *with* them, and soon you'll be working with them as well through the lessons to come. Once you start coaching, your child actually begins *using* the brain-based executive functions, and those skills begin to grow.

Pave the way for this conversation at least a week or two earlier by mentioning that you find some things harder than others, how that's only human—*we're all working on something*—and that when you need to learn something or do something new, you ask for help. Share an example from your experience.

When you're ready, have a conversation with your child about tackling the social challenge together:

- Show your child that social challenges are important and deserve special attention.
- Establish that problem-solving steps help develop essential social skills and strategies.
- Introduce the *Play Better Plan* as a fun way to use those steps to develop those skills and strategies using game-style levels of activities, practice, and rewards.
- Win your child's cooperation to work together with you as coach and to plan the next steps together using the *Play Better* playbook.

THE INTERACTIVE CONVERSATION GUIDE

STEP 1. Set the Scene

Pick a time and place most comfortable for your child to have this initial discussion. A half hour to forty-five minutes should be sufficient. Kids tend to be more receptive to conversation when they're physically comfortable, unhurried, and undistracted. Other helpful starters:

- Approach your child when he is in a pretty good mood, not on the heels of a blowup or meltdown. Talk together privately, without other siblings around.
- Pick a quiet place—no phones or screens to distract you.
- Make your point clearly and keep your tone warm.

You can say:

- I have something I'd like to talk with you about.
- You know how you are so good at maths and it's easy for you? And how some of your friends have tutors because it's not so easy for them? For some kids, being social is easy. It's not so easy for you, and I'd like to be your go-to person for that—your friendship tutor.
- You know how people take piano lessons and you take karate lessons? Well, I want to think about some friendship lessons. And we can do them right here at home—or anywhere we feel like it.

Suggest that you are going to have some fun times together practising social stuff so she can get better at it and then she'll have some playdates to practise. You might use a specific sport or activity she likes as an example. Say: "You know how Coach works on your swings in baseball, and how, if he didn't, you wouldn't know how to hit that curveball? Well, we are going to teach you how to get better at social stuff and I am going to coach you."

Other tips for setting the scene:

- Some children focus better when they have something to do with their hands—just not digital devices or games. Try giving your child a fidget toy or a notepad to take notes. If he reacts or overreacts to being approached about the subject, try to give him something comforting to play with or hold.
- Assure your child that you have plenty of time to talk so he doesn't feel as if he needs to rush through the conversation.
- Start the conversation with a discussion about your child's strengths. Use examples. Refer to one of his gifts and brag a bit to him about a special talent he has. Compliment your child on some things he does well, like asking for snacks politely or being gentle with his little sister.
- If you and your child have had disagreements about social skills in the past, then you can acknowledge that and you can apologise for not understanding. Repeat that you want to help her with this social stuff and now you know how.
- Refrain from using negative statements, such as "You're bad at sharing."

STEP 2. Use open-ended questions

By asking open-ended questions, you encourage your child to talk about his friendship situation. Open-ended questions use the words *who*, *what*, *when*, *where*, and *how*. Some conversation starters:

- Who are you playing with these days?
- How do you feel your friendships are going?
- What are you doing well as a friend?
- How can you be a better friend?
- I have noticed that sometimes you have a hard time with (identify a behaviour). What makes (name the behaviour) hard for you?

- When do you feel you have a hard time finding friends?
- How would you like your friendships to change?
- Where could you approach someone?
- How come that happened?

If your child resists, ask her, "What feels hard about this?"

If she denies there is any friendship problem, you can say, "Well, I have noticed..." and then name a few specific situations. Ask her what feels uncomfortable about changing. Share with her the positive things that could happen if she were willing to work on her friendship skills and ask her what *she* would like to be different. Share with her a picture of possibilities—what it could be like. Some phrases that may help soften resistance:

> I am curious...
> Tell me more about that.
> What is that like for you?
> What does that feel like?

STEP 3. Clarify concerns and express empathy

As your child responds to your questions, be sure to show that you hear his concerns by being a reflective listener: Listen closely, repeat back what you understand your child to be saying, and ask if you understand correctly. You can say: "Here's what I hear you saying...Is that right?" If your child feels that his concerns are heard and validated, he'll be more open to hearing what you have to say. Below are some tips on how to be a good reflective listener:

- Repeat back your child's statement without giving an opinion. By repeating his statement, your child also hears what he has said.
- Confirm with your child that you captured his thoughts and feelings accurately.
- Clarify your child's thoughts and feelings by asking questions.
- Express empathy and validate your child's feelings: "I hear you. I get it. That must be hard."
- Use *you* and *I* statements, such as "I notice you seem overwhelmed" and "I'm hearing you are lonely."

Here's an example of a conversation guided by reflective listening:

CHILD: I don't have any friends, and I never will. Other kids are mean.

PARENT: It sounds like you feel left out. And you think other kids are mean.

(Parent recaps the child's message and repeats it back to her.)

CHILD: There is no point in trying. No one gets me.

PARENT: It sounds like you feel that things can't get better?

(Parent clarifies the child's thoughts and feelings.)

CHILD: Yes. Things won't get better.

PARENT: I'm sorry you are feeling so frustrated. I want to help you with that.

(Parent expresses empathy and segues into the problem-solving part of the conversation.)

STEP 4. Problem-solve

Next, you want your child to brainstorm with you to help come up with solutions to his friendship problems, so he feels engaged in the decision-making process. Encourage some suggestions. Your child's suggestions may not all be helpful, but try to focus on the good aspects of his suggestions and then offer your own ideas. Discuss how changing his behaviour could bring about positive results in the future. Here are some questions to help him understand that accepting help would be beneficial for him:

- What gets in the way of you making friends?
- What do you think would have made this playdate better? (mention past playdate)
- What are your options for making your friendship situation better?
- What would it feel like if you could get better at making friends?
- What would it be like if you were happier?

STEP 5. Discuss the *Play Better Plan* and coaching approach

After brainstorming about the social situation and the desire for improvement, you can introduce the idea of the playdate coaching programme and incorporate some of your child's suggestions into the plan. You can introduce the programme with these conversation starters:

- What if we could work on being a better friend?
- What if we could work on helping you with (a problem behaviour)?
- Everyone needs to practise things sometimes. (Give an example of what you are working on in your life right now, like stressing out less about deadlines or eating more salad.)
- What if we could figure out a way to help you create stronger friendships?
- I think I know a way for you to find good friends.
- You told me before that you would like to have an easier time playing with kids at school. I have an idea on how we could work on that goal together.

COACH NOTES

- Don't be a historian. Recounting a long list of past mistakes only shuts kids down. If your child doesn't know what you're talking about, give one or two specific examples.
- Talk frankly with your child, but try not to shame or judge her.
- Do not get angry even if your child refuses to talk about hard things.
- Avoid words like *always* and *never*.
- Allow your child to express his viewpoint whenever he feels the need to.
- Allow for degrees of buy-in. A child does not have to say "Hooray, let's do it!" A shrug and "Okay, sure" might be her way of signalling she's willing to give it a try.

REWARDS AND INCENTIVES

We all appreciate a pat on the back for a job well done. Children do too, especially when they're tackling something that's always been hard for them. Incentives and rewards make hard work more fun. They add to a child's sense of purpose and their motivation to keep working, deepening the lessons learned. Do you *have* to include rewards and incentives for your child in this coaching plan? No. Would I like you to consider doing so? Yes. Here's why.

A plan for rewards and incentives gives you a simple, organised way to acknowledge your child's progress, boost motivation, enhance the sense of accomplishment, and provide a speedy source of gratification, when otherwise the bigger wins of social skills learning take longer to register for your child. This is also your hedge against the slippery slope into bribery. Bribery is a desperate effort to win your child's compliance when you're worried you can't or you're already in a tug-of-war over behaviour.

In a rewards system, you outline a reward for positive behaviour *beforehand* and outline clear criteria for what your child must do to achieve the reward. For instance, computer time might be a reward for participating during in-home coaching sessions. You might agree on favourite collectible cards or kits, or points towards the purchase of a Lego set. Rewards can serve as a reminder about practising a desired behaviour—*You don't want to miss out on your points today.* Mystery motivators, menu systems, and points menus are good ways to incorporate variety into a rewards programme if your child gets bored. Samples of each of these menu systems are provided in the worksheet.

The reward chart is a way to recognise your child's progress each day. In a reward chart system, you evaluate your child's overall behaviour at the end of each day instead of giving recognition for every positive behaviour throughout the day. You record their progress on a chart and award check marks or stickers for the behaviours and goals successfully achieved.

You might also tie additional periodic rewards and incentives to progress on the *Bridge to Betterment*. Although "practice" does not appear as a separate plank in the illustration, continued practice is what makes each step possible, so it makes a handy touchstone for the positive reinforcement of rewards.

HOW TO CREATE A REWARDS AND INCENTIVES PLAN

To start, explain the idea of rewards and incentives to your child. You can say, "I know sometimes when we work together on this it's going to be hard, but I am so proud of you and I was thinking if we had a little reward for your hard work it might add to the fun part of things. You could enjoy those rewards as we do the coaching and practice together. You help pick out the rewards and we'll change them up as we go along." Then:

- Choose behaviours that your child cares most about. That's a built-in incentive. Choose four or five and stack the deck in the child's favour. Two can be behaviours that they do some of the time, so they can get a head start on success.
- Be clear in your language about the behaviours on the watch-list for rewards. *Fight less* is vague and open to (endless) debate. Grown-ups tend to think in broad terms: *Be kind. Think of other people. Do your best.* Your child is thinking, "What does that mean?" Focus on something specific: *When Spencer asks you to stop, you stop. This is what I'm expecting.* Be specific about what you're looking for—what you *want* to see, not what you *don't* want to see.
- Agree on the expectations around a rule. For example: "You won't get rewarded if you only do this behaviour at the end of the day. I need to see it throughout the day."
- Establish a plan for follow-through. Make it part of your *Play Better* coaching schedule, so your child can count on it. How often will rewards payouts be made? Once a week? Twice a week? Decide together. If you don't plan the timing ahead, your child may feel a bit tricked: "Well, I didn't know I had to wait till Sunday."
- Pick the behaviour and reward together, ahead of time. Let your child lead the way on the choice of rewards, and think through possible side effects ahead of time. Some kids are hoarders and they'll simply stuff tickets or rewards away—perhaps their reward can be something they get to do that's a treat.
- Pick a system that works for you all. For example, a mother who spent hours a day in the car driving her kids around did the rewards time in the car and kept a folder there with rewards tickets. She and her child would review the day, note the *Play Better* successes on the checklist, and she'd hand out the tickets right then and there. Whatever you choose, just make it realistic for both of you.

Bottom line: Involve your child in planning, think about the details ahead, and keep the plan simple. You don't want to tack on an unnecessary complication. But a simple plan delivers a big upside.

But...isn't this just bribery?

No. A rewards plan makes good on a promise. Bribery is an act of desperation.

Here's the difference, in two familiar scenarios:

At the playground, a child is throwing sand at another child, and his mum asks him to stop. He keeps throwing sand. Mum tells him firmly to stop. He continues. Finally—and we've all been there, done that—she says, "If you stop, then I'll give you a cookie." That may get him to stop, but it rewards bad behaviour.

That's not like saying earlier, "Hey, you all want to go to Dunkin' Donuts, so if everybody gets ready and in the car now, then we can go to Dunkin' Donuts." That's a plan. The playground moment wasn't a moment for an incentive or reward. It was a moment to say, "This isn't acceptable." And implement the consequence. "I've warned you three times, and now we're leaving the playground."

The plan also eliminates an unnecessary power struggle. A rewards and incentives plan devised by the two of you makes you partners, and you're both accountable. Here's the deal, here are the criteria, and that's that. It's a completely different conversation—not bribery. In fact, it's a helpful feedback loop. If it's been a day or week without hitting the mark for a reward, then that's something to take up in your coaching session and conversation. In this way, the Rewards and Incentive Plan supports the larger *Play Better* goals that your child has set.

Comfort Zone: Cozy, Creative, Courageous

We all know how it feels to tackle something outside our comfort zone—all the more when it's something hard for us. Here's a low-stress way to engage the child who is struggling to keep an open mind or continue in the process:

1. Explain what a "comfort zone" is and what it means when something is "outside your comfort zone." To change and grow, we must be willing to lean into discomfort sometimes and engage in the process. Use examples from your own life: "I was nervous to learn to ski but I tried it, and it felt uncomfortable at first." You can prompt your child by asking questions about this idea of being uncomfortable and stretching to get beyond it. "Remember when you went to a new football team and felt like you wanted to stay with the old one?"

2. On a piece of paper, have your child draw a large circle to represent his comfort zone. Leave a margin around the circle—that's going to be the space for things outside his comfort zone.

3. Ask him to jot inside the circle things he does that are *inside his comfort zone*. These might include joining in with younger kids; staying out of the lunchroom; sitting with only one "safe" friend; playing with things

he loves, like Lego; going to a grandparent's house or after-school programme; eating favourite foods; playing with certain people or in the favourite places.

4. Then ask him to jot outside the circle some things that are *outside his comfort zone*. Let your child tell you what those are.

5. If your child's list doesn't include some behaviours you know are problematic, then you can ask, "Would _____ be inside your comfort zone or outside your comfort zone?"

6. When the drawing is done, chat about what it feels like to do things inside his comfort zone and outside his comfort zone. You might volunteer to pick something that's outside your comfort zone to try to do and ask your child to pick one thing he could try, too.

7. Ask your child to look for patterns: What does he notice about how many or what kinds of things he does outside his comfort zone?

8. Over the next few days, point out when something is outside or inside your comfort zone.

9. This activity helps your child become more aware that stretching is necessary and to think about his choices and activities. No change happens in the comfort zone. To develop new social behaviours, your child has to move out of his comfort zone and be open to a new way.

Reaching New Heights: Using Conversation to Elevate Our Self-Talk

Changing what you say and do can be like trying to climb the mountain to change. Everyone falls down sometimes, but do you try again? Reaching New Heights is a visual representation of the climb we all experience when moving from the closed "I Can't Mind-set" to the open "Possibilities Mind-set." The language becomes a shortcut you use to signal to your child (or others, including yourself) when she is demonstrating a fixed or closed mind-set. It's important for a child to understand that some choices, beliefs, and behaviours will not help her be successful, and in fact are holding her back. This is part of teaching children how to hold the mirror up to their own behaviour, their own mind-sets, and to hear their comments and self-talk—their inner coach—and how all of it expresses and shapes their beliefs about themselves.

Reaching New Heights

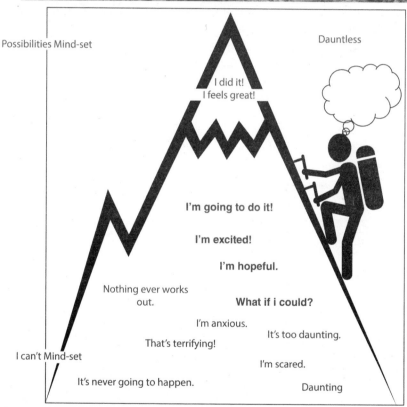

Possibilities Mind-set

Dauntless

I did it!
I feels great!

I'm going to do it!

I'm excited!

I'm hopeful.

Nothing ever works out.

What if i could?

I'm anxious.

It's too daunting.

That's terrifying!

I can't Mind-set

I'm scared.

It's never going to happen.

Daunting

You can start Reaching New Heights very simply: just post the visual on the fridge or the bulletin board. Then follow these steps to introduce the idea and make it an easy reference point in everyday life:

STEP 1. Show your child that there is an "I Can't Mind-set" **and a** "Possibilities Mind-set." Explain that certain things we do put us in the I Can't Mind-set, like when we give up easily or won't try new things. Other things we do put us in the Possibilities Mind-set, like when we try a little harder to overcome an obstacle or keep an open mind about new things.

STEP 2. Explain that some of the stories your child tells herself, her behaviour, and things she says are "Possibilities Mind-set" **behaviour and some are** "I Can't Mind-set" **behaviour.** Offer some examples of I Can't Mind-set behaviour, such as frequently giving up, saying "There's no point," or refusing to socialise with anyone new. Some examples of Possibilities Mind-set behaviour include being willing to try something that might not work out or seek new kids to play with. Discuss that to change, you have to make sure that your actions, and the stories you tell yourself, are in the Possibilities Mind-set. As you work with your child, if she says something in the I Can't Mind-set, point it out and say, "What I'm hearing is I Can't Mind-set talk." Of course, be quick to catch yourself when *you* slide into the I Can't Mind-set with your self-talk!

STEP 3. What direction do your words and actions take you? What are examples of things your child says or does that keep her in the I Can't Mind-set or in the Possibilities Mind-set? Be prepared with specific examples you have seen, to counteract shrugs and deflections like "I don't say stuff like that." Without shaming, simply identify times when, for example, your child has given up trying on something that mattered to her, or declared "There's no way this will work out." You may want to write down examples for a few days before this. Ask your child to share what choices she is making that are in the Possibilities Mind-set. Examples could include participating in the *Play Better Plan*, or anything you know she's doing that fits the bill. Remember that having your child reflect on this and bringing examples forward herself exercises executive function skills, so don't be too quick to fill in the blanks for her.

STEP 4. What's holding you back? Ask your child about choices, behaviours, stories that might get in the way of her success.

STEP 5. Ask directly about her feelings and validate her emotions. Ask your child how she feels about these experiences she has described. State clearly that you can appreciate her feelings: "I understand that this is hard and that it may be scary." Then make the connection between someone's self-talk and story, and discuss how much of her stories and behaviour are in the Possibilities Mind-set and how much are in the I Can't Mind-set. Brainstorm some specific actions your child could take to move more into the Possibilities Mind-set.

YOU'VE GOT THIS!

The ability to have a full conversation with your child on any topic is so important. It's also natural to feel overwhelmed as you set out to do it. Just remember, your parent/child relationship is strong and loving. These social skills–building lessons and coaching techniques make the most of that. When in doubt, be curious. Ask your child what he feels and why. Listen and allow him to tell you about his feelings. Remember that your child has been through a lot. He may be fearful, overwhelmed, full of feeling, and defensive—rationalising with a story. Acknowledge those feelings and help him give them a name. Then do what all good guides (and parents) do: try to provide perspective and influence to help him make good choices. Help him see that there *are* possibilities within his reach. And this coaching plan is a good one.

Home Advantage
In-Home Coaching and Practice Build Basic Skills

Give yourself a high five: you've now identified your child's high-priority needs for executive function social skills coaching (Chapter 7) and the corresponding EFQ Lesson Track (Chapter 8), and you've had the conversation with your child about starting. Now get out your day planner. All that's left is to plan the time for your in-home coaching sessions.

In-home practice is essential for success. In sports, practice is how you develop any new skill. The same goes for social interaction, from approaching a group to having a conversation. Practice helps the brain create new connections and then make those connections stronger and deeper, establishing robust neuronal pathways that support the new skill. Practice also helps children develop more ease with the physical moves—how to present themselves or comfortably handle transitions. Practice is doubly important when a child is trying to *unlearn* an entrenched behaviour and, at the same time, learn a new one. Talking about a new, desirable behaviour introduces it to the brain as an idea, perhaps even an attractive idea. But the old habit is reflexive until, with practice, the brain develops the new alternative pathway to support the skill. Then, with continued practice, reflection, and conversation—the core elements of this coaching programme—those pathways grow stronger. As they strengthen, so does the executive function hub for social skills. In the brain, that's how new habits are formed and old habits lose their grip.

Your in-home coaching commitment also sends your child a message. Time and attention are how we show our children what's important. We hound them about homework and family commitments. We arrange our lives around their drop-off and pickup times. We nag them to spend more time on things that matter to us and less time on things that don't. Our time and attention are how we show our children that *they* are important. *For the best results in coaching your child for behavioural change, start by making in-home coaching and practice sessions a top priority.*

Wherever your child begins on the learning curve, whatever the EFQ Lesson Track, your child will continue to engage in daily in-home coaching lessons and continue to "level up" in their tools. Check your child's progress against the *Bridge to Betterment* and *How Will You Know?* for signs that she's becoming proficient with a new skill in home sessions, before putting them to the test in other settings.

AS YOU START: FIVE STEPS TO OPTIMAL IN-HOME COACHING SESSIONS

Each lesson track has specific activities tailored for those skills and behaviours, but for all of them, these home practice steps are the same. This is how you guide your child through a coaching session and wrap it up when you're done. I've unpacked the steps here to explain and offer a few examples. But it's not a complicated setup. You've got this!

STEP 1. Plan the in-home coaching session

- Create a schedule that's consistent, yet adaptable if needed.
- Schedule it for a place and time of day with minimal distractions—no TV or sibling antics—and when he's usually able to listen and engage with you. Perhaps after he's had a chance to unwind from school, but before he turns to homework.
- Choose a setting that's calm and comfortable. Maybe the kitchen or a cozy spot in the study, maybe a walk outside.
- Ask your child for suggestions. If there is a time after school when he wants desperately to watch a programme or play a game, let him do that first so he doesn't see coaching as always taking away from his fun time.
- Prepare yourself, too, by shifting into coach mode so that your tone and presence are calm and welcoming.

STEP 2. Introduce the lesson

Welcome your child to the coaching session, introduce behaviour that's been identified for change—the undesirable behaviour—and present your child's lesson activity with instructions for this session and later practice. Each of the EFQ Lesson Track activities begins where you do: Setting up the lesson gives your child a clearly defined job to work on—a *mission*—during each skill-building exercise, and eventually in playdate settings. For example, the focus of the lesson might be: "I will pause and think before I react when I'm upset," or "I'll let my guest pick the activity," or "I'll try to hear when my friend is expressing her annoyance and stop before I go too far," or "I'm going to monitor how silly and goofy I'm getting and wind down." Having a mission helps direct your child's behavioural attention to her goal in clear and simple terms. You can also refer to missions in everyday situations as a way to help your child understand what's expected of her on an outing or at a social gathering, and translate the lessons from home to the outside world.

The mission is always to practise the new skill that you've identified together. For example, an identified behaviour for change could be your child's habit of impulsively grabbing toys from another child when he's feeling angry. He'll practise the new, desirable behaviour and other skills in the lessons at home. The new behaviour could be to take a deep, calming breath and choose to share, or at least choose not to grab. You'll talk with your child about what makes the new behaviour a more positive, friendly response. You can script it simply, for easier recall, in this case suggesting a question like "Can I take a turn?" Or ask your child to count to five and scope out what someone else wants instead of reacting impulsively. Practise this skill in advance of playdates.

STEP 3. Demonstrate and model skills

Show your child what it looks like to use the skill successfully. You can act out a skill yourself, or you may try some creative ways to show it. For example, you might read aloud from a script in the Who Is Your Audience? tone exercises to show your child what's needed. You might act out a desired skill as if responding to a challenging social situation. You can pretend a friend just took away your toy and model the appropriate behavioural response: "Can I please have my toy back?" or "It hurts my feelings when you take away my toy." Kids naturally learn social skills by copying parents' behaviour, so that's a built-in boost for making the lesson stick. Your role-play provides the words and actions your child can adapt for many other circumstances. Your example provides a helpful guide for your child to emulate.

STEP 4. Practice makes progress!

It takes repeated practice for kids working on new behaviours to really get the hang of them. Once your child understands the instructions for the lesson and you've shown what the new behaviour looks or sounds like, then all that's left is practice. Now your child is better able to understand what's expected in a social setting and can practise the skill.

For the lessons to really start to stick, you should practise five days a week—and don't panic at the thought! Practice sessions don't have to be long. In fact, don't push too long. If your child needs shorter lessons, that's okay. Everyone's attention span is different. Every single practice helps.

STEP 5. Wrapping up

Wrap-up helps your child cement what he has learned. A successful wrap-up session helps your child self-evaluate his own progress and witness his own actions so he can start building social self-awareness. You can say, "On a scale of 1 to 5, how would you rate your effort on that practice? What did you learn?" Share with him what you saw him do well. Praise anything he tried that is out of his comfort zone. Ask him to recap for you what he is working on and why. Reiterate his mission for the next day's practice or an upcoming real-life social setting.

BUT...I DON'T HAVE TIME TO FIT ONE MORE ROUTINE INTO OUR LIVES.

Yes, you do. You're holding this book because your child's social situation has demanded plenty of your time, attention, and emotional energy in the past—and it's still a problem. This programme and practice is going to change that. Is there some wiggle room to be flexible? Of course. Diet books say that if you're in an airport, you can expect to eat differently than if you're at home. Or you can take a cheat day and it's not the end of the world. But if you cheat every day, you won't see the progress you want, because progress comes from consistent practice. Neuroscience shows that coaching conversation and practice together create new neuropathways that change behaviour. So, if you wing it, phone it in, and are hit-or-miss about practice, then you're not going to get the results. Most importantly, your child won't get the results. There are so many ways to improvise *and* stay engaged. Stick with the basic *Play Better Plan* and the results will help motivate you both to stick with it.

YOU'VE GOT THIS!

It doesn't have to be a perfect session as if you're a professional. As long as you follow the directions and engage in this home practice and start to really spend time on this skill building, you are going to make progress.

PART III

The *Play Better* Executive Function Social Skills Tracks

11

The Starter Track for Everyone!

This lesson track presents the first lessons you and your child will complete in the *Play Better Plan*. All children benefit from these lessons regardless of their results from the Executive Function Questionnaire and the EFQ Lesson Track identified to follow after this Starter Track. It's important for your child to complete all of these Starter Track lessons to be prepared with the concepts and terminology woven into every tool going forwards in the *Play Better Plan*. If you believe that your child doesn't need support in one or more of these concepts, then spend less time on that lesson, but please don't skip it.

Have your child pick out a special notebook (you too!) for jotting notes and answers in the lesson exercises where they are indicated. The notebooks can be helpful—and fun—to refer to over time, and they give your child a way to see his progress.

LESSON: HOW TO SPY 101

The purpose of Social Spy

Throughout the *Play Better Plan*, your child will be asked to be a "Social Spy" to improve his ability to notice and observe the behaviour of people and groups. In this context, being a Social Spy simply means learning to watch and listen for social clues and cues essential for making more positive choices.

Social Spy helps your child to:

- obtain important information they lack about social interactions with their peers and within their school and play settings

- sharpen their understanding of how other children interact
- observe the unspoken rules of different environments
- learn to pause so that they can notice social cues
- watch positive social behaviour so they have a visual model to navigate towards
- compare their behaviour to others.

Social Spy can also reduce conflict. Rather than arguing about a behaviour, you can ask your child to spy and see for herself what other children do. This helps your child compare her behaviour to that of others. For example, a child may need to understand that she is louder than other children in public places. Social Spy encourages her to listen to how loudly other children speak in public places, and in this way, understand the need to adjust her volume. Or your child may need to watch the body language of other children hanging out after football practice, so that she can mirror that casual body language when she tries to relax with other kids.

© 2016 Maguire

Missions

Every spy needs a mission: a clearly defined job the child must complete during each skill-building exercise. For children, missions can be a playful way to help them engage in the lesson and have a clear understanding of what is expected of her in the context of each lesson. After completing her mission, your child records her observations in a spy notebook, via text or in a format chosen between parent and child.

Design your own Social Spy lesson

You can design your own spy mission when you need more intel to help your child move forwards or to bolster their understanding of a concept. Together, you can take a spy field trip to a mall or a shop, hotel lobby, coffee shop, bookstore, or museum, for instance, to practise noticing social cues or to watch specific social behaviours.

Materials

- Take a small notebook to serve as the Spy Log to record observations, or have your child text you notes from the mission, or, if it works for them, simply try to remember what they observe.
- A small spyglass can help make social spying fun and is fun to use in home play.

Setting up the lesson

Explain that social spying is a fun way to investigate other people's behaviour and get the information you need about social clues, language, and behaviours. Explain to your child that the mission is for him to gather information and report back to "debrief"—talk about what he saw and what it means to him. Decide together how to report his social observations—in a notebook, in a conversation with you, or perhaps via texts.

Activity

1. Role-play with your child to show how she can spy on her peers without being obvious. Practise spying with your child: show them how to observe someone without staring or pointing, how to listen for clues, and how to do this quietly, without hovering or leering or telling others about your Social Spy mission.
2. Partner with your child to pick a specific behaviour from this list: listen to someone's conversation, look at body language to detect who is angry or watch to see how people often show that they are in a hurry through their body language or voice.
3. Rehearse spying on your family or go to a public place so your child gets practice pretending to spy where she won't be noticed by other children.
4. Brainstorm with your child about how he will log his observations. Share his spy journal with him. Share an example of observations

that might be gathered and logged in a spy journal and discuss how he'll capture his observations.

Wrapping up

Ask what she has observed and, based on what she has learned, what new social behaviour(s) she wants to practise.

LESSON: UNSPOKEN RULES

Setting up the lesson

Each environment and situation has its own set of unspoken rules that dictate what behaviour is appropriate. Your child needs to learn to pause and interpret these unspoken rules and then adjust his behaviour to meet those expectations.

Activity

1. Read aloud with your child this description of unspoken rules:

There are millions of unspoken rules in everyday life. The rules are not written down or posted anywhere. So you must figure them out for yourself based on how others behave in each situation. How loud should your voice be in a certain place? How much information can you share with a new person? When is it okay to sit or stand? These are the kinds of social rules that must be learned so that you fit in and know how to act in any social situation.

Unspoken social rules are not absolute, but they are a guide to help us act appropriately, be polite, and fit in. You learn these rules by watching other people: their body language, their tone of voice, and their facial expressions. How people act in a quiet, sombre gathering differs from how they behave at a party or on the playground. So there are unspoken rules for most times and places. The more you learn about how people behave, the easier it is for you to feel comfortable around them. It is important to pause and think through the expectations of a social situation.

Read this scenario to help your child understand unspoken rules.

Scenario:

■ In a coffee shop, adult customers are sitting quietly at tables, working hard on their computers, many wearing earphones.

There is no noise and there are no children anywhere. There is a long line to order coffee and there are very few seats.

2. After reading the scenario ask, "What cues do you notice that tell you what the unspoken rules are?" Write those unspoken rules down.

3. After your child has had a chance to identify some unspoken rules, you may share others. A few might be: keep your voice low because people are working; mostly it is grown-ups, so kids need to sit still; do not hover when you want to grab a seat; know what you want when you are in line to order since other people are waiting; don't interrupt people wearing earphones because they are working and do not want to chat.

Wrapping up

Ask your child to tell you about some unspoken rules she has noticed in your household. In the house of a close friend? In her classroom at school?

LESSON: UNSPOKEN RULES FIELD TRIP

Setting up the lesson

Explain that unspoken rules can be different in different environments or different situations. Watching and listening for verbal and nonverbal cues help you recognise the unspoken rules in that place and situation. Tell your child that this activity will help her learn to pause and notice the unspoken rules in any situation.

Activity

1. Pick a location such as a mall, shop, restaurant, or a library and take a field trip with your child. When you arrive, find a place to sit out of the way. Ask your child to scan the environment and consider what she notices: "What do you notice about the people? What do you notice about the sound level and people's voices? Is it noisy (the mall) or quiet (the library)? Think about the unspoken rules and the expectations for behaviour here. What would some of those be?"

2. Then ask her about the social clues that tell her about the unspoken rules. Some other categories of clues would be how people are dressed, whether it appears to be a particularly family-friendly or child-friendly environment, and what that means.

3. Tell your child, "Look at the body language of the people here. What do you notice? What is everyone doing? What do their actions tell you about what you need to be doing? Are people busy or laid back? Moving slowly or hurrying along? Based on how they are acting, what actions can you take to help you fit into this environment?"

4. Finally, ask your child to list all of the unspoken rules at the location. At this point, feel free to help her with hints if she is missing some. Write down those unspoken rules.

Wrapping up

Ask your child to tell you what unspoken rules are and why they are important.

LESSON: UNSPOKEN RULES—PUBLIC RULES AND PRIVATE RULES

Setting up the lesson

People behave differently in public than in private (at home), where they may be more casual. This means that someone your child knows well may behave differently in a playdate at home, at school, or out in the community.

Activity

1. Discuss with your child the different ways that people behave in public and private settings. How well you know someone, whether that person is new to you, a close friend, or a family member, affects how you act. Pick someone you know well and someone who is just an acquaintance, and explain to your child that he is going to try to discover the unspoken rules for each person. These might reflect differences in personality, a more formal or more casual home setting, food sensitivities, or maybe the presence of pets and how they are to be treated. Ask your child to describe someone who is close—a family member or old friend. What makes them close? Ask him to think about the unspoken rules for each person's house based on how well you know them. Some questions to promote thought are: How well do I know this person? What do I know about them? How casual or formal should I be? Do they like their house neat? Do they have rules they have told you in the past? What are the rules for your body—okay to be active or to wrestle or roughhouse? What are the rules for your actions?

2. Write down the unspoken rules.

Wrapping up

Going forwards, you can ask your child to notice the unspoken rules when you enter a new place or situation. Make it a game and help him think about the unspoken rules and see if he can point them out when prompted.

LESSON: SOCIAL CUES AND SIGNALS

Setting up the lesson

Many children with social struggles have trouble interpreting social cues or do not pause to notice them. Throughout the programme, your child will learn to recognise that there is social information all around us. Our role is to pause to take in that information to help us be better friends.

Activity

1. Read the following introduction to social cues and discuss social cues to notice.

   Social cues are the verbal and nonverbal messages that tell us information about what people think and feel. In any situation you enter, you need to consider the social cues or signals to help you know how to act and what to say.

   A social cue can be a verbal or nonverbal hint and can be positive or negative. These cues can be signs of someone's emotional state, intentions, and the messages they want to convey.

2. Role-play and act out what each cue might look like. Tell your child, "Guess what message this person is trying to communicate in the scenario through her verbal and nonverbal cues."

   - **Tone of voice**: When a person says "yup," and then "I got it," in a sharp tone, what is the person trying to tell you with his tone of voice?
   - **Volume of voice**: What is a person trying to show you when he speaks in a muffled tone, nods, whispers, says "I got it," and holds up his hand as if to stop someone from talking? Ask your child, "What are they trying to show you with their voice?"
   - **Pace of language**: When people talk very fast on a mobile-phone, turning their body away and looking away from you as you are talking to them, what is the person trying to show with their behaviour?
   - **Language and word choices**: Someone says, "Okay, buddy, you can stop now," or "That was funny; we got it." Ask your child, "What is that person trying to tell you with her language?"

- ❏ **The speaker's energy level:** A person shows low energy and yawns and asks you no questions. Ask, "With that energy, what is the person saying with his body?"
- ❏ **Body language**: Someone stands with arms folded and shoulders turned away from you. Ask, "What is this person trying to show you with this body language?"
- ❏ **Personal space**: You lean close to someone and they step back and move away from you. Ask, "What are they trying to show you with their body about personal space? What do people feel when someone is too close to them?"
- ❏ **Eye contact**: Ask your child, "When someone walks with his head down with his eyes glancing away and his shoulders hunched, what is he showing you with his eyes and body?"
- ❏ **Facial expressions**: Ask your child, "What is a person trying to show you when she frowns and her eyebrows come together? What is she showing with her facial expression?"

Wrapping up

Continue to watch for cues in daily life with your child. From time to time, point out someone's cue and ask your child to decode the message.

LESSON: LIKE THIS, NOT THAT

Setting up the lesson

Learning from past experiences is critical because it helps your child make positive social choices. After all, every social situation can be figured out if she learns to pause and consider past experiences. With her experiences in mind, she learns to consider what is *similar* and *different* about new people, situations, and social challenges. Building on this, she can find ways to learn the unspoken rules for new situations.

Like This, Not That asks your child to consider how a person, place, or situation is similar to a past experience and how it is different from the past. This thought process is a helpful first step in any social situation.

Activity

1. Present the concept below of Like This, Not That and read the following introduction to the lesson.

    One quick way to figure out how to manage any new experience or person is to think about how you've handled a *similar* experience in the past. Next consider how the new situation or person is *different* from or *similar* to a past experience. So when you enter any new situation or meet a new person, think, "Is this Like This, Not That? *How* does the new person or situation differ from others before? In what ways are they similar?" For example, Danny enters a birthday party where they are playing laser tag. Danny has been to a party where they played laser tag before, so in that way the party is *similar* to one he has been to before; he notes that the cake is the same and even the decorations. There are *differences* too: the people who are there and how teams are picked.

2. Pick an upcoming event, situation, person, or even a group project at school. It can be both similar and different from the past. Ask your child, "How does your past experience with this differ from what you see now? In what ways are these (people, situations, groups) similar? Are there any things you learned from the past that might be useful as you think about how to be today?"

3. Some additional questions you can ask: How is this current place or situation similar to a past experience and how is it different? How is this environment like what you have seen before? How is the environment different from what you have seen before? What similarities and differences do you see in this situation? Based on those similarities and differences, what do you know about how you should act and talk? What do you think the social rules might be?

Wrapping up

Going forwards, practise with your child in any new situation or with new people, thinking about how it is Like This, Not That.

LESSON: THE IMPRESSION YOU CREATE IN THE WORLD

Setting up the lesson

Your child needs to understand that he makes social impressions through his actions, words, and body language. Often, he may not realise that how he acts towards others directly affects how people think about him and treat him later.

Activity

1. Read the following introduction and show your child the fossil image of the dinosaur in the rock.

Everywhere you go, you leave behind an impression, just like these dinosaur bones left behind an impression millions of years ago. It is important to be aware that through the things we say, our tone of voice, our body language, our facial expressions, and our actions, we leave behind an impression with everyone we meet. These impressions affect how people feel about us and how they treat us.

2. Ask your child: "What kind of impression do you want to make? What gets in the way of you making a good impression?"

Wrapping up

Discuss with your child the impressions that other children or adults have made on him and what they have said or done that left that impression.

LESSON: MAKING A GOOD IMPRESSION

Setting up the lesson

Now that your child knows what an impression is and understands that we control (to a great degree) the impression we create, it is time for her to understand more about what goes into the impressions we create and how she can change her social impression.

Activity

1. Ask your child: "What actions, words, and body language help cre-ate a positive impression?" Feel free to use some examples if she is stumped: giving friendly smiles, making eye contact, lending a help-ing hand, sharing, speaking in a friendly tone, compromising with

friends and letting things go, paying attention to what your friend cares about, and listening to what your friend is interested in.

2. Read aloud the examples accompanying the visual below for The Impression You Make in the World and ask your child what she thinks they mean. If she is confused, then clarify the meaning to her. If need be, act out what a negative scowl face looks like, what a sharp cranky tone sounds like.

3. Talk with your child about the list of things we do that might alienate other people and make a negative impression. Ask your child to point out the things she might do that could get in the way of making a good impression. Feel free to write down any that are not on the list.

Impressions You Create in the World

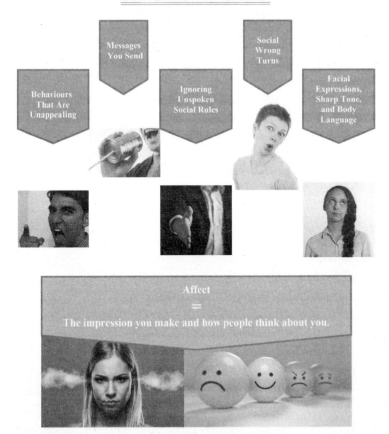

© 2018 Maguire

Behaviours that might alienate people:

- Show a negative, scary face and scowl
- Speak with a sharp, cranky tone of voice
- Ignore someone when I sit next to them
- Look all around rather than making eye contact
- Sit with arms folded over my chest
- Walk away when someone is talking
- Tell someone they are wrong all the time
- Ignore someone when they speak to me
- Hold up my hand to tell someone to shush
- Explode and get very angry at friends
- Ignore unspoken rules
- Blurt out and interrupt other people
- Brag all the time
- Hog toys and games
- Other _____

Pick two or three behaviours from the list and act them out for your child. Really play it up. Then ask your child, "What impression did I make? How do you feel about how you acted? What would happen if you act this way with friends?"

Wrapping up

Ask your child, "What impression do you want to make? What do you need to change to make a better impression?"

LESSON: FRIENDSHIP CHEMISTRY

Setting up the lesson

Many children lack self-awareness and can't realistically assess their social behaviour and the specific actions that may alienate their peers. This lesson is meant to help your child become aware of three things. First, that everything we do is noticed by other people and that they operate with the history of our interactions in mind. Second, it is important to make sure our actions reflect what we mean to do, our intentions. This should help children begin to make the link between how they act and how they are treated. Third, it is important to be aware that his peers are watching his behaviour, that they form an opinion about his actions, and that those opinions can affect how they react and treat him.

Activity

1. Show your child the Friendship Chemistry visual and read aloud the visual, including the bubbles. Ask your child what he thinks about the statement that people have thoughts about our actions, that these thoughts create a reaction, and that these thoughts affect how they treat us?

2. Walk through Friendship Chemistry using these scenarios so your child can bring this concept to life. Feel free to use the bubbles to fill in the actions and reactions of peers to the scenarios that follow. While you read and discuss the scenarios, ask your child such questions as the following:

   What are other people's thoughts about your actions?

   What is their reaction to you?

   How will they treat you after this event?

   What are the signals that other people are getting upset about or having feelings about your behaviour?

   What do you think your friends feel?

   What are the signals that your friend is getting annoyed?

Friendship Chemistry

Every action has a reaction.

People operate with your history of interactions in mind.

© 2017 Maguire

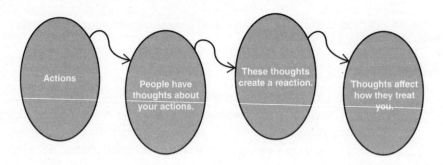

Actions → People have thoughts about your actions. → These thoughts create a reaction. → Thoughts affect how they treat you.

What do the signals tell me about other people?

Scenarios:

- Kate tells other people the rules. She feels, *If they are doing something wrong, I have to tell them.* Her friends often tell her they don't need a boss or that they do not like what she has to say. Kate does not know why people do not invite her to play at break time.

- Jamie nags his mother for something he wants on the sidelines of his football game. Over and over he asks for a treat. His friends are watching. After, they are very quiet and look away from him.

- Ozzy tells a story over and over or talks about his favourite subject all the time. His classmates often roll their eyes or walk away. Ozzy's classmates often seem frustrated with him out of the blue.

- Sofia is very shy. When someone sits next to her, she does not talk to them. She wants her peers to speak to her. She waits and often kids think she is snobby or rude for not speaking to them when they greet her with a smile. Eventually they stop speaking to her. Sofia does not know why.

Wrapping up

Going forwards, you can use Friendship Chemistry to help your child analyse any social problem. When you notice behaviours that may be causing a disconnect, discuss them with your child during your next coaching session. Ask her questions such as, "How did (insert actions) affect your friend? What did your friend feel about (insert action)?" When you use Friendship Chemistry, be sure to ask your child questions to help him reflect on his social role and his actions.

LESSON: THE POLITE PRETEND

Setting up the lesson

A Polite Pretend is the concept of acting polite and having positive social reactions even when you feel annoyed, irritated, hungry, tired, or bored. For some children, failing to show this simple social courtesy causes a Social Wrong Turn.

Activity

1. Read the following introduction to the Polite Pretend to your child.

   Everyone has moments when they feel annoyed, irritated, uncomfortable, overwhelmed, tired, hungry, bored, or they dislike the person speaking and they have trouble being polite. Even though you are *not feeling* polite, it is important to answer questions from adults and peers, show socially appropriate emotions, respond to others, and go along with the social rules of the situation.

2. Ask your child some questions about the concept of Polite Pretend: What do you think about a Polite Pretend? Have you ever struggled to be polite when you are uncomfortable, bored, irritated, tired, hungry, or upset? What makes a Polite Pretend important? What are some situations where you might struggle with Polite Pretend? What should you do?

3. Role-play by asking your child to show you what a Polite Pretend looks like in the following scenarios. What actions did the person need to do to perform a Polite Pretend?

Scenarios:

- Josh is tired and hungry and has been at school a long time. His mother is chatting with his teacher. But Josh wants to go.
- Annie is bored with the conversation with her uncle and she just wants it to be over.

Ask your child to tell you what gets in the way of performing a Polite Pretend? If he objects to performing a Polite Pretend, ask him: "Why? What do you imagine other people feel when you do not perform a Polite Pretend? What is the benefit of performing a Polite Pretend?"

Wrapping up

Ask your child to recap when and where he might need to perform a Polite Pretend. Brainstorm strategies to help him figure out how he can perform a Polite Pretend in the future. A code word you agree upon with your child could be a great way to prompt him to remember to perform a Polite Pretend in the heat of the moment.

LESSON: FRIENDSHIP IS A TWO-WAY STREET

Setting up the lesson

Friendship Is a Two-Way Street helps your child discuss a tough topic: Who are your friends? How do they treat you? How do you feel about the fact that friendship has to be based on mutual interest in being friends? This reflection and discussion gives your child some criteria to evaluate his friendships and his perception of friendships. The criteria for this evaluation are based on emotional intimacy, mutual interest in friendship, nonverbal cues, body language, and facial expressions. These all help your child examine who is really a friend and who is not close enough to your child to be truly called a friend.

Activity

1. Introduce the concept that there are different types of friends based on closeness, interests, and how receptive they are to you. Read the Different Flavours of Friendship description in the illustration that follows. Show your child the visual and read to him the criteria for the Flavours.

   Friends are like ice cream—there are different Flavours, but each is unique. People have different friends for different purposes. We have different levels of interaction with different people. There are stages of friendship, and there are people who are close with us and those who are not. It is okay to have people who are not our best friend in our lives. Sometimes the tough part is to really look at your friendships and know what you would like to change.

   This lesson is meant to help you understand your friendships and how you feel about them. How close you are to someone tells you how to decide what you share with them and how often you see them. Most people have different friends in different categories.

2. Discuss with your child the different people he knows. Refer to the visual Who Do You Know and Where Do They Fit? Ask your child to map out the different people he knows and have him consider who might be a friend and who is just someone to say hello to. If he plans to put too many people in the friend stage who are not

The Different Flavours of Friendship

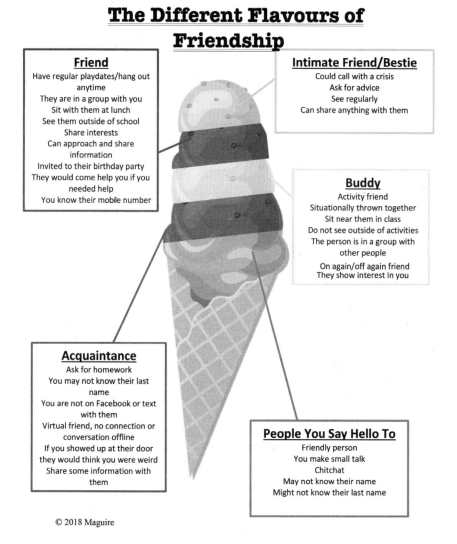

Friend
Have regular playdates/hang out anytime
They are in a group with you
Sit with them at lunch
See them outside of school
Share interests
Can approach and share information
Invited to their birthday party
They would come help you if you needed help
You know their mobile number

Intimate Friend/Bestie
Could call with a crisis
Ask for advice
See regularly
Can share anything with them

Buddy
Activity friend
Situationally thrown together
Sit near them in class
Do not see outside of activities
The person is in a group with other people
On again/off again friend
They show interest in you

Acquaintance
Ask for homework
You may not know their last name
You are not on Facebook or text with them
Virtual friend, no connection or conversation offline
If you showed up at their door they would think you were weird
Share some information with them

People You Say Hello To
Friendly person
You make small talk
Chitchat
May not know their name
Might not know their last name

© 2018 Maguire

close to him, ask him, "How often do you speak with them or see them outside school or an activity?" Remind your child of the criteria listed for each stage of friendship.

Wrapping up

Continue to discuss the Flavours of Friendship and refer to your own personal circle of friends and acquaintances to discuss the concepts with your child.

Who Do You Know and Where Do They Fit?

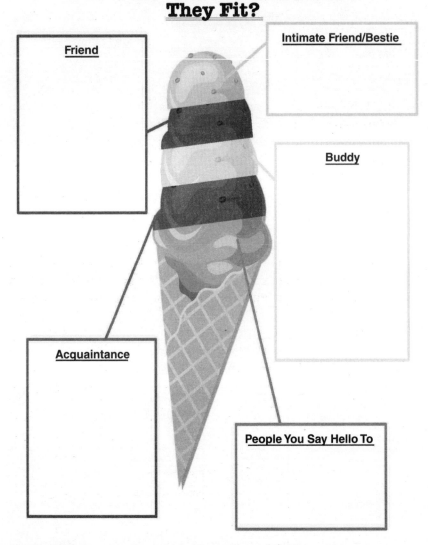

Friend

Intimate Friend/Bestie

Buddy

Acquaintance

People You Say Hello To

LESSON: SOCIAL RIGHT TURNS AND WRONG TURNS

Setting up the lesson

The Social Right Turns and Wrong Turns lesson can be used as a framework, so your child can consider her role in any situation. Your child can use this lesson to decode any situation and consider what she needs to do to comply with the unspoken social rules, to follow the social guide-lines, and to make a good impression on other people. The term *Social Wrong Turn* can be a little code between you and your child, a cue to remind her to think about unspoken rules and social guidelines in any situation.

Activity

1. Read the following description of Social Right Turns and Wrong Turns to your child.

   In every situation, there are unspoken social rules or expecta-tions known as *social guidelines*. They are the general rules that help you know what the polite, customary protocol is for any social situation. When you enter a social situation, you can have a Right Turn where you comply with the social guidelines and unspoken rules or a Wrong Turn where you misstep and do not follow the social guidelines and unspoken rules.

   When we ignore unspoken social rules or make a Social Wrong Turn, it makes an impression on other people and then they remember that impression and they react to us based on what they have seen in the past. We want to leave impressions that we are ready to play and that we are friendly and likable so people want to be with us and want to be our friend. You can change your impression and you can send a different social mes-sage. Everyone has bad days, but it is important to think about the impression you make on other people. Following the Social Guidelines (see table below) can help you better manage that impression.

Social Guidelines	
The Right and Wrong Turns of Social Behaviour	
SOCIAL RIGHT TURNS **Using Unspoken Rules**	**SOCIAL WRONG TURNS** **Ignoring Social Guidelines**
1.	1.
2.	2.
3.	3.

2. Show your child the table above, then ask her to tell you about Social Right Turns she has made recently. Ask, "Why was using the unspoken rules important in that situation?" Then ask her about a time when she made a Social Wrong Turn and what happened.

3. Read aloud the scenario and help your child walk through the Social Right Turns and Wrong Turns of the situations. Identify the Right Turns and Wrong Turns in the scenarios by writing them in your lesson notebook. Ask your child, "What social choices did you make and what happened as a result? What unspoken rules were supported or violated?"

Scenarios:

- Frank was feeling angry and irritated and wanted to leave a family party. His uncle tried to ask him questions about his baseball team, but he just shrugged and didn't really look at his uncle. After this his uncle never really approached Frank again.

- Jane went to school and discovered that the kids in a neighbouring classroom were having a party. She sneaked into the party and took some doughnuts. Other kids glared at her; her teacher found out. The kids from the neighbouring classroom ignored her on the playground later. Her teacher reprimanded her and seemed very angry.

Wrapping up

Discuss with your child how she can use the Social Right Turns and Wrong Turns lesson to figure out social problems. Whenever she faces a social dilemma, she can consider what Social Guidelines are, and how she can make a Social Right Turn.

LESSON: FRIENDLY, AGREEABLE SNAPSHOT

Setting up the lesson

Part of learning to make friends is understanding that we all have social choices and that we need to choose behaviours that are agreeable and friendly. Your child benefits from understanding that there is a relationship between how we act, the nonverbal messages we send, and the impressions we make.

Activity

1. Present the concept of friendly and agreeable behaviours. Describe to your child that we demonstrate friendly and agreeable behaviours or

disagreeable behaviours through our actions, what we say, our tone of voice, our facial expressions, and our body language. For instance, scowling is unappealing, while smiling is appealing. Share with your child that the benefits of friendly and agreeable behaviours include:

- ❑ making a good impression
- ❑ demonstrating to people that you are friendly
- ❑ showing other children you are ready to play
- ❑ encouraging other kids to seek you out
- ❑ creating positive thoughts about you in other people
- ❑ creating positive reactions to you from other people.

Share with your child the visual of the Friendly, Agreeable Snapshot and the list of friendly and agreeable behaviours that follow. Have your child pinpoint on the Friendly, Agreeable Scale any behaviours he demonstrates that are friendly and agreeable. If your child is unable to think of some friendly, agreeable behaviours, feel free to bring up some positive behaviours you have seen. If he cannot think of any disagreeable behaviours, prompt him or delicately suggest some examples, saying, "What about…" or "I have noticed that…"

Friendly, Agreeable Snapshot

What are my behaviours on this scale?
What makes someone agreeable?

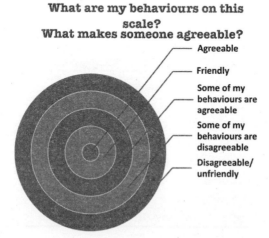

- Agreeable
- Friendly
- Some of my behaviours are agreeable
- Some of my behaviours are disagreeable
- Disagreeable/ unfriendly

Friendly and agreeable behaviours:

- Patience with others
- Good listener
- Flexible and able to cooperate with others
- A good sense of humour
- Aware of body language
- Compromises with a friend
- Takes turns
- Shows interest in a friend
- Manages his feelings and upset
- Shows his good mood
- Recognises that he is not always right
- Lets go of grudges and hurt feelings
- Manages impulses
- Approachable and friendly, smiling often
- Adapts to changes in routine or playmate's desires

Present the concept of behaviours that are unappealing to your child. Share with him the list of unappealing behaviours and have him pinpoint on the Friendly, Agreeable Snapshot any behaviours he demonstrates that are unappealing.

Disagreeable behaviours:

- Showing a negative, scary face and scowl
- Speaking with a sharp, cranky tone of voice
- Telling someone they are wrong and reprimanding them about the rules
- Ignoring someone
- Looking all around rather than making eye contact
- Sitting with arms folded over your chest
- Walking away when someone is talking
- Telling someone they are wrong all the time
- Ignoring someone when they speak to you
- Holding up your hand to tell someone to shush
- Exploding and getting very angry at friends
- Ignoring unspoken rules
- Blurting and interrupting other people
- Bragging all the time
- Hogging toys and games
- Badgering and nagging peers to get your way

- Telling someone the same story or topic over and over again
- Other _____

Wrapping up

Ask your child to describe what overall impression he makes. Allow your child to write in any specific behaviours that make him less agreeable on the graph and any behaviours that he knows cause social problems.

LESSON: LEARNING TO WALK IN SOMEONE ELSE'S SHOES

Setting up the lesson

Learning to Walk in Someone Else's Shoes is meant to help your child create an experience where she takes the perspective of other people and thinks about their feelings, her impact on them, and their reactions to her behaviour by stepping into their shoes. This activity creates a neutral way to help your child consider the feelings of others and look at both sides of an issue without you telling her the other person's perspective. She'll be able to role-play and really consider the feelings of other people. The Learning to Walk in Someone Else's Shoes mat creates a three-dimensional dress rehearsal and experience for a future conversation and problem-solve, an event to help your child really consider the perspective of other people.

**LEARNING TO WALK IN
SOMEONE ELSE'S SHOES**

© 2016 Maguire

Activity

1. Copy the Learning to Walk in Someone Else's Shoes mat or draw the mat on craft paper. At any time, your child can pretend to walk in the shoes of multiple people in a situation.

2. Start by sharing the concept that it's important sometimes to consider how other people feel, who they are, and to walk in their shoes. Explain that throughout the lessons in Learning to Walk in Someone Else's Shoes, your child will put herself into the shoes of specific people and think about how they might react and how they would feel about a situation. Discuss the fact that sometimes people are hard to figure out and their reactions seem to come out of nowhere. Walking in someone else's shoes means you think about how you would feel in the same situation. You may never fully understand how someone else feels, you may not know everything about the person's circumstances, but it is important to try to think about both your perspective and other people's.

3. Present the scenarios below. Ask your child to step into the shoes of the people in the scenarios below by stepping onto the Learning to Walk in Someone Else's Shoes mat. For fun, your child can select special shoes to wear on the mat or take off her shoes. After you read the scenario, ask your child, "What does the main character feel?"

Scenarios:

- Keton's mother stays up very late making him a costume for the school play. She works every night for weeks. When she picks him up from school, she tells him she has a headache and she is really worn down from working on the costume. Without responding about the costume, Keton asks her, "Did you bring me a sandwich?" How did Keton's mother feel? What makes asking about the sandwich a Social Wrong Turn? Step into Keton's mother's shoes—what would she have appreciated hearing from Keton? Why does it matter what he said?

- Mrs. B is willing to help you with your science work, but you have not shown up to meet with her nine times. Today you ask her to meet after school and she says, "Sorry, I can't today." Step onto the mat and think about what Mrs. B feels. How do you think she felt in the past when you didn't show up? What has her experience of you been?

Wrapping up

Discuss the different scenarios and ask your child to detect what key social cues and signals tell her how the characters feel.

LISTS FOR EVERYONE!

These are lists that your child will reference in multiple tool tracks and across multiple lessons. The lessons will direct you to find the specific list here in the Starter Track for Everyone!

Things that make me experience big emotions

- Social problems
- School or academic problems
- People who bug or irritate me
- Homework
- Losing a privilege like computer time
- Break time
- Lunchroom
- Losing a game
- Boredom
- Waiting
- Changes in schedule, plans, or activities
- Worrying about something I said or something said to me
- Too much noise, crowds
- Someone telling me what to do
- Breaking the rules or having other people break the rules
- My siblings
- My parents

Calm-down strategies

- Blow bubbles
- Chew gum
- Complete a puzzle
- Use the Blue Sky Breathing lesson in Chapter 19
- Use stretchy resistance bands
- Listen to music or audiobooks
- Do some yoga

- Sing the ABCs forwards and backwards
- Swing
- Go for a walk
- Draw with chalk or colour ten pictures
- Play hopscotch, skip, or bounce on a trampoline
- Take a bubble bath
- Look at a lava lamp or hourglass
- Pop bubble wrap
- Go to a calm-down tent or area
- Read a book
- Trace your hands
- Do a craft
- Draw ten pictures
- Wear a weighted vest

Signs of Interest

Signs of Interest in a Conversation:
Smiling
Saying supportive comments
Saying yes in a supportive tone
Leaning forwards in a chair
Making eye contact and looking directly at you
Laughing
Asking questions of the speaker

Signs of Boredom with a Topic:
Sighing
Shrugging
Yawning
Turning away
Giving short answers
Asking no questions of the speaker
Not responding with words or your body
Not making eye contact
Staring off into the distance
Having a sharp tone or a tone that is flat

What other signs of boredom with a topic do you notice? _____

12

Flexible Me

Flexibility/Adaptability

Note: All of the EFQ Track chapters (11-19) begin with Level 1 lessons. As your child progresses, advance to Level 2 lessons, which are labelled "Level 2" and are designated by the light grey background.

LESSON: WHAT DOES IT MEAN TO BE FLEXIBLE AND WHY IS IT IMPORTANT?

Setting up the lesson

This lesson is meant to help your child identify what being flexible means and what makes it so important to friendships. Your child comes to understand what behaviours are flexible and why being flexible is a key element of friendship.

Activity

1. Introduce Flexible Me characteristics to your child and share that being flexible is what is expected during play. Read aloud the list of Flexible Me expectations below. Ask your child to identify the flexible characteristics he struggles with. Discuss: What do you think the trait means? What do you notice about the character? Share the two lists below with your child. Does anything sound familiar to him?

Flexible behaviour:

- Think how friends feel and adapt your behaviour
- Shift when a routine or plan changes
- Meet people halfway
- Adjust thinking and mind-set when needed
- Let go of old hurts and blame

- Know you are not always right
- Compromise with friends
- Understand rules are not absolute; they are guidelines
- Refrain from "my way or the highway" behaviour where your agenda and intention are the only ones that matter
- Hear out other people's ideas

Inflexible behaviour:

- Getting stubborn when things are not what you want
- Bossing other people around and making them do what you want
- Campaigning to get your way
- Arguing with everyone
- Correcting other people
- Sharing your ideas and never hearing other people's ideas
- Feeling you are always right
- Feeling rules are absolute and unbending
- Ignoring how people feel and pushing your own agenda
- Not shifting when plans change

2. Ask your child what it feels like when he is being flexible. What does being flexible look like? Why is being flexible important? Ask your child to imagine that he is playing with someone and no one shares with him and everyone corrects him and tells him he is breaking the rules. What would that feel like?

Wrapping up

Continue to talk about why flexibility is important to friendships by asking your child questions about other people's feelings. Talk about your child's friendship role, such as: "What do your friends expect when you play? What do you think your friend feels about (insert behaviour)?" When your child demonstrates flexible behaviour, celebrate that behaviour and say, "I love how flexible you are being."

LESSON: THE RULE POLICE

Setting up the lesson

Rule Police lessons help demonstrate to your child that constantly reprimanding other children and acting as the Rule Police alienates her peers. Rule Police activities also help your child identify her stories about rules and help her understand the benefits of being more adaptive.

Activity

1. Explain to your child that many rules of play are guidelines. Guidelines are advice to help you make choices, but they are not always absolute. Remind her of her social role and the Social Right Turns, Social Wrong Turns exercise. Ask your child, "How is being flexible a Right Turn or a Wrong Turn and why? How do you feel about rules?"

2. Explain to your child that there are some rules that must be followed because ignoring them is dangerous or harmful. Make a list of those rules. As you make the list, challenge any rules she feels are important that will not result in a dangerous situation and chances of the negative consequences are slim. To do this, you can ask her why she thinks the rule is important and why it is important to her. Ask her what the chances are of her prediction happening.

3. Discuss with your child what rules can be compromised. Hint: if she struggles with this question, some examples include the number of people who can participate in a game, when two people have been taught two different ways to play a game, places where you can play, when you play, and so on.

4. Share with your child that sometimes rules can cause friendship problems. Present the concept to your child that constantly correcting other people about rules makes you the Rule Police. Read this Rule Police description aloud.

The Rule Police means you:

- demand that other people follow the rules
- feel rules are absolute and unbendable
- feel rules are more important than anything
- let everyone know there is a right way to do things and a wrong way
- leave games if people don't follow your rules
- tell other kids to play your way
- reprimand other kids or adults for rule violations
- tell on kids to teachers, coaches, and adults if they break the rules
- demonstrate know-it-all, smarty-pants behaviour
- boss other people around.

Wrapping up

Examine with your child: What does it mean to be the Rule Police? What are the consequences? What do friends feel about Rule Police behaviour?

LESSON: RULE POLICE SCENARIOS

Setting up the lesson

The Rule Police scenarios hold a mirror up to your child's behaviour and allow him to see how Rule Police behaviour looks and feels when demonstrated by other children.

Activity

1. Read aloud the scenarios to your child.

    After each scenario, ask your child, "What do you think about the rule enforcer? Do you like that person? How would you feel if you were the rule enforcer? What if you were the other person and the rule enforcer was wrong? Would you want to play with the rule enforcer? How do you think onlookers felt about the rule enforcer?"

    #### Scenarios:

    - Marta is receiving an award, and she is on the podium with her head teacher. Kids in the auditorium are laughing and talking. They are not supposed to be loud. Marta tells them to shush from the podium. The chatty audience members visibly move their heads back in their seats and frown.

    - Billy takes his bowl of cereal to the basement even though they have a new sofa and his mum told him not to eat on the new sofa. His brother Owen tells his mother and Billy gets caught. Owen says, "I feel like if someone is doing something wrong, I need to tell them it's wrong." While Billy and his mother are in the other room having a discussion about the incident, Owen interjects himself over and over into the discussion. He interrupts the conversation and repeatedly tells Billy the rule and why Mum did not want him to eat in the basement. Later when Owen wants to play, Billy says no thanks.

2. Discuss the concept that in each of these scenarios there are signs that tell us how the person feels about the Rule Police character. Ask your child, "What are the body and vocal cues that tell you how the person feels who was 'policed'? What do you think is their reaction? How do you think they will treat the rule enforcer if they see him again?"

Wrapping up

Discuss what your child has learned about Rule Police behaviour.

LESSON: STICKY BRAIN

Setting up the lesson

Does your child struggle with interests, obsessions and rumination top-ics, problems, and mistakes? Do comments from classmates get stuck in her brain? This creates a big emotional reaction, making it hard for her to read social cues, remember the unspoken rules, and generally pro-duce the behaviours she wants. When things get stuck, they become a distraction, something that creates emotions and causes rumination, meaning—it causes you to think the same negative thoughts over and over. The concept of things getting stuck and rumination is an impor-tant topic for your child to understand. Creating a visual representation of things that get stuck can help your child witness this process of hav-ing a Sticky Brain.

Activity

1. Present the Sticky Brain image and share with your child this Sticky Brain list, that sometimes things get stuck in your brain:
   - ❑ Thoughts
   - ❑ Things you said
   - ❑ Things you did or did not do
   - ❑ What you want
   - ❑ Feeling unhappy
   - ❑ Big feelings
   - ❑ Something you are interested in
   - ❑ Things other people said
   - ❑ Problems

   When I am stuck, it's hard to:

   - read social cues
   - shift
   - think about how friends feel about my actions
   - think about how my message was received
   - think about what impression I am creating
   - be flexible and adapt to changes in my routine

- listen
- learn new information
- pay attention
- realise how big worries are affecting me
- cope with my emotions
- think about other people's feelings.

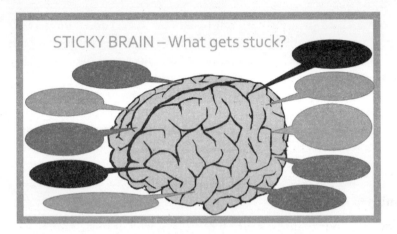

© 2016 Maguire

2. Share with your child that when things get stuck, it's hard for anyone to be Flexible Me. After showing your child the list, ask her if she ever has things get stuck. Then ask your child how she feels when things get stuck and what behaviour occurs as a result of her having Sticky Brain. What does it feel like to be stuck? How do other people feel about that behaviour?

3. Take the blank Sticky Brain and use Post-it notes or strips of paper to represent the thought bubble. Have your child write down the things that cause her to have Sticky Brain and paste them or tape them on the brain. Discuss with your child the emotions, stuff that bugs her, body signals, and feelings she experiences when she becomes stuck on a topic. If she cannot think of any, share a personal example or something you have noticed when she is stuck.

4. Read aloud the strategies for being stuck.

Strategies to cope with being stuck:

- Interrupt the pattern and go somewhere else.
- Take a step back.

- Go for a walk or exercise.
- Journal or talk to someone.
- Say to yourself, "I am stuck; I have to get out of the loop."
- Replace the thoughts from something negative to something positive.
- Take a shower or a bath.
- Pet a dog or cat.
- Listen to music or an audiobook.
- Do sit-ups or push-ups.
- Put an elastic or rubber bracelet on and twist it lightly.

Wrapping up

Create a plan for strategies your child can use when she gets stuck. Cue your child to use those strategies when you notice she is stuck and cannot go forwards.

LESSON: GETTING UNSTUCK

Setting up the lesson

Now that your child is aware that he may sometimes experience Sticky Brain, this exercise helps him practise using strategies to shift and get unstuck. Kids love it when you "explain the brain." It can be a game changer when they realise that it's the architecture of the brain—a bit different in each of us—that makes it harder for some people to get unstuck when they're stuck on a thought.

1. Read aloud the following concept of the gearshift of the brain to your child.

    Like a car, every part of your brain helps your brain go, shift, stop, and think. There is a part of your brain that is like a gearshift in a car and is called the *cingulate gyrus*. The gearshift of the brain helps you shift, move from thought to thought, let things go, and be flexible. So when your brain's gearshift gets stuck, you may feel stuck on a thought and have a hard time shifting your thinking or your behaviour. When your brain is stuck, one way to shift is to change where you are or what you are doing—that interrupts your brain and interrupts the thinking that is stuck. This change is called a *pattern interrupt* and it's the best way to "reset" your brain so it can shift gears. Sometimes your brain's gearshift just won't move on its own. Everybody's brain is a little bit different this way, and some get stuck more easily than others.

2. To practise getting unstuck, ask your child to pick one of the things on the Sticky Brain list (see previous lesson) that gives him trouble.

That's the one he'll work on in this exercise. Now read aloud the list of pattern interrupts below. Have your child choose two strategies to practise in the future. Act out a scenario in which he has been stuck recently and what using this pattern interrupt would look like.

3. Create a cue or prompt with your child so that the next time he is stuck, you or the prompt can remind him to try using the pattern interrupt.

Pattern interrupts:

- Distract yourself and do something new.
- Write down solutions for your problem.
- Start doing something you find fun.
- Slip an elastic band on your wrist, and every time you think a negative thought, flick the elastic.
- Take a walk.
- Exercise.
- Paint or draw.
- Go see a friend or loved one.
- Consider whether there is evidence for the negative thought you are thinking.
- Create an alternative thought for the negative one bugging you.

Wrapping up

Continue to prompt your child to try using a pattern interrupt when he experiences Sticky Brain. If he is ruminating and thoughts are getting stuck, work on seeing what evidence there is for the negative thought and what he could think instead.

LEVEL 2 TOOLS (CHALLENGE STEPPED UP)

LESSON: MY WAY OR THE HIGHWAY

Setting up the Lesson

Forming friendships involves adjusting what we say and how we say it based on the comments we get from the other person. When some children struggle with flexible thinking and behaviour, they also struggle to think about other people. Although they do not intend to, they can make people feel that they are constantly pushing their own agenda, getting their own way, and failing to compromise. I call this My Way or the Highway behaviour. It is important for your child to come to recognise this behaviour and to be able to learn the impact of this behaviour, the impression it creates, and the disruption it imposes on play.

Activity

1. Read the following introduction of My Way or the Highway.

   When we do not think about our impact on other people and we only focus on our needs or agenda, we are demonstrating My Way or the Highway behaviour. It may not be what we mean to do. But My Way or the Highway behaviour means that we are not sharing, cooperating, and listening to friends. We are making a Social Wrong Turn.

   In a friendship, it is important to meet people halfway. We need to think about what they want to do, too. We need to remember not to get stuck in the My Way or the Highway mind-set, where we push our agenda, campaign for an activity, a food, a place where we want to go, and refuse to listen to other voices. When we make all the choices for other people, the friendship is out of balance.

2. Read and discuss the list of common My Way or the Highway behaviours to your child:

Common My Way or the Highway behaviours:

- Always making the choice or deciding what she will do with friends
- Nagging other people or campaigning to get her way
- Grabbing what she wants without worrying about other people
- Deciding what activity or choices
- Making it all about what she wants.

Ask your child, "What does My Way or the Highway behaviour look like? What do people feel about this behaviour? What are the consequences?"

Wrapping up

Discuss occasions when your child might exhibit My Way or the High-way behaviour. Ask him what other people feel about this behaviour.

LESSON: MY WAY OR THE HIGHWAY SCENARIOS

Setting up the lesson

In order for your child to better understand that My Way or the Highway behaviour is a problem, he has to first experience some-one using it on him. This experience helps your child to under-stand why shifting this behaviour is so important.

Activity

1. Read the scenarios, then ask your child the questions provided. If need be, role-play and act out what the scene might look like. After each scenario, ask your child the following ques-tions: What was the My Way or the Highway behaviour the person demonstrated? What impression did he or she create? What were people's thoughts about him or her? How did other people react? How do you think they will treat him or her?

Scenarios:

- Jay loves pizza. He comes from a large family. When pizza arrives, he rushes in and grabs an entire pizza box for him-self. He takes what he wants. He does not worry about any-one else. Later that night, he wants to play video games with his brother. His brother says, "No thanks," and slams the door in Jay's face.

- Cary is frustrated that Lilly always decides what to do. If they go to the movies, she insists on seeing her first choice and nags over and over until she gets her way. If Cary picks a song, Lilly asks over and over to pick her favourite song. Lilly nags Cary, saying, "Oh, come on, it's better. Pick this one," and then two seconds later, "I have such good taste—you'll love this." If Cary has a different opinion about something than Lilly, she won't let go and feels like she can-not fight Lilly all the time. After a playdate, Cary tells her mother, "It is easier to just give in."

Wrapping up

Discuss why the characters grew frustrated with the My Way or the Highway behaviour. Role-play the scenarios with your child. You play the main character, and your child experiences the My Way or the Highway behaviour in the scenario. After, ask him what it felt like. Discuss how it felt when someone pushed *their* agenda and controlled *his* actions. Then ask your child to demonstrate what actions the main character needed to demonstrate to be more adaptive.

LESSON: PILE OF CHOICES

Setting up the lesson

During play with other children, often inflexible children are rigid and dominate the play agenda. They may remain unaware of their behaviour and its impact on their playmates. The Pile of Choices creates a visual representation of each choice your child makes on a playdate and how this creates an imbalance in her relationship with friends.

Activity

1. Show your child the visual of Pile of Choices and read the following introduction.

   This is a pile of all the choices that someone made over the course of a playdate. Each time the child pushed what she wanted, she made a choice. Notice that the ball is rolling towards the person who got to make all the choices.

2. Ask your child what she sees in the image. Who made the majority of choices? What does it feel like to hold back or to allow a friend to make some of the choices? What do you notice about the pile? What does the pile look like to you?

Note: If your child continues to deny My Way or the Highway behaviour, add this to the game: Ask her to take a challenge. With a sibling for one day or with a carefully selected friend during a playdate, ask her to put a poker chip or a piece of paper in a jar every time she demonstrates My Way or the Highway behaviour. This can occur subtly. No mention of it needs to occur during the playdate. If she feels uncomfortable, you can keep track of the behaviour. Then take a look at the visual image (the jar of chips) of her behaviour after the playdate when you can do it together.

Pile of Choices

My Way or the Highway Choices

Watch my video

Eat when I want

Listen to my music

Play my video game

I choose the game

I make the rules

I choose what we do when

Friend's Pile of Choices

I went along

Keep It Even. Meet People Halfway.

© 2018 Maguire

Wrapping up

The Pile of Choices is a symbol of one-sided My Way or the Highway behaviour. Continue to help your child by asking him how high his pile of choices is or when his friend gets to make a choice.

LESSON: MY WAY OR THE HIGHWAY AND SOCIAL GUIDELINES THE RIGHT AND WRONG TURNS OF SOCIAL BEHAVIOUR

Activity

1. Refer back to the My Way or the Highway scenarios. If your child has not read them for a few days, read them again.
2. Using the Social Right Turns tool in the Starter Track, ask your child to pinpoint what Social Right Turns the characters made. What Social Wrong Turns? What are the unspoken rules the main character ignored?

Wrapping up

Discuss the way Social Right Turns and Wrong Turns make other people feel and discuss what My Way or the Highway behaviour your child would like to shift to help create a positive impression.

LESSON: WHAT DO PEOPLE FEEL ABOUT MY WAY OR THE HIGHWAY BEHAVIOUR?

Setting up the lesson

My Way or the Highway scenarios help your child really understand what My Way or the Highway behaviour looks like, and it allows him to understand how other people react to this behaviour. Experiencing the behaviour and seeing models of My Way or the Highway behaviour often pinpoints for children why exactly this behaviour needs to change.

Activity

1. Discuss with your child how important other people's reactions are to his My Way or the Highway behaviour. Ask your child to role-play with you at each point in the scenario. Ask your child, "How do you feel? How does the other person feel? How does My Way or the Highway behaviour affect friendships?"

Scenarios:

- Kathy reminds everyone of things they need to do. When there are sweets or a treat she wants, she reminds everyone it's hers. On the way home from the supermarket with her four siblings, Kathy claims the red Tootsie Pops. When they get home, she reminds everyone they are hers. When the sweets come out of the shopping bag, she runs over to snatch them up.

- When you play with Matt, there is always a problem. Eventually the game or play skit falls apart because Matt won't compromise and has to have his way. He argues about everything. Then if everyone refuses to cave to him, he storms off. So no one wants to include him in a group or work with him on a project because they see the problem as inevitable. They secretly make plans and hope he won't find out.

Discuss the scenarios with your child. Ask your child to identify what the main character could have done to make a Social
Right Turn in the scenario. Continue to talk about what other people feel about My Way or the Highway behaviour and how that
makes them treat him.

Wrapping up

Point out any examples of this behaviour you notice in daily life
exhibited by other people. Create a plan with your child of specific behaviours and situations where he can be more flexible and
what he can do instead. Discuss why this may be hard for him.

Mind Your PEAS and Cues

Reading the Room

LESSON: READING-THE-ROOM ROLE-PLAY

Setting up the lesson

The first lesson helps your child understand all the elements of the process to read the room. This lesson brings the process to life, so your child can understand the concept and how all the pieces come together.

Activity

1. Read the following introduction to Reading the Room.

   The ability to interpret the unspoken rules and social cues in any situation or environment is called *reading the room*. This means scanning any place you enter or any situation you are in to see who is there, what the unspoken rules are, and to understand any social guidelines.

2. Explain to your child that today you'll go over the whole process to read the room and then during your *Play Better* in-home lessons, you'll work together on learning this skill lesson by lesson. Read aloud the visual with the steps to read the room.

3. Demonstrate to your child the steps to read the room at home by standing at the door of your space, narrating each step with the explanation. Act out the process as much as possible.

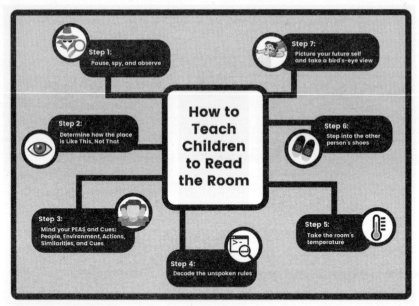

© 2016 Maguire

STEP 1: Pause, spy, and observe

When entering a space, people observe the surroundings, situation, people, and circumstances. In every social situation, it is important to observe and notice social cues, such as tone of voice, people's body language, and their facial expressions.

STEP 2: Determine how the place is Like This, Not That

Pausing and considering these similarities and differences of an environment and the people there is a quick, useful way for you to figure out the Social Guidelines and Unspoken Rules for the situation. It helps to try to remember past situations and experiences in order to notice the similarities and differences to your current situation.

STEP 3: Mind Your PEAS and Cues

To help you remember what to think about when you enter any situation, there is a little mnemonic: Mind Your PEAS and Cues. PEAS stands for *p*eople, *e*nvironment, *a*ctions, and *s*imilarities. *Cues* means to remember to read the social cues.

STEP 4: Decode the unspoken rules

Remember to interpret the unspoken rules in each situation so you can quickly identify the Social Right Turns you need to make.

STEP 5: Take the room's temperature

Within the situation, evaluate the people's mood, emotions, and energy, and then adjust your behaviour to meet that mood. Taking the room's temperature also helps you understand the unspoken rules and social guidelines.

STEP 6: Step into the other person's shoes

When you enter any situation, think about how your behaviour and messages will be received. Thinking about other people's feelings helps you know when you need to adjust your approach to meet the unspoken rules of a situation.

STEP 7: Picture your future self and take a bird's-eye view

Taking a bird's-eye view of any situation means scanning the situation and imagining your future self and how your choices will impact you, what other people will think of your actions, and then adapting your behaviour accordingly.

Wrapping up

Ask your child why reading the room is important. Then go and spy on members of your family and ask your child to notice one social cue. Tone of voice, body language, and facial expressions can tell him what might be going on within your family.

LESSON: HOW TO TEACH CHILDREN TO READ THE ROOM SCENARIO

Setting up the lesson

This lesson is meant to guide you and your child through the process of reading the room—what the process looks and feels like and how the steps come alive, so it is clearer to you and to your child.

Activity

1. Read this scenario and walk through the steps of reading the room with your child. You may wish to pick a place your child is familiar with to make the activity more real. You may also want to have your child hold the visual of the steps to reading the room as she reads through this scenario with you.

Scenario:

■ Gwenie steps into a large gift shop that has cards, gifts, handbags, jewellery, trinkets, and gift wrap. Gwenie's mother asks her, "What do you notice here?" Gwenie then uses the steps, as follows:

STEP 1: Pause, spy, and observe. Rather than rushing into the shop, she stops and tries to look around. She notices that there are many breakable holiday decorations. She tells her mother, "There are a lot of breakable things here, it is crowded, and I have been somewhere like this but not here before."

STEP 2: Determine how the place is Like This, Not That. Gwenie looks around. She notices the shop is similar to one she visited with her grandmother last year but different since this shop is larger and there are more people in it.

Gwenie's mum asks her, "How will you use Mind Your PEAS and Cues here?" Gwenie pauses and thinks about…

STEP 3: Mind Your PEAS and Cues. She notices the people, environment, actions, and similarities. Gwenie may notice how loud people are speaking in the shop, whether or not there are children, elderly people, young adults, or teenagers there. She may note that people are deep in conversation, if their energy is high or low, if they seem hurried or stressed. She may notice the environment, how crowded the aisles are in the shop, how people show they are ready to check out, whether people wait to be served to look at items in the cases—do they drape themselves on the cases or remain calm with their hands folded?

Actions: How do people pay when they are hurried? What does their tone of voice sound like when they are hurried? Would the people in line mind this or feel annoyed?

Similarities: What is similar about this situation to one you have been in before? What body language and facial expressions are similar to what you have dealt with before?

STEP 4: Decode the unspoken rules. Gwenie states, "Things are breakable and so you should not touch." She says she notices that it is very quiet, so the rule is not to shout or be loud, not to horse around and to stick close to Mum. Next, Gwenie's mum asks her to look at what the people might be thinking about a group of kids coming to the shop. What does she notice about the body language, facial expressions, and energy of the people in the shop?

STEP 5: Take the room's temperature. Gwenie says that the lady behind the counter is moving very fast, that the customers are also moving fast and seem in a hurry, that no one is making eye contact and that everyone is being quiet. Gwenie's mother asks her to consider taking the perspective of the customer service people and customers—stepping into their shoes. To prompt Gwenie, her mother asks, "What do you think they need from us to make their job and shopping experience easier?"

STEP 6: Step into someone else's shoes. Gwenie says, "Well, the cashier is busy, so she might want us to have our money ready and not tell long stories but to be ready to check out. The customers might want us to stand in the queue and be ready so they can get on their way." Finally, Gwenie's mother asks her how she wants to feel about her behaviour when she leaves. What would behaving well in the shop look like? What are the Social Right Turns and Wrong Turns she can make here?

STEP 7: Picture your future self and take a bird's-eye view. Gwenie answers her mother's questions. She says she cannot be selfish and take the last of something if another customer is reaching for it, and that she would like to think about other people in a crowded shop.

Ask your child what she notices about the process Gwenie used to read the room. What social cues told Gwenie about the Unspoken Rule and Social Right Turns in the story? How did Gwenie figure out how to act? If your child is stumped, share with her key cues that gave Gwenie information.

Wrapping up

Ask your child if she is willing to spy and read the room with you the next time you are in public. If necessary, continue to practise being spies in a way that won't draw attention to you and your child.

LESSON: DEVELOPING CHAMPION NOTICING SKILLS

Setting up the lesson

A key skill that will help your child learn to read the room is the ability to pause and notice social information. The more you engage your child in this game and ask him what he notices and what that information tells him in daily life, the more your child's reading-the-room skills will improve.

Activity

1. Read the following introduction to developing champion noticing skills.

   It is important to become a champion observer in order to make sure you are able to notice all the social cues and information to help you become a better friend. Each social signal, each piece of social information about someone is a clue that can tell you more about the PEAS and the Social Guidelines and the Unspoken Rules of any situation. Then you can use these cues and signals to figure out how to adapt your actions to meet the needs of the situation.

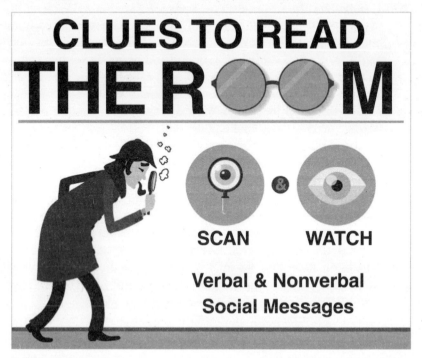

© 2016 Maguire

2. Read your child the scenario and act it out. Remind your child to take note of these cues in his Spy Log and ask him to notice the social cues in the situation that help the character read the room.

Scenario:

- Everyone in Joe's class is ready to leave for a field trip. The teacher asks if there are any questions. Joe asks a question, and then continues to talk after he gets an answer. Kids in his class groan and glare at him but Joe does not notice. People are packing up their bags and one person even says, "If people are going to talk endlessly, then we'll miss the bus." Joe does not seem to connect the comment with his behaviour. The teacher continually tries to interrupt Joe.

After you read the scenario, ask your child, "What cues did Joe miss? What do the cues tell Joe about how he should change his behaviour? What are the unspoken rules in the story?"

Wrapping up

Discuss the idea with your child that as a Social Spy, his job is to look for clues that tell him how people feel based on their facial expressions and body language. Continue to prompt your child to spy and notice in daily life.

LESSON: SPY ON YOUR SURROUNDINGS

Activity

Take a field trip with your child to a public place like a mall, a big shop, or a large shopping plaza and spy on shoppers and workers in the shops. Explain to your child that her job as a spy is to notice social verbal and nonverbal cues and to collect information. After the trip or subtly during breaks, have your child record her findings in her notebook or other Spy Log.

- Practise being observant about details. Notice all the entrances, exits, and toilets. Draw a map of them. How many are there?
- Do employees wear uniforms? What do the uniforms tell you about who is doing what job? Based on what you observe, who is in charge in this shop?
- Who is a grumpy employee? What verbal and nonverbal cues make you believe that?
- Who is not formally in charge—they are not the boss but they think they are in charge or they seem to be running the show?
- Who is in a hurry? What social cues tell you they are in a hurry?

Wrapping up

Discuss your field trip with your child. Each time you enter a situation with her, ask her to notice who is there and what social cues are demonstrated.

LESSON: SPY ON PLACES I KNOW

Mission

Go to a friend's house and discreetly spy. Your job as a spy is to notice details and collect information. After you leave the location, write down all of your observations and report back to your parent.

- Is the house casual or formal? How do the members of the family treat the furniture?
- Are they tidy, messy? Do they like things organised and neat? What is important to them?
- Should you touch items in the house or keep your hands to yourself?
- Would it be okay to fool around and jump on the furniture? Or no? How do you know this?
- What do they eat? Health food, goodies?
- What are the hobbies of the people in this household?
- What are the unspoken rules of the house?

LESSON: READING THE ROOM AND LIKE THIS, NOT THAT

Setting up the lesson

Read the introduction to Reading the Room and Like This, Not That below. Remind your child of the Like This, Not That lesson in the Starter Track.

Everywhere you go and with everyone you meet, there are similarities to somewhere you have been or people you have met. When you are trying to read the room, it can be really helpful to consider what *similar* and *different* situation to use in order to figure out what the unspoken rules for the current situation are or what you might already know about the situation or person from past similar experiences.

Activity

Read these scenarios.

Scenarios:

- Finn shows up for a meeting with a teacher. The teacher's door is closed and the teacher is deep in conversation with another student who is often in trouble. Finn is not sure what to do. Should he enter, wait in the hallway, knock, or simply leave?
- Henry is making jokes about being really bad at sports. Francis is not sure if she should join in. Everyone seems to be having a good time and Henry is doing impressions of his latest dodgeball game. But she is not a close friend to Henry and they do not joke around.

After you read the scenarios to your child, ask your child to think about entering a situation where he was unsure what to do. Ask him, "How can you think of the similarities and differences in the situation to help you figure out the unspoken rules and the social guidelines you need to follow?" Some examples of what your child might observe: energy, mood, body language between people, unspoken rules for that space. What social cues tell someone how to react?

Wrapping up

Talk about Like This, Not That and reading the room. Discuss that, given what your child has observed, what choices about his behaviour could he have made? How could/should he adapt to meet the needs of the situation? What makes these choices important? Discuss how thinking about past situations could help your child know what to do in the future.

LESSON: MIND YOUR PEAS AND CUES

Setting up the lesson

Mind Your PEAS and Cues breaks down the large concept of reading the room into smaller pieces that show how to do it. This method gives your child a rhyme or catchy phrase she can say to remember a systematic method to read the room in any situation.

Activity

1. Read the descriptions of each element of PEAS and Cues that follow and show her the visual. Start with this introduction:

     When walking into a new space, you can notice the verbal and nonverbal cues and unspoken rules that dictate the social guidelines for that situation.

2. Discuss with your child how in any room you have ever entered or any situation you have been in, there are always people, there is a specific environment, and people are taking actions. There are ways in which that situation or place is similar to one you have been in before. Ask your child if she can think of a recent place where there were all the elements of PEAS and Cues.

People

Most of us want to blend in with people and mirror the way other people are behaving when we are in public. Fitting in requires reading cues from the people around you. When you enter a new space, notice who is there and think how well you know them. What can you do to mirror the people in the group? Identify whether people's bodies are stiff, relaxed, or silly. What are people talking about? What is their tone? If you were to join the group, what might you ask or say to build on that topic?

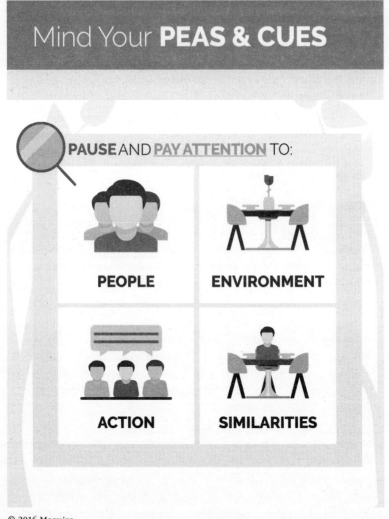

Mind Your **PEAS & CUES**

PAUSE AND **PAY ATTENTION** TO:

PEOPLE

ENVIRONMENT

ACTION

SIMILARITIES

© 2016 Maguire

Environment

When you pay attention to the immediate physical and social setting, you get clues to help you identify what behaviours are expected in that particular situation. What is the mood or energy in the room? Is everyone serious or are they laughing? Notice whether people are standing close to one another or further apart. Does the space encourage one-on-one conversations or does it promote mingling about?

Actions

People's actions can tell you a lot about unspoken rules and expectations in a specific social situation. What is everyone doing? How are people treating one another? What do their actions tell you about what you need to be doing? Based on how others are behaving, what actions can you take that will help you to naturally fit into the group?

Similarities

Comparing and contrasting different social situations can help you understand how your social behaviour needs to change in various environments. Recognising the similarities and differences allows you to blend into a group and get comfortable quickly. Is this situation like one you have experienced before? How is the current situation similar to your previous experience and how is it different? Based on what you know about the hidden rules in similar situations, how do you want to talk and act?

Cues

Social cues are the verbal and nonverbal messages people use to express their emotions, what they want, what they are thinking, and what they want to do. Social cues are expressed through tone of voice; pace of language; and a speaker's energy, body language, eye contact, and facial expressions. Recognising the cues from the people in any situation can help you interpret what the unspoken rules are, how you should behave, and signals you need to pay attention to in order to understand if what you are doing and saying will help you fit in and to figure out what you should say and what you should hold back.

Wrapping up

Go on a field trip, even if it's just somewhere in your house where people are gathered. Ask your child to read the room using skills from PEAS and Cues.

LESSON: PAUSING TO NOTICE

Setting up the lesson

The purpose of this lesson is to help your child learn to pause in any situation, scan the environment, and notice the social information using the Mind Your PEAS and Cues mnemonic. Plan a field trip with your child to a play space or playground. The trip should be somewhere your child needs to rehearse pausing. Additionally, as you go through your week, subtly point out moments where your child can practise reading the room.

Activity

1. Take a field trip to a shopping centre, play space, or playground. Remind your child to pause and notice his social cues in the space. At the end of the visit, debrief with your child privately and write down his observations with him. Ask him what he noticed: What were the unspoken rules? What made pausing to mind his PEAS and Cues hard? What was important about the people and actions and the environment in terms of telling him the social guidelines?

2. Have your child record observations in his Spy Log.

Wrapping up

Use Pausing to Notice in a playful way throughout everyday activities. The point is to make pausing and noticing a habit. Noticing that the world around you is inherently interesting can help a child enjoy the practice—and the habit!

LESSON: DECODE THE UNSPOKEN RULES

Setting up the lesson

Understanding in every situation that there are unspoken rules is a key component of reading the room. By incorporating those rules into daily life, you help your child gain situational awareness—picking up on what's going on around her, including the people, the setting, her role in it, and what it means.

Activity

1. Remind your child of the fact that in every situation there are unspoken rules that help you determine what the Social Guidelines are and

what Social Right Turns she needs to make. Explain to your child that by spying and being a champion "noticer," you can figure out the unspoken rules. Remind your child of the Mind Your PEAS and Cues mnemonic.

2. Take a field trip to a public place like a hotel, coffee shop, department store, or library and act as a Social Spy to notice the unspoken rules.
3. Have your child write down her observations in her Spy Log—what are the unspoken rules of that space and how does she know that?

Wrapping up

Continue to talk about unspoken rules in everyday life. Discuss how you have household rules, and some are posted or discussed and some are not. The more you ask your child what social cues would tell a stranger about those unspoken rules and ask her to guess, the more she develops this skill.

LEVEL 2 TOOLS

LESSON: READING THE MOOD

Setting up the lesson

Evaluating the atmosphere of a situation requires understanding the energy, mood, body language, and context of that circumstance.

Reading the mood, made up of facial expressions, body language, and unspoken messages, is hard for some children. Your child must first learn that he needs to read the mood. Next, he will practise pausing to notice and to identify the emotional state of other people. Finally, he will learn to adapt his behaviour to that mood.

Activity

1. Role-play how people show their mood through their body language, tone of voice, what they say, and what they do. Ask your child to guess your emotion. Demonstrate to your child how you show anger about a common topic like missed homework or chores or a big mess.
2. Present the idea to your child that he will engage in a little fun game for one day. Your child will pick two members of the family and social-spy on them. He will try to identify what they express with their body and voice, what they

say, and what they do to demonstrate that they are experiencing the moods listed in the table below. Have your child use this table to log the behaviours he sees that show what mood the person is experiencing.

Emotion	Family Member 1	Family Member 2
Nervous		
Confused		
Frustrated		
Hopeful		
Excited		
Stressed		
Uncertain		
Confident		
Overwhelmed		
Growing annoyed		

3. Go to a shopping centre, supermarket, school, hotel, coffee shop, or bookshop and social-spy on two specific people. Try to identify what they do in their body and voice, what they say, and what they do when they are in the moods presented in the table. Use the table to log your findings.

Emotion	Person 1	Person 2
Nervous		
Confused		
Frustrated		
Hopeful		
Excited		
Stressed		
Uncertain		
Confident		
Overwhelmed		
Growing annoyed		

4. Back at home after the spy session, discuss how your child would alter his behaviour to match the atmosphere, mood, and emotions a person displays. If your child struggles with the general question, offer these scenarios:

Scenarios:

- Your child enters a quiet office where people are working. Ask: Would he be loud and silly? If he is loud and silly, how would he need to change his behaviour to become (1) quieter and (2) have his body and energy feel calmer?
- Your child encounters someone in a moment when they are intensely busy or concentrating on something—maybe hands full, organising papers, or in a conversation with someone else. Ask: If the person is feeling hyper or overwhelmed, should you pause and allow the person to finish before asking for a snack? What would you do to alter your behaviour?

Wrapping up

Discuss your child's observations with him.

LESSON: HOT AND COLD BEAR HUNT

Setting up the lesson

The Hot and Cold Bear Hunt* allows your child to practise reading facial expressions in a fun way. This exercise can be repeated, and parent coaches can also have scavenger hunts to detect mood and facial expressions in daily life.

Activity

Before today's lesson, select a stuffed animal and hide it in one specific room before your child enters.

At the start of the lesson, explain that you are going to have a bear hunt and your child will find the stuffed bear by guessing whether

---

* Adapted from Dana Maher, 2017; Jed Baker, 2003.

or not she is hot or cold by reading your facial expressions. Then show your child two facial expressions. One facial expression will demonstrate "hot" to her when she is close to the bear, and the second facial expression will demonstrate "cold," when she is far away from the bear.

Then ask your child to hunt for the bear and read only your facial expression with no words to find the bear.

Wrapping up

Once your child finds the bear, ask her how facial expressions can tell her what actions she can take when she reads the room. Continue to practise reading the face!

LESSON: READING THE ENERGY

Setting up the lesson

Someone's energy or the vibe or atmosphere that people exude is a key indicator of the mood of any situation. Learning to pause and understand this energy will help your child become more situationally aware.

Activity

1. Read the following description of Reading the Energy to your child.

   An emotion is a feeling you have about a person or situation. When people have an emotion inside their minds and bodies, it shows up in their energy, meaning how powerful or big their expression is, the activity they show in their body, and the actions they take that show their emotions. For example, when someone is tired and sleepy, they have low energy and this shows up in how low-key they are, how slowly they move. People's energy can help you figure out what they need from you. People expect and want you to shift and adapt your own behaviour depending on their energy.

2. Present the chart with the kind of energy people show and what that means in terms of how you adjust your behaviour when you are reading the room and reading the mood of the people in a situation.

Remember when you read the room, a big piece of what you are trying to detect is what other people in the situation are doing, and how they expect you to behave. To figure that out, it helps to be someone who scans the room and then adapts their behaviour to match the mood of the people and situation encountered.

Energy	Behaviour Needed
Stressed	
High energy	
Low energy	
Anxious	

Wrapping up

Continue to discuss that someone's energy and mood affects how we react to them. Ask your child to read your energy throughout the day. Prompt your child if necessary to read your energy!

LESSON: READ THE ROOM AND STEPPING INTO THE OTHER PERSON'S SHOES

Setting up the lesson

Part of successful situational awareness is the ability to interpret the feelings and perspective of the other people in the situation. Once you can do that, you can adapt your behaviour to mirror the atmosphere and expectations of the situation. The ability to interpret the inner emotional life, context, and nuances of a situation will help your child present the kind of adaptive behaviour he needs to create socially appropriate behaviour anytime, anyplace.

Activity

1. Explain to your child that he needs to think about what other people will feel about his actions, and then adapt his behaviour to meet their expectations.
2. Using the Learning to Walk in Someone Else's Shoes mat from the Starter Track, have your child step into the shoes of the characters from the scenarios that follow. Discuss with your

child some scenarios. As they step into someone's shoes, they need to adapt their behaviour based on how the other people will feel and then how they will react. Explain that by stepping into other people's shoes, you can more readily predict what you need to do to match the energy, mood, social guidelines, and unspoken rules of the situation.

Scenarios:

- There is a long line at a soft drink dispenser at the cinema. You want to try each type of soft drink, since you are not sure what soft drink to choose. The people in line behind you are shifting from foot to foot and it's hot. They are glaring at each other and rushing to the soft drink dispenser the minute one person is done, not even letting him put the lid on his drink before the next person is filling his cup. What should you do?
- You love to do voices and pretend to be people from other countries. You are in a crowded space. What should you do?
- A friend of yours is upset; they received bad news when you entered the lunchroom. You got good news. What should you do?
- Your father has lost his keys. You know he loses them all the time. He is frantically looking for them and his energy is very high. You want to say that he never puts the keys back on the hook. What should you do?

For each scenario, ask your child, "What are the unspoken rules? What are the social guidelines? What will other people feel? What do their faces tell you? What does the tone of the people in the room and what they are saying tell you about their mood? What is their energy like? High? Low? How well do you know the people in the space? What do the people's actions tell you about the Social Guidelines?

Wrapping up

Ask your child to observe and practise identifying people's energy and mood and then adapting his behaviour to that mood.

Who Is Your Audience?

Shifting Communication to Meet the Needs of the Audience

LESSON: FILTERING INFORMATION

Setting up the lesson

The ability to filter information means the ability to scan the environment and to adjust what one says based on the situation and people, your relationship to them, and information that could offend other people or that is meant to be private. This exercise is meant to demonstrate in a very visual way the process of filtering information that will stick with your child.

Materials

- One pasta strainer or a coffee filter
- One small ball

Activity

1. Share with your child that there is always information that we have to hold back and cannot share because it would hurt someone's feelings, the information is a secret, the information is private for just a few people to know, or the information is not on topic and does not fit into the conversation. There are people we are close to and people we are not close to. What information we share depends on how close we are to the people we are speaking to.
2. Put a small ball into a strainer and stand at the sink with your child.

3. At the sink, pour water into the strainer over the ball. Show your child how the water goes through the holes of the strainer, but the ball does not.

4. Discuss with him how strainers are like the human brain—some information stays in, and some information comes out.

5. Ask if he feels like his words tend to spill through his brain filter, or if his words stay inside. Discuss with your child how he felt after he realised the effect his words had.

6. Ask your child to think about the filter and the ball again. Ask, "What are things that would be okay to get through the brain filter (e.g., compliments)? What are things that should get stopped by the brain filter (e.g., talking out of turn, interrupting someone, saying something mean)?"

Wrapping up

Have your child draw his brain filter. Ask him to show you what gets caught in his filter and what gets through. Continue to discuss filtering with him and debrief with him when he filters information and when he does not.

LESSON: FILTERING SOCIAL INFORMATION

Setting up the lesson

This lesson will bring to life the need to filter and how it impacts your child's friendships. Bring out the pasta strainer from time to time and role-play specific situations where your child is unsure what to filter or where she needed to filter but did not.

Activity

1. Start by talking about filtering and asking your child why it is important.

2. Read the scenarios one at a time and ask your child to react to them. Then using the questions as her criteria, ask her to share with you whether or not the person was filtering information. Discuss the scenario and the consequences of not filtering.

Scenarios:

■ Jessie is the top swimmer on her team and in the state. In a swimming competition, her friend Calvin did very poorly; while she was first, he was last. Calvin is huddled by the pool and is upset. Jessie tells him all about her victory. She speaks about how her goggles fell off but she still touched the wall seconds before the other swimmers. Is Jessie filtering? Why is it important for Jessie to filter? What should Jessie hold back and what should Jessie share?

- Winnie's father got a new job. Her parents have discussed it in the car and in front of her. Her father will make significantly more money and Winnie knows the exact figures. Winnie's father said it's good he is leaving his firm because his boss was an immature man. At a party with mixed friends, including some who work with Winnie's father, Winnie shares what her father said. Is Winnie filtering? Why is it important for Winnie to filter? What should Winnie hold back and what should Winnie share?

- Mike does not want to go to a birthday party with his uncle and his cousins. They often brag and do not treat Mike well. When his uncle asks why Mike is not coming, Mike says that he is pretty busy and

Filtering Social Information

© Maguire, 2018

would love to come next year. Is Mike filtering? Why is it important for Mike to filter? What should Mike filter and what should he share?

Wrapping up

Ask your child what she has learned about filtering. Why is filtering important?

LESSON: TOPICS TO BE FILTERED

Setting up the lesson

This lesson is meant to help your child witness what public and private information looks like and what information he should hold back.

Activity

1. Read the following introduction to Topics to Be Filtered.

    Everyone has topics that they should not discuss in public. This lesson introduces the concept of public and private topics and the fact that we do not share some information in order to spare someone's feelings, nor do we share secrets that someone has asked us to keep confidential, bring up sensitive topics that will offend someone, or bring up topics that are not central to the conversation.

2. Discuss that there is public information and private information that should be filtered so you do not offend, hurt, or upset someone.

3. Make a list of topics that should be filtered and write it down in the chart. If your child is stumped and cannot come up with a topic that should be filtered, gently share some examples you have observed by saying as neutrally as possible, "I have noticed that" or "Remember the time when…" Do not launch into the consequence of not filtering. Ask your child: "What was the situation? What information could have been filtered? What did the other person feel like? What would you do differently next time?"

My list of information I should filter

Hurts Someone's Feelings	Secret	Private Information
Sensitive topic	Off topic of the conversation	Other

Wrapping up

Ask your child to share with you what he will filter going forward and what people's reactions are to unfiltered information. Continue to practise filtering in daily life with your child.

LESSON: FILTERING PRACTICE ALL IN THE FAMILY

Setting up the lesson

Learning to filter information takes repeated practice and awareness of how your information is received and what information needs to be held back.

Activity

1. Present the fact that learning to filter takes practice. Collaborate with your child to pick an event involving your immediate or extended family to engage in a fun game.
2. For an hour, your child will go about her daily life, but she will practise filtering information based on what she has learned about filtering out comments that would offend someone, are private, or are not relevant.
3. After the event, ask your child to share with you what information she decided to filter and why. Then ask her what it felt like and what she would do next time. Ask her if she struggled with this process, or if there were times when she did not filter, but wishes she had?

Wrapping up

Continue to pick events, people, and situations where your child agrees to practise filtering. You may ask her to practise for an hour at a time, so it is more manageable. But the practice will raise your child's awareness and ability to filter.

LESSON: WHO IS YOUR AUDIENCE?

Setting up the lesson

Your child will use the different faces to learn to adapt information based on who he is speaking to. The faces (see Appendix) represent people such as: teachers, coaches, parents, and friends. You can also use photos of key people in your child's life. You may also photocopy the image and have your child practise speaking to the different people by placing their faces in the empty circle.

© 2016 Maguire

Activity

1. Show your child the Who Is Your Audience visual. Explain that we adjust how we approach other people, depending on who we are addressing.

   Explain to your child that the different faces provided with the tool represent people in his life and the different audiences he encounters. Explain that everyone needs to adapt their stories, what they say, what they share, and what they hold back based on who they are speaking with and where they are.

   Discuss with your child that whenever we are speaking to someone, we should consider:

   ❏ Who is your audience?

   ❏ What do you know about the audience?

   ❏ How will your message be received?

   ❏ What information do you need to give?

❏ What do you want your audience to feel?
❏ How do you decide what to share?

Demonstrate the concept of adjusting your message by presenting the scenarios. Allow your child to choose the face to represent the characters in the scenarios. Then read the scenario.

Scenarios:

■ Two friends, Kendall and Abby, are at a beach with their parents. Kendall asks her father if she can have something from the ice cream van; he says no. Abby's father says that Abby may have something from the ice cream van. Abby then turns to Kendall and says in a braggy tone, "I'm going to have a slushy *and* a Ring Pop!"

■ TJ is talking to his father's boss at a picnic. His father's boss is a mature man with grey hair and is very important. TJ tells his father's boss about an episode of a favourite TV programme in detail with exact quotes from start to finish.

■ Manny says he is "just really blunt and to the point." So, he goes up to someone at a science fair at his school and says that their project "needs some help."

■ Fred is very sick and has been in bed all day. Jason comes home from school and he wants to play video games. Fred is lying in bed and has been throwing up into a rubbish bin. Jason enters his room to talk about the new video game. He ignores Fred's signs of distress and talks to Fred about the video game.

2. After you read the stories, ask your child to consider how the information will be received. Did the character adapt his or her message to meet the needs of the audience? What did the audience or person being spoken to feel about what was being said? Have your child replay the scenario so your child tells you how the character should have adjusted his or her message to the audience. What specific words and actions should the character change?

Wrapping up

Continue to talk about who your audience is in daily life. As your child encounters people, discreetly ask your child how he will shift his message to the specific audience he is encountering.

LESSON: WHO IS YOUR AUDIENCE—WHAT IS THE CONTEXT?

Setting up the lesson

Context is a key concept many children struggle with and one that greatly affects how your child shifts her message to her audience. Understanding context will help your child in many social arenas to present as someone who can scan a situation and adapt her behaviour to the context.

Activity

1. Read aloud the following introduction of the concept of context to your child.

    Context means what is happening all around you when you speak to someone. Context is the situation, the environment, the mood, the circumstances, and what has been going on. Thinking about context means thinking about what is going on for the audience you are speaking to. For instance, are they sad? Did they just get bad news? Interpreting the context can help you adjust your message to the audience you are speaking to. Wherever you go, it is important to pause and think about three things: where you are, who is there, and what the situation is.

2. Share the following list with your child of different situations or contexts that would change your message and actions to meet the audience.

Contexts to pay attention to:

- Someone is really busy.
- Someone is trying to go somewhere.
- Someone is sad and received bad news.
- Someone is happy, and you are in a bad mood.
- Someone uses body language to tell you they do not want to talk.
- You have been lucky and they have not.

    Ask your child to tell you some situations or contexts where people would not want to hear good news. Or they would not want to hear about a sad situation.

3. Read the scenarios and ask your child to think about how the message should be received and how they would adjust their message based on the context for the audience.

Scenarios:

- Your teacher is packing up her bag alone in her classroom with the lights off. She is slamming her books and papers into a briefcase. She keeps checking her watch and her mobile phone is beeping. You need to talk to her about a paper, and you do not have an appointment.
- Richard's parents have received bad news and it seems like they are saying a big trip to Disney World is off. His parents are talking quietly and he notices they look like they might cry. His mother is twisting a tissue over and over in her hand and her face looks intense. Richard wants to ask them if the trip is off and to campaign to ask them not to cancel the trip.

    After you read a scenario, ask your child, "What is the context? How should the character shift his or her message based on what is going on?"

Wrapping up

Discuss situations where your child thinks she should shift her message based on context, and spy on context with your child going forward.

LESSON: ANTICIPATING PEOPLE'S MOTIVES—WHO ARE THEY AND WHAT WILL THEY DO?

Setting up the lesson

Some people, very automatically, create an analysis of each individual they encounter, thinking about personality, patterns, and characteristics. Other people struggle with this. The more your child can think about people's motives, perspectives, values, interests, and history, the more he can predict how his audience will react.

Activity

1. Read aloud the following description of people's motives and reasons for their reaction to what we say and do:

    Motives are someone's reason for taking action or for wanting certain things. They are hidden and not always obvious, and they are something that helps you understand why people do the things they do and why they say the things they say. Learning who someone is and predicting what they will do comes from stepping into their shoes and noticing a million little details about that person. Stepping into their shoes will tell you about their personality and what is important to them, and it can help you predict what choices they will make.

2. Explain to your child that in order to help him predict what people will do, he has to notice the small details, such as their interests, pet peeves, touchy subjects, what is important to them, and the choices they make. Their personality also gives you hints so you can predict how someone will react in a situation. Details can create a picture of someone and allow you to anticipate what they will feel about your messages.

3. Create an inventory of specific people in your life by spying on them and gathering information to answer the questions about their interests, personality, and preferences. Hint: if your child cannot answer these questions, have him spy to help flesh out this information.

   Create an inventory of the following people:
   - ☐ Favourite teacher
   - ☐ Teacher you struggle with
   - ☐ Close family friend
   - ☐ Authority figure

   Answer the following questions for each person:
   - ☐ What interests this person?
   - ☐ What are their favourite TV programme, games, hobbies, music, sports teams, and movies?
   - ☐ What do they value?
   - ☐ Are they sensitive to a topic?
   - ☐ What motivates them?
   - ☐ What evidence or little facts do we have about their personality?
   - ☐ Are they someone in authority?
   - ☐ What is their history with you?
   - ☐ What are their likes and dislikes? Do they have any pet peeves?
   - ☐ What kind of sense of humour do they have?
   - ☐ What have they told you about what is important to them?
   - ☐ What is fun for them?
   - ☐ How much energy do they have when they speak?
   - ☐ Is there a topic that makes them speak with more energy and passion?

4. Once you are done gathering information, ask your child to tell you what they have learned about the people. Discuss with your child what the information he obtained tells him about the person.

   Then ask your child to predict how each person would react to:
   - ☐ hearing a long story
   - ☐ hearing a goofy joke

- ❏ making excuses and blaming other people
- ❏ skipping their event or activity
- ❏ making a mistake
- ❏ eating junk food
- ❏ running in their house
- ❏ receiving hugs and physical contact
- ❏ questioning their plans
- ❏ eating healthy food
- ❏ hearing stories about specific interests of yours.

Ask your child to predict how the person will feel based on the information he has gathered. If your child struggles, prompt him with questions about the person and remind him of the information he found. What does the information you learned reveal about the person and how you would approach them?

Wrapping up

Continue to suggest your child spy on people and their information and use it to predict their reactions. If your child struggles with social dilemmas, remind him to construct an inventory about the person, and if necessary, help your child use that information to solve his social problem.

LESSON: LISTENING FOR SOMEONE'S TONE OF VOICE

Setting up the lesson

The tone of voice you use greatly affects how messages are received by your audience. A sharp, stinging tone can alter the way people feel about your child. Often people who struggle with a sharp tone do not hear their own tone of voice or recognise its impact. This lesson will help your child begin to recognise the importance of tone on her messages.

Activity

1. Read the following introduction of the tone of voice concept to your child and show her the chart that follows.

   Tone of voice is the way we say things and how it changes the meaning of our words. It can sometimes make our messages come across differently from what we mean to say. Tone is the pitch in your voice and how you stress certain words. There are different tones to describe different emotions, including showing frustration, mocking, and making fun of people.

For example, if someone says, "Can you hurry up?" Tone transforms a neutral comment to a rude, disrespectful, offensive, insulting, or even happy comment. A good way to understand the tone of what we say is to remember that it can be personal (P), offensive (O), and terrible (T); remember the acronym POT.

2. Read aloud and act out the different comments, showing how a neutral comment transforms into a zinger, a snide remark, a snarky comment, or a one-liner due to the tone of voice used. After each example, ask the child, "Why did it change? What did you hear?"

Neutral Example	Sarcastic Tone Version
Said with a neutral, flat tone: "I just love your scarf."	Read so that you highlight the word *love* differently with your tone. "I just *love* your scarf."
Said with a neutral, flat tone: "Champ, the major leagues are waiting for you."	Read so you highlight that this is an over-the-top comment, making your voice snarky so that you are using a negative tone and are clearly running down the person and using a sarcastic tone of voice: "Champ, the major leagues are waiting for *you*."
Said with a neutral, flat tone: "That is SOOO nice."	Draw out words and use a sharp tone: "That is SOOO nice."
Said with a neutral, flat tone: "You are a real genius."	Place the emphasis on the words *real* and *genius* to show they are the opposite of a genius and use a sharp tone: "You are a *real genius*."

3. Explain that body language can also transform comments from a neutral comment to an offensive comment. Role-play and act out each comment—first neutrally and then using the instructions and body language.

Neutral Comment	Comment with Body Language and Tone
Said with a neutral tone of voice: "Sorry I can't talk right now."	With a smirk, rolling your eyes, and using a sarcastic, taunting tone, say, "*Sorry,* I can't talk right now."

Say this with a smile in your voice, upbeat as if it is just what you need: "That's just what I need!"	With a sideways glance and a frown, cross your arms and say in a sharp, derisive tone, "That's *just* what I need!"

Wrapping up

Ask your child to collaborate with you to notice and spy on tone in daily life. Create a code word to discreetly remind your child of her tone when she gets off track.

LESSON: HEARING YOUR OWN TONE

Setting up the lesson

This activity will help your child hear and understand the impact of zingers and sarcasm by experiencing how that tone affects even simple phrases. Your child will continue to develop his self-awareness and will learn to hear and adapt his tone. This exercise will help your child become more aware of his own tone.

Activity

1. Explain the process of thinking about how people feel and learning to hear your tone of voice. Using a smartphone, record or take a video of your child acting out the phrases provided using the instructions.

Type of Comment	Examples	Act It Out
Zingers	"You are a real genius."	Place the emphasis on the word *real*; sharply and cuttingly say *genius*.
Sarcasm	"Champ, the major leagues are waiting for you."	Say this with a flat, dead tone that indicates that you are mocking the listener and that the majors are not waiting for him.
Snide and snarky comments	"You have the best clothes. You should be a fashion designer."	Place the emphasis on the word *best* and create a tone that shows that you feel the opposite of what you are saying.

2. Play back the recording of your child acting out the phrases and ask him, "What does the tone sound like? What do other people feel? What do you mean to sound like?"

Ask him: What message do you want to send?

Ask your child to step onto the Learning to Walk in Someone Else's Shoes mat. How does a snarky comment or potshot make other people feel? How will a zinger or sarcastic comment be received by other people? How will they treat you if you use zingers all the time?

Wrapping up

Ask your child to use the audience tool and to continue to practise shifting his tone. Role-play with your child to adjust his tone for key phrases from your daily life.

LESSON: SOCIAL MEDIA, TEXTING, EMAIL, AND YOUR AUDIENCE

Setting up the lesson

Many children do not recognise how important it is to adapt their written communication with others. Emails, texts, and social media can create a problem for children who do not recognise how their tone, punctuation, or use of emojis can change the way that they are perceived. This lesson will help your child adapt her written communication to her audience.

Activity

1. Read through the steps below to think about your audience when you are sending a written communication.
   - ❏ Pause and think before you type.
   - ❏ Before you say something or send an email or a text, think about how it will be received.
   - ❏ Picture the person receiving it—who are they and what do you know about them?
   - ❏ Read the message aloud and think about how a change in tone or emphasis on certain words would change the message.
   - ❏ Think, What did I say? What did I mean? What was my tone?
2. Pick a specific teacher or friend to think about as you role-play and act out how the message might be read by following the instructions for tone of voice.
   Say the phrase:
   - ❏ Are you *ever* going to post the homework? (Place the emphasis on *ever* so it sounds snide and accusatory.)
   - ❏ Oh, is this *really* true?

❑ I think you are *wrong* about that. Let me check your facts.

❑ You didn't ask *me* how it went?

❑ It was a long shot—about something *you* wanted.

Then ask your child, "How would your audience receive this information? What could you do to prevent a message that is offensive?"

Wrapping up

Practise working on written communication and thinking about what you know about who the specific audience is and how the message would be received.

15

Build on That

Friendship Communication

LESSON: A RECIPE FOR A CONVERSATION

Setting up the lesson

A Recipe for a Conversation helps your child understand all the parts of a conversation that create two-way, reciprocal discussions. To develop reciprocal conversation skills, your child needs to understand the flow of conversation and why such behaviours as off-topic comments, blurting, interrupting, and monologuing make it hard to have a reciprocal conversation with him.

Activity

1. Read this introduction to your child and read each part of the Recipe for a Conversation.

   Every conversation has different parts. Some are about speaking, some are about listening, and some are about thinking how you will respond. A conversation starts with a greeting, followed by each person's comments as they speak. Then interpret the verbal and nonverbal signals. You could be speaking to one person or a group. A conversation is a bridge between the initial comment and the thoughts of each person in the group. You build on it by adding to the conversation.

2. Role-play and act out each part of the conversation and discuss what each piece means.

A Recipe for a Conversation

Parts of the conversation:

RECIPE

- Greeting
- Topic
- Building on topic
- Holding back off-topic comments
- Interpreting verbal and nonverbal signals
- Listening
- Making supportive comments and gestures with my body

- ❑ **Greeting**: "Hello" or "How's it going?"
- ❑ **Topic**: A recent break or summer holiday, or a popular sports game
- ❑ **Building on topic**: Add comments about the topic, building out from yours and from the ones your conversation partner has made. For example:

    Speaker 1: This summer I want to camp more.

    Speaker 2: Me too. I love camping. Where do you go?
- ❑ **Holding back off-topic comments**: Filter out or set aside comments that are off topic, those that could be hurtful to your conversation partner, or others that interrupt the flow of the conversation and are *dis*ruptive rather than *con*structive in building the conversation. For example, in the summer camping conversation, it would be off topic to begin talking about what you want for dinner or a funny joke. It would be hurtful to say something

negative about the person you're talking with. It would interrupt the flow to suddenly shift to a complaint about your teacher or someone else you know.

- ❏ **Interpreting verbal and nonverbal signals**: This tells you how the speaker feels about a topic. Are they interested? If someone sighs and yawns or turns their attention elsewhere, they are telling you with their body language that they are not interested in the topic.

- ❏ **Listening**: This means attentively taking in information. It is important to both *be* listening and to *look like* you are listening.

- ❏ **Making supportive comments**: These are short comments that help the speaker know you are listening and interested in what they are saying. These comments can show happiness or interest. For example:

    "I hear ya."
    "Uh-huh."
    "Oh, wow."
    "Mmm."
    "Whew."

    Supportive comments can show sadness or upset or that you feel for the person. For example:

    "Oh, wow, that is tough."
    "Oh, how is that?"
    "That must be hard."

- ❏ **Gestures**: Use body language to help build a conversation and show interest and enthusiasm for the speaker. For example, a smile can help the speaker feel you are interested and friendly.

    Gestures that suggest interest are smiling, nodding, and leaning forward in your chair.

Wrapping up

Act out any pieces of the conversation your child may not understand.

LESSON: LISTENING LOOKS

Setting up the lesson

Listening and responding are important social skills. It is important to not only listen to other people but also to look like you are listening to others. Listening Looks helps your child to both listen and demonstrate his listening to others. Your child will learn that it is important to show you are listening to your peers.

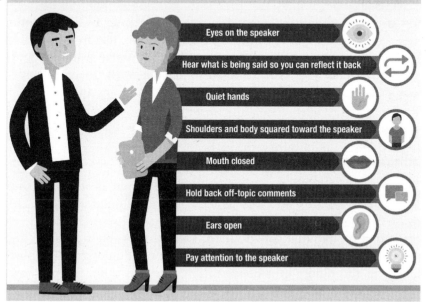

© 2016 Maguire

Activity

1. Begin by asking your child: "What does it look like to appear to be interested and attentive to a speaker? Why is listening important? Why is it important to look like you are paying attention and are in sync with the conversation? What do other people think when you do not make eye contact, walk around in circles, or cannot follow the conversation and therefore lose track of what is going on?"

2. Role-play for your child what a good listener looks like. Show her how to place her eyes on the speaker, how to reflect back what is being said, have quiet hands, have her shoulders squared toward the speaker, with ears open. How does your body demonstrate that you are paying attention to the speaker?

3. Explain to your child that when you carry on a social interaction with someone, you use body language to relate to them and to communicate with them. Demonstrate to your child what it looks like when she doesn't appear to be listening to the speaker. If you turn

your body away from them, look down at your shoes, and walk around while you are supposed to be listening, what does that say to others? Ask your child what she feels when you turn away from her.

Wrapping up

You can remind your child to show you a Listening Look throughout your work. As your child engages in conversation, feel free to help her both look like she is listening and practise her active listening. If this is a challenge for your child, ask her to practise at set times throughout your daily conversations.

LESSON: BUILD ON THAT

Setting up the lesson

Creating a reciprocal back-and-forth conversation is a major social skill. To develop this skill, you as the coach must first make your child aware of what a reciprocal conversation looks and sounds like, the elements that go into that conversation, and the elements needed to keep a conversation going. To help your child notice how each comment builds on the others in a conversation, you can build a Jenga tower with your child, play catch, stack building blocks, or place marbles in a jar. Each time your child builds on a topic, she can add a Jenga piece or toss the ball back. This gives your child a visual representation of how a conversation grows. Each comment in a conversation builds on the last comment. If your child strays off topic, don't add a block or marble; this shows her that only reciprocal building comments develop a conversation. This will signal to your child that they are off track.

Activity

1. Explain to your child that a conversation is reciprocal when comments go back and forth and each comment builds on the comment before it. Refer to the list of possible conversation topics. Feel free to add to this list with your child. Note there are topics your child may favour, but you have noticed that her peers aren't interested or show that she talks about the topic too much. For this exercise, suggest that your child pick a different topic.
2. Together with your child, choose a topic from the topic list and explain that you are going to role-play a conversation.

Building on That

Build on a conversation by picking one topic. Then, every time a person builds on the conversation topic, mark it by adding blocks or a marble to a jar. This gives the child a visual representation of how a conversation grows and that each comment builds on the last comment. With each comment add another block to the pile or put another marble in the jar.

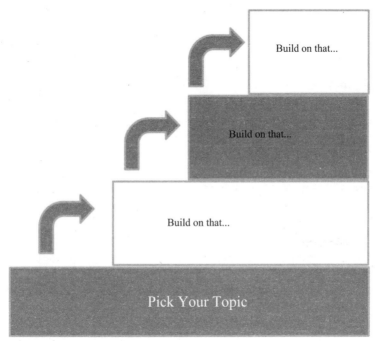

© 2016 Maguire

Topics of Conversation	
School	Teachers
Favourite subjects	TV programmes
Games popular at school	Pets
Cartoon characters	Movies
How was your weekend?	How was your holiday?
What do you like to eat for lunch?	Sporting heroes
What did you do this summer?	What are you going to do this summer?

3. Engage in a Build on That conversation on the chosen topic. Ask your child to try to hold back side comments.

Wrapping up

If she struggles to have a back-and-forth conversation, ask, "What makes that hard? What are you noticing about how side comments affect the back-and-forth conversation?"

After the conversation, discuss what that felt like and what your child would like to change.

LESSON: THE EMPTY CHAIR ACTIVITY

Setting up the lesson

For many children, identifying that they are in a monologue—talking about things that interest them and not others—is a problem that they don't realise. They must first experience what it is like to have someone talk *at* them. That will be your job, Coach. This method is meant to help your child experience being talked at. Another method is to ask them to tell a story that you have seen them tell this way, as a monologue. Record them as they talk, either audio or video. This must be done carefully, so as not to shame your child but to help him step into someone else's shoes, helping him understand what talking too long and being interrupted feels like. In order to highlight to your child what it feels like to be talked at and not to engage in reciprocal conversation, he must experience what it feels like and understand how his peers and others feel and what monologuing looks like.

Activity

1. You will begin your session with a skit. As your child comes to sit down in the session, you will start to talk at your child, giving him no chance to speak. Talk at your child as if he is an empty chair and choose a topic you love to talk about and give lots of detail. Do not allow him to speak or fully participate in the conversation. If necessary, interrupt your child and continually say what you want to say without allowing him the space to speak. If he gets up or asks questions, ignore him. This is meant to be a vivid demonstration of how talking at people feels.

2. After a few minutes, stop and ask your child if he has noticed anything about how you are speaking to him. What does it feel like to have someone speak at him rather than with him? What do other people feel when he talks too long?

Wrapping up

Discuss with your child why conversations are back and forth and ask him to give an example of a time when he may have spoken for too long. If this is not a problem for your child, ask him about someone else he knows who monologues.

LESSON: TELLING A TIGHT STORY

Setting up the lesson

Some children tend to monologue, dominate conversations, or tell stories that never seem to end. This game can help your child learn how to tell a tight story that does not meander. Your child will learn the value of telling stories in a way that engages her peers while, at the same time, she will practise reading social cues, so she can alter her approach or self-regulate her emotions. Learning to tell a tight story and talk about topics interesting to peers will help your child make a favourable impression and have reciprocal conversations. Your child must learn to consider how much information she should provide to the listener.

Activity

1. Introduce the concept of telling a tight story to your child, and refer to the visual explaining that a story should include who, what, and why.
2. Act out and narrate a story that goes on too long by reading the scenario.

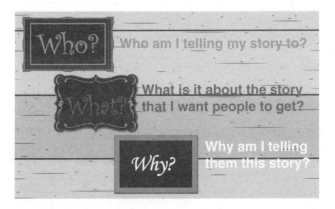

Who? Who am I telling my story to?

What? What is it about the story that I want people to get?

Why? Why am I telling them this story?

© 2016 Maguire

Scenario:

- "So, I went on a school trip to Washington, D.C., and Washington, D.C., is great. It's full of lots of history. I had this hotel room with a soft drinks machine and we ran around the halls. We went to the Smithsonian. And when we went, lots of us ran up and down the escalator until a security guard yelled at us. On the coach on the way down we had fun, too. D.C. is hot in May and we had lots of slushies and flavoured ice to help us cool down. We sat by shady trees when we could. I counted fifty trees near the Vietnam War Memorial on that big open green space. Well, maybe fifty—I lost count several times."

3. Ask your child to choose what details could come out of this script to make it a tight story. Discuss how removing these details would change the story. Ask your child to read the story without the extra details, and then discuss what makes this a tight story and what makes this story feel and sound different from the previous version.
4. Ask your child to practise introducing a concise story. Ask her, "Who are you telling the story to? Why are you telling the story and why does the person need to know this information?"
5. Ask your child to pick one or two stories (especially stories she likes to tell) and tighten them up by revising the story with your child. She may narrate the story out loud and you can help her by timing her and by helping her consider details, tone of voice, and content that makes the story too long. Ask her to choose one or two events in her life to tighten and have available if someone asks a question.
6. Model introducing and delivering a short, concise story so your child learns what it looks and sounds like.

Wrapping up

Ask your child what went well and what she learned. Ask your child if she is willing to agree to a cue, a shorthand reminder, so she can tell a tight story.

LESSON: STAYING ON TOPIC

Setting up the lesson

Conversations are ever changing. They are a back-and-forth between people building on a topic and attempting to respond to the other people in the group.

Activity

1. Ask your child to tell you what it means to be off topic and what it means to be on topic.
2. Using the script below, demonstrate how a conversation should flow so that the speaker and listener build on a topic. Then, using this script, demonstrate where someone is off topic and makes comments that are out in left field.

Script

SPEAKER 1: Do you watch football?
SPEAKER 2: Yeah, I like the Patriots. What about you?
SPEAKER 1: So I am really into my dog. I like to take him for walks.
SPEAKER 2: What?

Ask your child what he hears.

3. Share with your child that sometimes we all get off topic. Ask him to play Build on That and discuss a topic of his choosing with you. Ask him to try to hold back off-topic comments and to try to stay on topic. During a Build on That conversation, if he gets off topic, ask, "Why is it important to you to say that?" Have him ask himself if his comment makes sense. Does it build on the conversation?

Wrapping up

Ask your child to tell you what other people feel when he makes off-topic comments.

LESSON: LISTENING ACTIVITY—DRAWING A MARTIAN

Setting up the lesson

Improving your child's listening skills will turn her into someone who can listen carefully and remember information. It will help with your child's memory and her attention to detail, and it may prompt the realisation that she needs to be a better listener.

Activity

1. Give your child a pencil and a blank piece of paper. Let her know you are going to read aloud instructions to draw a Martian.
2. Read the instructions twice. Your child should draw the Martian while you narrate. She may not ask questions to clarify the information, and she may not ask you to draw the Martian.

Describe the Martian

- The Martian has a big, round head and a small body.
- The Martian has two antennae that look like lightning bolts on his head.
- The Martian has two eyes on the top of his body.
- The Martian has big feet with six toes.
- The Martian has two hands with gloves on them.
- The Martian has one big mouth that is open in an oval and he has three jagged teeth and four square teeth in his mouth, which is open.

Picture of the Martian

- Then compare her creation to the instructions. Ask her to rate her listening on a scale of 1 to 10 based on how she carried out the instruction in the drawing on the page. Ask her, "What made this activity challenging?"

Wrapping up

Discuss listening and what your child learned from the activity.

LEVEL 2 TOOLS

LESSON: BUILD ON THAT SIGNS

Setting up the lesson

This lesson is part of the practice to eliminate blurting and to learn to hold back comments and wait to speak. You and your child will have signs during the conversations in this lesson. The signs are not meant to shame your child. Instead, they are meant to signal to him that he is off topic or that you would like him to hold back a comment.

Activity

1. Photocopy the signs that follow and glue them to ice lolly sticks. Laminating them will make them last longer.

   Introduce the concept of the Build on That signs to your child and read this introduction to him:

   There are some comments that are off topic and do not add to a conversation. And sometimes everyone needs to hold back or filter information, so you do not hurt someone's feelings or add information that does not contribute to the conversation. To build on a conversation, it is necessary to stay on topic, hold back off-topic comments, and take turns letting the other person speak.

2. Explain to your child that when you make comments, he should build the conversation. It is important to think about whether comments are important for the other person to hear, make sense in the conversation, and help you build the conversation so it's reciprocal. Ask your child, "What does it mean to be off topic?"

3. Give your child his Build on That signs and explain that the signs are meant to cue him and remind him to think about his comments and to help him recognise when he is off topic and when he is on topic. The signs can also be held up by your child to demonstrate that he is holding back or he is on topic.

4. Suggest to your child that he enter the Build on That conversation by considering this: Am I hijacking the conversation? Am I filtering what is off topic? Are my comments relevant? Am I

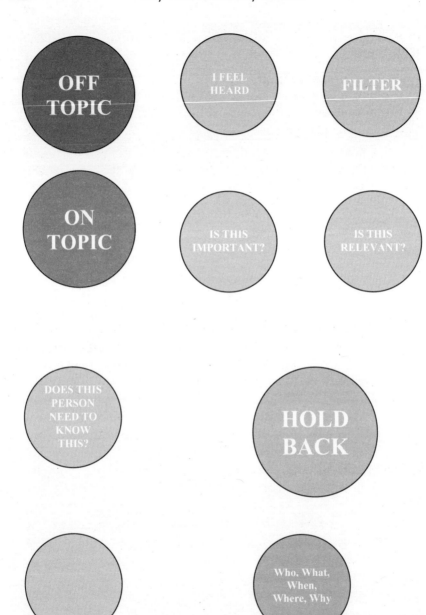

reading the speaker's mood and face? Am I able to reflect back pieces of the conversation to the speaker?

5. Engage in a Build on That conversation using a topic of your choosing. If your child gets off topic, hold up the OFF TOPIC sign. If he asks to share "just one thing" or an off-topic comment, show the IS THIS IMPORTANT? sign or the DOES THIS PERSON NEED TO KNOW THIS? If he is listening well, the I FEEL HEARD sign. Or use the blank to make your own.

6. Your child's job is to hold back comments and to stay on topic. If he is off topic, hold up the OFF TOPIC sign.

7. The goal is to practise this exercise repeatedly until your child begins to identify when he is off topic, when he is on topic, and when he demonstrates that he needs to hold back comments.

Wrapping up

Ask your child what he learned from using the Build on That signs. Ask him what happens when he is off topic and how other people feel about it. Brainstorm solutions to any dilemmas involved in holding back comments.

LESSON: SOCIAL DATABASE

Setting up the lesson

To have reciprocal relationships, children need to learn to notice and gather information about their peers. This means recalling interests, preferences, history, likes and dislikes, their peers' sense of humour, their pet peeves, so they can recall the important information in the moment. Social Database is meant to help your child realise the need to gather information about friends and to help her learn to create an invisible social database to house her peers' information.

Activity

1. Read the introduction in step 2 to the Social Database and read it aloud.

2. Our job as a friend is to find out about our friends' interests, preferences, history with other friends, likes and dislikes,

and sense of humour, and to remember that important information during a conversation. This does not mean we interrogate other people, but it means we learn to be curious and to ask people about their interests and not just our interests. Knowing information about people, trying to remember it, and showing interest in other people are parts of being a good friend. In your brain, you keep a social database of this information. The social database helps you when you have conversations with people. You can make sure you do not talk about a touchy subject, you show interest in them, and you can build a closer friendship because you know more about them.

3. Suggest that your child pick someone you know and try to list everything you know about that person. Think about someone you would like to get to know or someone you know less about. Role-play having a conversation with that person to discover more about their interests. Some suggested questions include: "What have you been up to? What is fun for you? What are your favourite TV programmes, games, hobbies, music, sports teams, and movies?" Have your child say whether her friend is funny, silly, or serious. Ask her how close she is to this person. What does this person like or dislike?

Wrapping up

Ask your child how she plans to use the social database. Is she concerned about how to gather information and implement using it? If so, brainstorm strategies.

LESSON: SPY MISSION TO BUILD THE SOCIAL DATABASE

Mission

Go to school or an activity and listen closely to collect information about a specific person you would like to know more about. Listen and learn: What are they interested in? Games, TV programmes, music, sports teams, movies, hobbies? Report back to your parent what you learn about this specific person.

Setting up the lesson

Since relationships are mutual, your child must understand that when he does not recall these details, other people may be offended. The social database will help your child learn that making these social connections forms the basis of a friendship.

Activity

1. Pick someone who might be receptive to your child practising developing his social database. Ask for your child's permission to share his goals and his journey through the *Play Better Plan* if the person is not part of your immediate family.

2. Let the person know what your child is trying to accomplish—he is working on trying to get to know someone. Discuss the idea of practising to develop the social database and to learn more about the person who is willing to practise with him.

3. Instruct your child: Pick a specific time or opportunity to speak with this potential friend. Find out more about what activities, sports, or clubs they enjoy. What are their likes and dislikes? What is their family like? What is fun for them? If they could spend a day doing anything, what would it be? Some questions you can ask are: What have you been up to? How was (insert event or activity)? What do you like about (insert activity)? Tell me more about (insert interest).

Wrapping up

Ask your child what he learned from this process. Brainstorm strategies to address any bumps in the road.

16

Friendship Is a Two-Way Street– How Fast Do You Go?

Cooperation, Participation, and Problem-Solving

LESSON: HAVING TWO-WAY-STREET FRIENDSHIPS

Setting up the lesson

Friendship needs to be reciprocal, and this means the child needs to show her intention to be friends, return gestures of friendship, and initiate and participate with other children. Cooperation is not just about compromise. It is about understanding that friendships are a two-way street.

Activity

1. Read aloud the following description of Having Two-Way-Street Friendships to your child.

   Friendship should be a two-way street. It should be balanced, so each person gets some of what they want. Meeting people halfway means that if someone approaches you, you greet them; if someone smiles at you, you smile back. If someone offers a compromise, you look for ways to agree. If someone shows you that they want to play with you, you invite them to play. If you went first last time, your friend goes first this time. If someone asks you to stop, you stop.

   Ask your child to tell you what meeting halfway looks like in each situation. What specific behaviours would she need to demonstrate to meet people halfway?

- ❏ Picking games
- ❏ Someone smiles at you
- ❏ Someone offers to play
- ❏ Someone makes a gesture that they would like to participate in your activity
- ❏ Deciding the rules of the game
- ❏ Participating and joining in with a group

2. Read the following friendship role description to your child:

My job as a friend is to be agreeable, to be willing to do what my friend wants to do, to compromise, to meet people halfway, and to consider other people's feelings. My role is to think about how my friends feel and to adapt my behaviour, so they know we are cooperating.

Then ask your child, "What is your job as a friend when you play with someone? What do you think about the way being a good friend is described? Where do you struggle with your friendship role?"

Wrapping up

Continue to discuss the concept of meeting halfway. Whenever possible, ask your child what she needs to do to meet people halfway.

LESSON: LIVING COOPERATION

Setting up the lesson

This activity is meant to practise meeting people halfway and to incorporate this behaviour into daily life. This will give your child the chance to move from a concept to practising the skill.

Activity

1. Discuss with your child why it is important to meet people halfway, to take turns, and to look for compromise in friendships.
2. Ask your child to pick five to ten times this week when he will give a little to get a little, and where he will compromise and meet people halfway.
3. Create a subtle cue your child can hear to remind him of this intention, like a nod or a code word. If your child is willing, keep track of his "meeting people halfway" examples by hanging up a chart. If he finds that embarrassing, you can track this in a smartphone or

simply write it down in your lesson notebook using the following chart as a guide.

Feel free to offer your child an incentive or points on his reward chart for this game.

MEETING PEOPLE HALFWAY LOG		
	Where I Met People Halfway	**Circumstances**
1		
2		
3		
4		
5		

Wrapping up

Go over the list of times when your child met people halfway and celebrate. Ask your child what it felt like. What was hard about meeting people halfway? Ask your child to continue to practise going forward and even make a game within the family where everyone can practise meeting people halfway.

LESSON: MEETING PEOPLE HALFWAY PUZZLE

Setting up the lesson

This lesson is meant to help your child act out compromise and cooperation in action. During the game, your child will not be able to complete the puzzle without cooperating with you. The test is to see how long it takes her to realise that she is stuck and that without cooperating with each other, neither of you will be able to complete your puzzle.

Activity

1. Get two paper jigsaw puzzles and then deliberately mix up the pieces beforehand, so each person has one or two of the pieces that actually belong to the other person's puzzle.
2. Share the jigsaw puzzle with your child and explain you will work together to complete a puzzle. Explain that the goal is to put together the simple puzzle. Explain that there are no rules. You can help each other to complete the task.

Wrapping up

After the puzzle is complete, ask your child, "What made it possible to complete the puzzle? What do you think the jigsaw activity shows us?"

LESSON: BUILDING THE TOWER

Setting up the lesson

Playing the tower building game* will allow your child to practise cooperating and participating with other people. To build the tower, compromising, meeting people halfway, and using collaboration skills are necessary. This lesson mirrors many collaborative activities that children engage in every day. If your child struggles with these skills, continue to practise this activity more than once.

Materials

- Blocks or Tinker toys
- Timer

Activity

1. This activity requires more than one person. If possible, have siblings or other members of the family play. The idea is that your child will work with a group and will have to compromise and collaborate and meet people halfway.
2. Before you start, privately discuss with your child that the mission of the exercise is to practise cooperation and meet people halfway. Discuss what behaviour he needs to demonstrate to show collaboration and to successfully build the tower.
3. Make it clear to your child and other participants that only the time keeper can enforce the rules. Using Tinker toys or blocks, tell the group they are going to build a tower. The goal is to create the tallest tower and to work together as a team.
4. All parts of the building and planning process will be timed.

---

* Adapted from Donald E. Gibson, PhD. Exercise available from the author at dgibson01@manhattan.edu.

5. Teams have ten minutes to create the tallest tower they can. To win, the tower must be the tallest. And it must be able to withstand someone poking it or blowing on it.

6. Each team builds its tower. Select a winning tower.

7. Now privately debrief with your child and ask, "What went well?" If he had trouble allowing only the facilitator to enforce the rules, ask him why he did not let the facilitator enforce the rules. What did he feel about rule breaking?

Wrapping up

Discuss with your child what is important about cooperating. If any Social Wrong Turns occurred during the tower building, ask him, "What did the other player feel?"

LEVEL 2 TOOLS

LESSON: BUILDING THE TOWER WITH NO RULES

Setting up the lesson

Building the tower with no rules will help your child learn to collaborate and compromise with other players. This may create a big emotional reaction for your child. But this activity allows her, in the safety of your home, to practise how to collaborate and work with a group.

Activity

1. This activity requires more than one person. Ask friends and family to play who will be accommodating and safe and who will allow your child to learn and grow.

2. In advance, explain that there will be no rules and the goal of the activity is to simply build the tallest tower in ten minutes. Explore with your child what strategies she needs to use to cope with an activity with no rules, and discuss her mission to manage her feelings and not reprimand others.

3. Explain to the group that you will play the tower game with Tinker toys or blocks, but with no rules.

4. Set a timer for ten to fifteen minutes and allow teams to play.

5. Teams build their towers. Select a winner.

Wrapping up

Now privately discuss the tower activity with your child and ask how she feels. Brainstorm strategies to manage any challenges that may have come up.

LESSON: STEPS TO MIX IN AND JOIN IN

Setting up the lesson

This lesson is meant to help your child identify a process to join in and participate with large and small groups of children in any circumstance.

Activity

1. Introduce the concept that this activity will help your child plan his approach and join a group at play, at break time, at parties, on a playground, or anywhere he goes. Role-play for your child how your body looks when you are opened up, how you look when you lurk near a group, and how you look when you enter a group.

2. Using stuffed animals, or involving other family members, ask your child to role-play and act out approaching a group, picking someone who is physically opened up, choosing where to stand to enter a group, and determining what closed-off bodies look like. Remind your child about the signs that someone is interested in being a friend.

3. Next, narrate and act out the steps to join a group in a play space for your child:
   - Pause and scan the play space
   - Think how the situation is Like This, Not That (similar or different)
   - Figure out the group's unspoken rules
   - Think about who you know, what they are interested in
   - Notice the social cues, body language, facial expressions
   - Make eye contact with the group and initiate a friendly gesture like a smile
   - Approach

Wrapping up

Continue to rehearse, and by taking field trips to activities, play-grounds, and play spaces, practise this skill. Create a plan and rehearse joining a group with your child.

LESSON: FRIENDSHIP: HOW FAST DO YOU GO?

Setting up the lesson

Approaching new friends and figuring out how to join and integrate into groups is hard for some children. This exercise will help your child examine her approach and to calibrate if she is moving too slow, too fast, or just right.

Activity

1. Read the following introduction to approaching friends to your child.

    When you are approaching new friends and trying to move through the stages of friendship, it is hard to know how much

to share and how fast to go. Different people with different personalities struggle with when and how to approach new friends and join a group. Some people go fast like a rabbit and have no brakes, and other people go slow like a turtle and make no moves. The task is to find the right balance and to go just right. What you do depends on how well you know the person, nonverbal cues people send, shared interests, and how often you speak with the potential friend.

2. Show your child the visual and read aloud the descriptions of moving too fast like a rabbit, too slow like a turtle, and just right.

What does too fast like a rabbit with no brakes look like?

- Rushing into a group
- Barging in with what you want to play even when the group is already playing a game
- Telling everyone how to play
- Going to many different groups and, like a firefly, joining and leaving
- Hugging people and getting in their personal space
- Asking someone to play all the time when you just met
- Taking over every conversation you are a part of

What does too slow like a turtle look like?

- Walking up to another person and quietly tapping their shoulder and whispering, "Can I play?"
- Hovering or standing near the group but not saying anything and then walking away
- Walking around the perimeter of the room but not moving towards the group in the centre of the room
- Following kids around, but on the edge
- Leaving play constantly to go to the loo, take a break, or check on something
- Ignoring other people
- Not responding when someone approaches you and makes gestures to play
- Thinking about approaching and planning it but never giving it a try

What does just right look like?

- Meeting someone and finding out about them
- Sharing common interests with someone and chatting when you see them
- Figuring out what other kids are doing at break time and joining the game
- Physically mixing in
- Playing the games that potential friends play
- Paying attention to what other people want to talk about
- Planning to approach a group and then doing it
- Playing with different friends and different groups, not just one friend

Wrapping up

Discuss which character your child resembles the most. Ask her what it feels like when she tries to approach a friend or a group.

LESSON: ACTING OUT YOUR APPROACH

Setting up the lesson

To help your child understand how to approach other children to play, your child will act out his approach. This will help the process come alive for your child. Additionally, rather than telling your child he needs to revise his approach, practicing his ways of approaching others will help your child evaluate actions that do not work.

Activity

1. Refer to the lists of behaviours for too fast like a rabbit with no brakes, too slow like a turtle, and just right from the previous lesson. Role-play and act out how to approach other children at play if you are too fast, too slow, or just right.

2. If possible, involve one other family member or more to demonstrate approaching a group of children. Pick family members who will be supportive and will help him act out his approach. Or place stuffed animals in a cluster to represent your child's friends so your child can practise approaching

a group. Rehearse each approach, then discuss why those approaches may not help your child to mix in and join a group.

Wrapping up

Discuss how your child would like to change his approach to making friends. Ask him if he would like to be more like a rabbit, like a turtle, or if there are specific behaviours he would like to shift.

LESSON: STAGES OF FRIENDSHIP

Setting up the lesson

The process of meeting someone new is presented in the Stages of Friendship graphic that follows.

This visual is meant to help your child evaluate where she tends to get stuck and to highlight to your child that the process of moving from saying hello to having a friendship occurs in stages.

Activity

1. Read aloud the following description of the stages of friendship to your child and show her the visual.

   Making friends does not happen in one day. There are stages of friendship, and at each stage you try to get to know the person and learn more about them. You seek people who are interested in the things you are interested in. When you skip a step, you don't get to learn more about someone. Instead, you rush like a rabbit with no brakes, or move too slow, like a turtle.

2. Remind your child of the Flavours of Friendship from the Starter Track and the fact that there are people we say hello to and people we consider true friends. Ask your child to notice the stages of friendship and discuss the fact that friendships develop over time. Ask your child to pinpoint in the diagram where he gets stuck. Ask him what gets in the way of his developing deeper friendships.

   Think about what gets in your way from moving from seeing someone you like at Stage 1 to seeing potential friends outside of school. Ask your child where he gets stuck. What gets in the way of joining a group at break time or after school?

Wrapping up

Discuss what challenges get in the way and where and how your child could approach them.

Stages of Friendship

Where Do You Get Stuck?

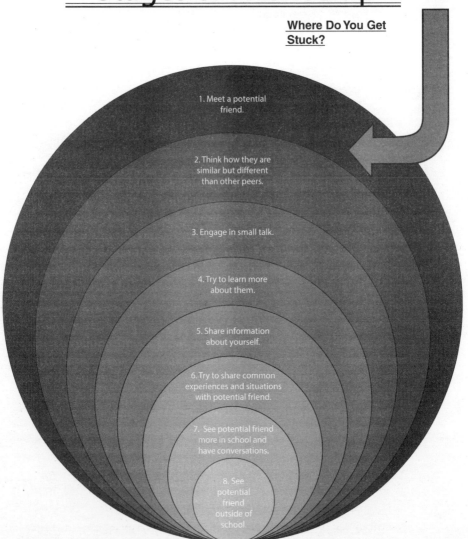

1. Meet a potential friend.

2. Think how they are similar but different than other peers.

3. Engage in small talk.

4. Try to learn more about them.

5. Share information about yourself.

6. Try to share common experiences and situations with potential friend.

7. See potential friend more in school and have conversations.

8. See potential friend outside of school.

LESSON: KINDNESS AND FRIENDLY BEHAVIOUR

Setting up the lesson

Some people are friendly and kind. They are polite and show your child the kind of courtesy that everyone should be accorded. But when children are perpetually left out, they often mistake this kindness for an invitation to seek a deeper connection to become friends. This lesson helps your child look at the signs of real encouragement to become a friend versus just kind and friendly behaviour to include someone in an activity. If necessary, create informational missions to help your child pick out people who encourage him versus people who are kind to him at school.

Activity

1. Read aloud the following introduction to Kindness and Friendly Behaviour.

    There are nonverbal cues that demonstrate that someone is encouraging you to become better friends. Often, it's hard to tell if someone is just friendly or if they are encouraging us to become better friends.

    Sometimes people are being kind and friendly, but because they are an acquaintance or a person we say hello to, these people are not seeking to move through the stages of friendship and become closer friends. We have different friends for different reasons. It is okay for people to be pleasant and yet not seek to have playdates or get closer.

    There are signs that someone is making overtures and trying to encourage you to seek them out to play more. Knowing these signs can be really helpful as you try to make new friends.

Signs someone is encouraging you to become friends

- They say things like, "Hey, we should get together sometime!"
- They continually seek you out and come to sit with you.
- They seek you out to share information or chat about a common interest.
- They ask you to have a playdate.
- They repeatedly request you as a partner in a game, project, or activity.

- They ask you questions about your interests.
- Small talk quickly moves to deeper conversations about your life.
- They invite you to sit with them, swing with them, and be with them.
- They introduce you as a friend.

Ask yourself, how much interest are they showing in you? What information about themselves have they shared with you? What does someone seeking you out look like?

Signs someone is just pleasant and kind

- They smile at you.
- They never ask you questions about your likes and dislikes.
- They run hot and cold—encouraging one day and not encouraging the next.
- They never get excited about your interests.
- The conversation never goes beyond saying hello.
- They never seek you out to play.
- When you approach them, the conversation with other kids always stops.
- Conversation stays at hello even when you try to chat.

Ask your child, "What does too eager look like? What does it mean to get to know someone?"

Wrapping up

Ask your child how he can figure out who might be an acquaintance and who might be a potential friend.

LESSON: FORMULA FOR MOVING FROM SMALL TALK TO CONVERSATION

Setting up the lesson

For some children, moving from saying hi to making small talk to having a deeper conversation can be a struggle. Often your child's nerves and anxiety make it difficult for her to figure out an approach

Formula for Moving from Small Talk to Conversations

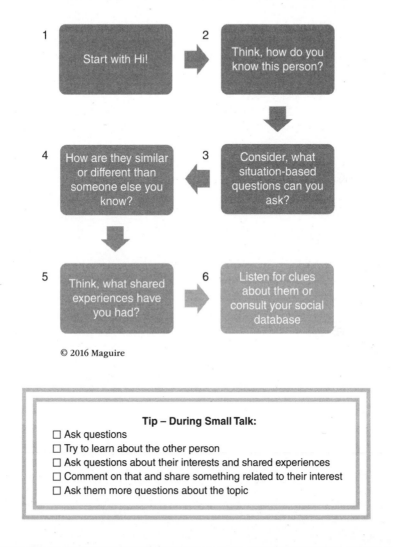

© 2016 Maguire

Tip – During Small Talk:
- ☐ Ask questions
- ☐ Try to learn about the other person
- ☐ Ask questions about their interests and shared experiences
- ☐ Comment on that and share something related to their interest
- ☐ Ask them more questions about the topic

---

to facilitate having deeper conversations, making connections, and making friends.

If bridging from saying hi to having a full conversation seems a mystery to your child, then this exercise presents her with a framework to use in every situation. The next few lessons break down the process of meeting a new person or trying to bridge from hello to a deeper conversation with any person your child encounters.

Activity

1. Introduce the concept: It can be hard to move from saying hello to someone to engaging in small talk and then having a longer, deeper conversation. Ask your child, "What does it feel like when you try to chat with someone else? What do you feel and what gets in the way?"

   Discuss the idea that the formula for moving from small talk to a conversation offers a process she can use in any social situation.
2. Read aloud the steps of the process in the visual.
3. Discuss the scenario. Explain to your child that curiosity is a great ally in any situation where you meet new people. People love to talk about themselves. Once you have information and clues about them, you can use those clues to help you build a conversation. While we do not want to interrogate people, trying to learn more about them is a useful skill. Ask your child, "What questions can you ask Bobby about himself? What would you like to know about him?"

Scenario:

■ You meet a new child at a play space. You have never met him before. The child tells you he is Bobby and is in year three. He lives in a town near you with a winning football team. He is wearing a T-shirt with a logo from a popular movie. He tells you he "loves this place and comes here all the time."

Ask your child, "What clues about Bobby do you hear?"
List the clues in your notebook.

Wrapping up

Continue to pick situations and people in your child's life and role-play this process.

LEVEL 2 LESSONS

LESSON: LIKE THIS, NOT THAT AND MEETING SOMEONE NEW

Setting up the lesson

Thinking about how someone is Like This, Not That gives your child a good starting point and will help him frame questions to meet the person's interests and background. This exercise will help your child in any new situation have a starting point to scan the room and determine how to move through the stages of friendship.

Activity

1. Remind your child of Like This, Not That from the Starter Track. Discuss the fact that in any situation, your child can consider how the new person they meet is *similar* or *different* from other people he knows. Present the fact that when you meet someone new, the things they say, the clues in their body language, their facial expressions, what they talk about, and their actions present you with key information you can use to get a clearer picture about them. This information gives you a launching point to create new conversation.

2. Read the scenarios to your child and ask him to consider how the person is similar or different from someone else he knows. Then, based on the information in the scenario, ask him/her what he knows about this person that could help him approach him/her, chat with him/her more, and move through the Stages of Friendship.

After you read the scenarios below, ask your child what questions he could ask the person in the scenario to learn more about him/her.

Scenarios:

- You meet a new person on the beach. She seems to be about your age, and she seems to love swimming and has been in the water for hours. You have been to the beach many times, and you notice she gives someone directions to the snack bar.

- You take a field trip and sit with someone on the coach on the way to the museum. You both used to have the same gymnastics teacher. You know she also loves the floor routine at gymnastics although she now goes to a different gym.
- You have lunch break without your friendship group. There are people you know in the lunch room, but you do not know them well. One person is Corey, and he is in your class and was on your robotics team last year, but you rarely talk.

Wrapping up

Pick a time in the near future when your child will meet someone new. Ask him prior to this meeting to think about how they are similar or different from other people he has already encountered. Ask him to consider any clues the new person presents about his likes, dislikes, and background.

LESSON: LIGHTS, CAMERA, ACTION

Setting up the lesson

This lesson helps the process of building your child's ability to create a mental dress rehearsal of her future self as someone who joins in a group at play. Ask your child to make a little video and actually walk through the spaces where she needs to fit in and join kids at play. This video will help her create a mental picture of the real-life scenario she needs to enter.

Activity

1. Explain to your child that she gets to make a movie. Then take a field trip, at a time that won't embarrass your child, to specific locations where she typically has to join in a group. Take a video of the space and how your child will navigate this space. Have your child walk through the actual space, if possible, to create the best mental image of her future self. Tip: To protect people's privacy, ask anyone there if it's okay to make a short video, or simply wait until the space is empty. Consider places to video, such as tables in the lunch room, play areas in the park, or the side wall of the playground.

2. Once you have the video, watch it with your child as you talk about her plan and rehearse joining in. Ask your child to think about her future self while watching the video. Ask, "What do you look like? What does it feel like? What are you doing?" Have your child narrate and role-play her physical steps and specific movements to approach and join a group. Ask your child to visualise where other kids usually play, and how they play. Where are they in the space? Ask her what specific movements she would have to make to go from Point A to Point B in the space.

Wrapping up

Collaborate with your child and pick a specific time to practise approaching and joining in with a group. If she needs a fresh start, she can go to a play space where she does not know the children.

LESSON: BRIDGING QUESTIONS

Setting up the lesson

Many children struggle with what to say and how to start a conversation with someone new. This exercise will give your child a process to move from hello to a real conversation.

Activity

1. Read the following introduction to the concept of Bridging Questions and show your child the visual of bridging questions.

    Conversations require bridging questions that link topics together. You need to learn to create questions to initiate a conversation and ask questions to keep the conversation going and encourage the other person to share more information with you. If you picture an old wooden bridge, each of these elements helps you build on the conversation.

2. With your child, role-play a conversation using the conversation topics suggested. Discuss the fact that when anyone tries to build on a conversation, they have to think about questions that build the conversation. Present your child with these questions you can use anytime, anywhere:

> ❑ What have you been up to?
> ❑ How is your day going?
> ❑ What was that like?
> ❑ What is your favourite game?
> ❑ What is the best part of your favourite TV programme?
> ❑ What did you do this weekend?

Bridging Questions

Topic the Speaker Brings Up:
Sports
Teachers
Time of day
Games
Hobbies
Favourite food
I don't love our teacher.
I think coach was mean last game.
I am so done with school; it's time for the holidays

Comments You Can Make to Bridge:
Oh, interesting.
Mmm, I don't know about that.
I would love to know more.
I hear ya.
Tell me more about that?
Interesting.

What Can You Say?
How is your day going?
Do you like (insert teacher, situation, activity, coach)?
How was that (insert situation)?
What was that like?
Hey, I noticed (insert something you noticed that is public and not going to lead them to feel weird).

Wrapping up

Continue to role-play with your child the concept of reaching out and initiating conversations with other children. Allow your child to take his time and to practise. Plan opportunities with your child and design missions to help him practise this skill.

LESSON: BRIDGING PRACTICE

Setting up the lesson

Practice makes better. The more your child gains confidence and practises bridging from hi to a more substantial conversation, the more she will thrive.

Activity

1. Sit next to your child and pretend you are strangers. Remind your child of the concept of bridging and the questions she can use anywhere, anytime.
   - What have you been up to?
   - How is your day going?
   - What was that like?
2. Role-play with your child. Prompt her by saying hello and allowing there to be silence. If it helps, assume the role of someone she knows peripherally.

Wrapping up

Ask your child what went well and what she struggled with. Continue to practise and suggest that your child practise using these skills at school.

17

Learning to Walk in Someone Else's Shoes

Taking Another Person's Point of View

LESSON: WALKING IN THE SHOES OF PEOPLE YOU KNOW BEST

Setting up the lesson

The Learning to Walk in Someone Else's Shoes lessons are meant to help your child learn to take the perspective of other people and to develop more empathy. The Learning to Walk in Someone Else's Shoes lessons here will help your child understand who people are, what motivates them, and how to anticipate their reactions and emotions. Your child will work on taking information from the past, examining it, and then using it to take a bird's-eye view of a situation, problem-solve, and make future social decisions. Your child will continually work on evaluating the impact of his behaviour and how other people will feel about his behaviour, so he can make decisions that help him make friends and demonstrate that he considers the feelings of others.

Activity

1. Privately, make a list of behaviours that may make your child present as selfish or that might demonstrate his need to learn to walk in someone else's shoes. For instance, taking the last piece of pie when someone loves that pie and it is not your child's favourite, or ignoring signs of distress in a family member because he does not take the perspective of others. Be very delicate; if this approach will upset your child too much, you can reference a fictional similar experience that you "noticed in a friend."

2. Next, ask your child to use the Learning to Walk in Someone Else's Shoes mat from the Starter Track and walk in the shoes of each family member. Present him with the examples you have collected. Rather than telling him why he was wrong, shift to use your coaching questions. For instance, saying, "I notice you took the last piece of pie the other day. What did your brother feel about blueberry pie?" Ask your child to role-play and pretend to be his brother. Have him walk in his brother's shoes and to explore what his brother feels.

Some conversation starters:

- What did (person) feel about (behaviour)?
- What was the impact of (action) on (person)?
- What were the signs that (person) was (emotion or physical state)?
- What made (topic) important to this person?
- What did (action) make them feel?

Wrapping up

Continue to use the phrase *Let's step into the other person's shoes* in daily life. When you notice your child needs to take the perspective of other people, you can ask him to step into their shoes.

LESSON: TAKING A BIRD'S-EYE VIEW—ANTICIPATING REACTIONS

Setting up the lesson

To help your child learn to understand and anticipate how other people will react to him and his choices, it is important to help him develop perspective, consider another person's point of view, and think about the person's past history, patterns, motivations, and hot buttons. Even if considering someone's point of view is difficult for your child, these lessons will help him understand that someone's past history helps us predict their future actions and reactions.

Activity

1. Discuss the concept that to really walk in someone's shoes, you have to think about how they have felt in the past, consider how they have reacted to your behaviour in the past, and take a bird's-eye view of their situation. Meaning, to step back and be able to see everything about the situation just like a bird flying overhead.

2. Read aloud the scenarios. After you have read the scenarios, ask your child to think about what is important to the characters in the scenarios. What has been their reaction to similar situations in the past?

Scenarios:

■ Every day, Toby helps his friend Nick. He gives him pencils when Nick has none. He invites him to his birthday party and always offers Nick some of his sweets. Toby is very faithful to Nick. Nick sometimes forgets to thank Toby, and he plays with Toby on Tuesday at an after-school programme where there are no other boys to play with. But when they are at break time during the week, Nick often doesn't think about Toby and goes to play Knock Out with other kids. Toby is not as good at sports and Nick always wants to win. Today there is a field day at school and Toby won a prize and gets to choose his field day team. Toby is wondering if he should choose Nick.

■ Julia is not sure how her friend Amy will react to the fact that she won a coveted spot on a gymnastics team and her friend did not. Julia is not sure if she should tell her friend and she also is not sure if her friend will come see her during a big sporting event. Last year Amy told Julia that being a good friend is most important to her. Amy does not love sports and likes gymnastics, but not like she loves football. Last year when Amy did not get a spot on the gymnastics team, she focused on football instead.

3. After your discussion about the scenarios, ask your child to step onto the Learning to Walk in Someone Else's Shoes mat, and have him pretend to take the viewpoint of each character in the scenario. Have him act out and narrate how each of the characters feels.

4. Choose a specific friend or situation your child has encountered where he did not take a bird's-eye view and where thinking about his friend's history may help him figure out what to do right now. Discuss that situation with your child asking, "What are the patterns here? What do you know about how your friend typically behaves?" If need be, have him role-play and step onto the Learning to Walk mat.

Wrapping up

Ask your child to brainstorm and take a bird's-eye view with you the next time he has a social problem.

LESSON: READING BETWEEN THE LINES

Setting up the lesson

Some children have trouble interpreting verbal and nonverbal communication and do not understand that most communication has two layers—what we say and the inferred meaning that comes from tone of voice, body language, facial expressions, and the context of a situation. This lesson helps your child begin to learn to read between the lines, so she can fully understand the nuances of what someone is saying and then adapt her behaviour to meet the nonverbal messages they are sending.

Activity

1. Read aloud to your child the following introduction to the concept of Reading Between the Lines.

    When people communicate, they use both words and tone of voice, body language, and facial expressions to tell you what they want to communicate. What people communicate in those ways can be either verbal (spoken) or non-verbal (unspoken). Interpreting this information is called *reading between the lines*, and it means that you are decoding what someone says and what they really mean.

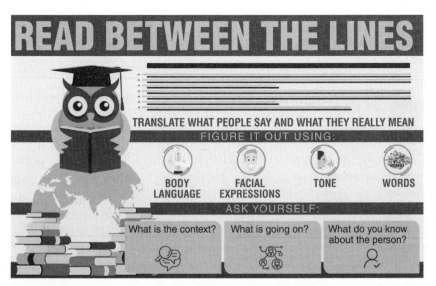

For example, if someone says, "Yeah, you're *so* right," with a sharp tone, they are using words that indicate you are correct, but their tone changes the meaning—what they really mean is, "You are wrong."

2. Introduce the visual of Reading Between the Lines and read it aloud.

3. Discuss the fact that translating these messages to figure out what people are trying to tell you is hard work for some people, but it can be practised.

Act out the examples to demonstrate the concept of reading between the lines. You read the line, then act out the signs. Then ask your child, "What is the person really trying to say?"

Example	Act It Out
Seriously?	Have your voice go up at the end in a way that shows that you are so surprised that someone has done the opposite of what is expected.
I am SOO happy right now.	Emphasise the word *so*—use a sarcastic tone to show you are not happy.
You are such a character.	Have an edge to your voice and emphasise the word *such*.
I'm fine.	Use a sharp hard tone to symbolise shutting down.

Wrapping up

Continue to practise reading between the lines in daily life with your child. Make it a game and ask your child, when appropriate, to read between the lines.

LESSON: SPY ON READING BETWEEN THE LINES

Mission

Go to school and try to read between the lines for a specific person, teacher, or coach you and your parent choose ahead of time. Especially if they are someone who often seems to stump you and uses a lot of confusing communication. After you spy, write down how they use nonverbal communication. Take what that person says, and then translate it to what that person means. Record your findings in your Spy Log.

LESSON: WHAT DO PEOPLE REALLY MEAN?

Setting up the lesson

Decoding what people mean can be overwhelming to children who do not easily read between the lines. Understanding that people use other nonverbal forms of communication like tone of voice to convey their intended meaning is an important realisation and helps your child improve his ability to adapt his behaviour to the expectations of any situation.

Activity

1. Read the following introduction to What Do People Really Mean?
   What people say is often different from what they mean. The tone of voice they use, what is happening, your past history with the person, and the body language they use change the meaning of their words. It is important to pause and notice that often someone is sending you signals with their body and tone of voice to tell you what they mean. Learning to read between the lines comes from learning to pause and figure out not what someone says, but what they really mean.

2. Act out each of the statements with the tone and body language instructions for your child. After you act it out, ask your child to read between the lines and think about what the person means and what the person is not saying here. This will help him figure out what they really mean. Discuss with your child that each of these phrases can change, depending on the body language and tone of voice the speaker uses.

What People Say	What People Mean	Act Out Role-Play Instructions
Whatever.		Have a sharp, dismissive tone to indicate you couldn't care less.
You are so funny.		Emphasis on the *so*—make it drawn out and use a snide tone to suggest they are not funny.
Oh, you should come, too.		Pause after the word *oh* and convey with a tone that they are not invited.
I don't mind.		Said with a tone that suggests I do mind.

Wrapping up

Point out examples in daily life where body language changed what someone said, and it was necessary to read between the lines. Have your child
spy on specific people in his life with whom he struggles to communicate.
Role-play with him interpreting what the person said and what they mean.

LEVEL 2 TOOLS

The next few lessons are about creating the impression you
intend to be positive and friendly. I call it the Public Relations
Campaign.

LESSON: WHAT IS YOUR BRAND?

Setting up the lesson

The Public Relations Campaign lessons can help a child look at
areas of her life where she needs to change the impression she
creates in the world. Using these lessons, she can address areas
of her life where she needs to promote a more positive image
or show her intentions, desires, and the messages she wants to
convey. This campaign begins with a discussion of her brand and
how each of us has a brand in the world.

Activity

1. Explain the concept to your child that everyone has a
   brand, just like a product you see in a shop has a brand.
   Read the following description of a brand.
        A brand for a product tells us what the product stands
   for and what the brand is all about. Brands are known for
   reputations and characteristics. For example, Disney, Nick-
   elodeon, McDonald's.
2. Discuss with your child that each of us has something like
   a brand, too—what we stand for, our values, our reputation, and the impression we make on other people. Share
   with your child that just like you buy certain products
   based on what you know about them, bystanders have

thoughts about her brand based on what they see, what they hear, and their perception of her brand.

3. Ask your child to think about three or four product brands, or a specific sports figure or movie star she likes and why she thinks they are special, unique, or reliable. Ask your child, "What comes to mind about this person's brand? What is their brand?"

4. Examine with your child what she wants her brand to be. Have her draw a logo or image that represents her chief characteristics and her brand. Suggested questions include: "What do you want your brand to be? What do you want people to know about you? Think about your strengths: What do you know about what you are good at? What do you have to offer the world?" Read from the List of Personal Brand Characteristics below and refer to the Strengths/Interests Matchmaker in Chapter 6. Have your child circle any characteristics she wants to include in her brand logo.

List of Personal Brand Characteristics

- Integrity
- Open-minded
- Authentic
- Energetic
- Reliable
- Kind
- Forgiving

- Good leadership
- Friendly
- Funny
- Wise
- Brave
- Curious
- Other _____

Wrapping up

Continue to refer to your child's brand and incorporate this topic into your daily life by spying on brands and pointing them out as you go through your day. As you encounter different brands, ask your child, "What do they stand for and what impression does the brand make?"

LESSON: PUBLIC RELATIONS CAMPAIGN

Setting up the lesson

Part of understanding other people's inner emotional world is understanding that your actions impact other people and inform how other people feel and react to you.

The Public Relations Campaign is meant to help your child understand "What I do impacts other people and what they do impacts me." Then to contemplate that: "Other people have thoughts about my actions and I have thoughts about their actions." It is a chain of thought that helps your child understand "public relations," or the understanding that other people can only know what you show them.

Activity

1. Read aloud the Public Relations Campaign visual to your child and explain the concept that people have thoughts about his actions, and he has thoughts about their actions. Ask your child, "What are areas you mean to do well in but need to show it?"

2. Discuss each of the statements in the visual and help your child understand what each statement means. Ask what impact his actions have on other people. Explore the fact that, despite our best intentions, people only know what they see. Share some concrete examples, such as ignoring someone because you are shy or saying something that should be filtered. Ask your child what specific behaviours he needs to show to make a good impression and to create likable, appealing behaviours.

3. Replay a scenario where the child did not have good public relations and explore what he wants to do differently next time. How did the other people in the situation feel about his behaviour?

Wrapping up

Create a time frame for a Public Relations Campaign using information from the Public Relations Problem-Solver chart that follows. Ask your child to begin his campaign.

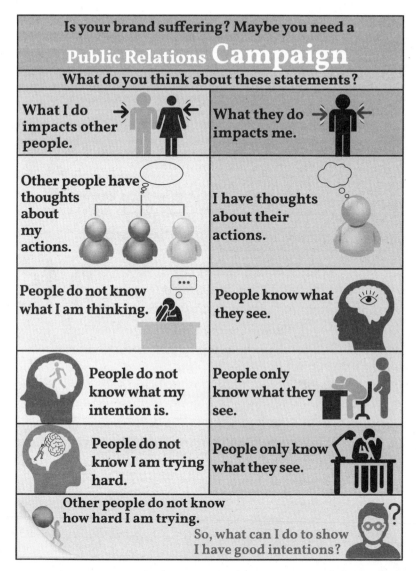

Public Relations Campaign
Problem-Solver

 **What do people think about
me/my brand right now?**

Where do I need to improve my brand?

 **If I ran a public relations campaign,
what would I want people to think
about me afterwards?**

**Where could I start my
public relations campaign?**

 **What could I do to demonstrate
or show my good intentions?**

What could I say to explain my intentions?

 **What past situation would I like to replay and
practise showing my intentions differently?**

**How could I demonstrate my good intentions
in new situations?**

 **What is my public relations
campaign action plan?**

© 2016 Maguire

LESSON: CAMPAIGN PROBLEM-SOLVER

Setting up the lesson

This exercise gives your child an active process to help her improve her brand as she develops her social skills. The Public Relations Campaign Problem-Solver provides an objective way to evaluate her own brand without making her feel bad.

Activity

1. Explain that public relations is a series of activities and actions that are planned to advance the reputation of a brand and make people have positive impressions of that brand. Discuss that people have feelings and reactions to how we act, and by creating a plan to change your brand, it can help your child make a better impression on her peers and help her as she tries to make new friends.

2. Show your child the Public Relations Campaign Problem-Solver and read aloud the questions it contains. Have your child answer each of the questions and jot down the key points in your notebook.

3. Create a Public Relations Campaign Action plan by identifying specific situations where your child could change the way she presents herself to others.

Wrapping up

Discuss the impression your child wants to create in the world and the way she can change her brand.

18

Once Was Enough

Self-Regulation

LESSON: HYPED UP WITH NO BRAKES

Setting up the lesson

Self-regulation is the ability to manage stress and energy levels to maintain a state of calm, alert awareness. There are different levels of activation in the brain and body, meaning that we move from lower energy to higher energy as we transition from a sleepy or calm state to an overwhelmed and dysregulated state. I call that overactivated state Hyped Up with No Brakes. When your child can't self-regulate, then he loses control. By helping your child understand the connection between physical and emotional feelings, activation levels, and his behaviour, he can start to better understand how to self-regulate.

Activity

1. Read this introduction to Hyped Up with No Brakes and show your child the visual.

    When you feel a big emotion, you can get excited or you can feel stressed. Your brain sounds an alarm and you become very activated and energised. It affects your mood and how you behave. Your body has different levels of activation. Sometimes you are sleepy and drowsy and in a state of Too Slow, No Go. Sometimes you are Calm-A-OK. Sometimes something starts to bug you, excite you, or stress you out and an alarm goes off in your brain. You feel stress rising, causing big emotion and big excitement inside your brain and in your body. When this happens, your rising activation is like an lift going up floor by floor in your body and mind. With each floor that your internal lift goes up, your emotions grow bigger and rise inside you, too.

First you might feel antsy or edgy—we'll call that state Things Are Bugging Me. As activation in your brain and body rises beyond what you can manage, it means that you are losing control and you are not able to manage what you do and what you say. That's Hyped Up with No Brakes.

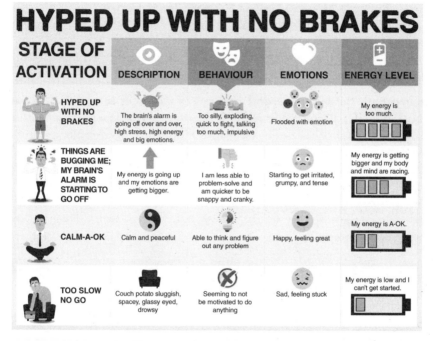

© 2016 Maguire

2. Read the description in the visual of how each state of activation changes your child's behaviour. Explain to your child that each level of brain activation changes his energy, his behaviour, and his emotions. Review the description of behaviour and emotions and energy and how it is affected by your level of activation found in the visual above.

When your brain and your body are Hyped Up with No Brakes, then your behaviour is too silly, too goofy, too quick to act, too angry, too quick to fight, or too quick to say something without thinking it through. Everything about your behaviour is just too much. Once you are overactivated and in a hyped-up state, your internal lift does not stop. It keeps going. It goes up and up and up as you lose control. To self-regulate and manage your body and your mind, you have to do something to be less activated. This means moving your internal lift down each level of activation from hyped up, to Calm-A-OK using calming strategies in the Starter Track.

3. Ask your child what Hyped Up with No Brakes behaviour looks like. Ask him, "What happens when you are in each state?" Have your child role-play and act out which behaviours occur when he is in the Too Slow, No Go; Calm-A-OK; Things Are Bugging Me; and Hyped Up with No Brakes states. Talk about how your child's internal lift and levels of activation change his behaviour.

Wrapping up

Incorporate the language and concept of different levels of activation into daily life. When your child is moving up in levels of activation, point it out and collaborate with him. Find a way to discuss his different activation states.

LESSON: GOOD WINNER, GOOD LOSER

Setting up the lesson

A quick and easy way to help a child who struggles with self-regulation when playing games with friends is to experiment with her activation level and her emotions in the safety of a coaching session. This lesson is meant to help your child expand her self-awareness about the levels of activation that occur and the emotional reaction that leads to her being a poor winnner or a poor loser. Your child will engage in this lesson often, so she can practise coping with emotions and activation in a safe setting.

Materials

Board games or games of chance such as tic-tac-toe; four square; Simon says; red light, green light; Pictionary; Operation; or any athletic game.

Activity

1. Read the following description of Good Winner, Good Loser.*

---

* Adapted from Baker, 2003.

Sometimes it is hard to control your emotions and your level of activation when you are playing games and having fun. When your internal lift goes up and you become hyped up, then your emotions bubble up and can become too much. That makes playmates have a reaction to you, and it can take away from the fun.

This lesson helps you learn what being a good winner and a good loser looks and feels like. You will also learn to notice your body signals (or tells) and warning signs when your emotions begin to get out of control. After playing this game, you will have some strategies to cope with big reactions and will know how to manage your feelings, so they don't become too much.

So, let's practise being a good winner and a good loser!

2. Ask your child to role-play and act out being a good winner or loser and what a poor winner and poor loser look like. Ask her to demonstrate behaviours that are too much and what level of behaviour and excitement is just right. Explain that as you play the game, she will be practising managing her feelings, her levels of activation, and her excitement. Discuss body signals and warning signs and how your child feels when she's about to lose control.

3. Invite your child to select a game to play. As she experiences winning or losing, point out when she needs to hit the pause button and how she might recognise her own signals.

During the game, notice her body signals and warning signs and when her emotional reaction is becoming too much.

This is a simulation practice. If your child struggles with self-regulation when she wins, then she needs practice: let her win. If she struggles with losing, play to win. Allow your child to experience a hyped-up state.

4. While she is in that state, interrupt with a coaching cue to pause the action and draw her attention to her emotional state and ask her to name the emotion. She needs to connect to her power to make a choice. You can say "I notice..." Then discuss the game and how your child felt as she played. Help her connect the dots between what she experienced, her body's signals, and what she can do the next time as she notices she's beginning to lose control. Brainstorm together to create strategies she can use when she recognises that her activation and emotions are becoming too much.

Wrapping up

Continue to play games and work on being a good winner and a good loser. If possible, involve other family members and play as a group. Help your child prepare strategies to cope with her reaction and allow her to learn to manage her real activation and real emotions with you so she can change her approach.

LESSON: BODY SIGNALS TELL YOU WHEN YOUR INNER ALARM IS SOUNDING OFF

Setting up the lesson

Part of what allows your child to have good self-awareness and to identify his level of activation is the ability to identify his emotional and physical state based on body signals. Learning to identify those body signals can be a key warning system to help your child understand his levels of activation so he can learn to self-regulate.

"Tells" are the body signals or physical sensations that are produced when your child experiences an increase or decrease in his levels of activation. Your child's internal alarm is sounding off and his levels of activation are moving from Things Are Bugging Me to Hyped Up. The brain creates these physical sensations as an automatic result of your child's reaction to a specific situation. These physical sensations or body signals are a key alarm that your child is growing upset and that his levels of activation are spiralling from Calm A-OK to Hyped Up.

These tells show that your child is becoming activated—that his lift is moving up. This lesson helps your child learn to notice body signals as a warning system that he is losing control. Tells help him become aware of his emotional, physical, and activation state. They show up in your child's body and mind. Being aware of his tells allows your child to identify what he is feeling, then practise calming strategies to down-regulate.

Activity

1. Read the following description of body signals and the example of common tells to your child.

    When you experience big emotions, you become stressed or excited, and your level of activation moves from Calm A-OK to Hyped Up. When this happens, your body signals and physical sensations show you that your activation is increasing. These physical sensations or body signals are your body's warning system—an alarm that tells you that you're growing upset, getting too much energy, becoming too stressed.

2. Review these with your child:

Examples of possible tells:

- Feeling hot and flushed
- Churning in the stomach
- Experiencing back pain
- Feeling jittery
- Feeling queasy
- Buzzing in the ears
- Feeling like he could jump out of his skin
- Having restless fingers
- Bobbing up and down
- Experiencing physical discomfort
- Breathing rate is higher
- Having tense muscles
- Experiencing increased sweating
- Getting red in the face
- Feeling body getting hot
- Crying
- Slurring speech
- Pulsing temple
- Rising blood pressure
- Feeling irritable and grumpy

3. Ask your child: "What tells do you have that signal you're becoming too hyped up? How does your body feel when you begin to lose control? How does (insert emotion) make you feel physically? Does waiting to do what you'd planned (insert activity) make you feel like you are going to jump out of your skin?"

   Your child may not be able to identify tells. If he cannot, then explain what these tells look like in later lessons and continue to bring up the topic.

Wrapping up

Continue to discuss tells and ask your child what a good cue would be for you to signal him when he is showing visible signs of rising activation. Collaborate with your child to see how you can help him witness this without making him have an emotional reaction. A good neutral question is, "How do you feel right now?" or "What tells do you feel?"

LEVEL 2 LESSONS

LESSON: SILLY-GOOFY SCALE

Setting up the lesson

Your child may become too silly, too goofy, too impulsive, and too out of control compared to her peers. This kind of impulsive behaviour gets your child in trouble at school and during activities, and eventually causes peers to grow tired of her behaviour. The Silly-Goofy Scale allows your child to simulate the behaviour of losing control and then to strategise with you so she can learn how to down-regulate when she becomes too silly and goofy.

Activity

1. Share with your child that sometimes behaviour becomes too silly or too goofy, especially if you are in a hyped-up state. Ask your child about a time when she became too silly or goofy. Ask your child: What level of goofy is too much? Have your child act out and role-play what being too silly or goofy looks like.
2. Show your child the Silly-Goofy Scale and read to her what happens in each stage, from totally in control to totally off the charts. Role-play what each stage of silly-goofy looks like, having your child act out the stages.

Wrapping up

Ask your child, "What happened as a result of being too goofy? What level of goofy would have been socially acceptable?"

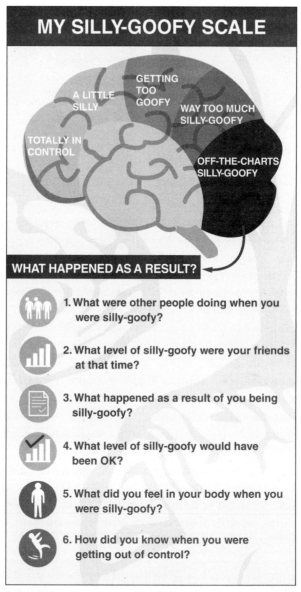

MY SILLY-GOOFY SCALE

GETTING TOO GOOFY

A LITTLE SILLY

WAY TOO MUCH SILLY-GOOFY

TOTALLY IN CONTROL

OFF-THE-CHARTS SILLY-GOOFY

WHAT HAPPENED AS A RESULT?

1. What were other people doing when you were silly-goofy?

2. What level of silly-goofy were your friends at that time?

3. What happened as a result of you being silly-goofy?

4. What level of silly-goofy would have been OK?

5. What did you feel in your body when you were silly-goofy?

6. How did you know when you were getting out of control?

© 2016 Maguire

LESSON: SILLY-GOOFY SCALE IN ACTION

Setting up the lesson

These games help your child reproduce what it feels like in the stages of activation, and notice what he experiences in his body and mind. In a safe space, take your child to do an activity that might make his levels of activation go up. Pick a specific place where he typically becomes hyped up and can experience what it feels like to be at the highest level of activation. Be a very active guide to help him understand his levels of activation. What tells show up when he loses control and what happens to his behaviour?

Activity

1. Remind your child of the Silly-Goofy Scale and explain that you want to help him have a real experience where he is hyped up so he can learn how to bring his internal lift down to Calm-A-OK. Explain that you are going to get him revved up by engaging in a play activity that may make him too silly-goofy. Tell your child in advance that when he becomes hyped up, you will step in, ask him to freeze the action, and ask him questions about how he feels in his body so he can practise using strategies to diminish his state of activation and move from hyped up to Calm-A-OK.

2. With your child, choose a place to practise these skills, somewhere you know is likely to make his activation level rise. Possible activities include having a (play) sword fight, bouncing on a trampoline, running around with a dog, playing red rover, running and jumping on a Slip 'N Slide, wrestling, or playing tag.

3. At the point where he is in a hyped-up state, step in and ask your child to freeze. Ask your child, "How do you feel? What is happening right now? What do you feel in your body right now? When did you feel you were becoming too silly-goofy? How excited are you on a scale of 1 to 5?"

4. If your child is not able to identify his body signals, you can share with him what you notice and ask him if he agrees. Giving him some suggestions can help.

5. Next, tell your child you are going to help his internal lift go from hyped up to calm down. Using a calming strategy from the Starter Track, help him down-regulate.

Wrapping up

If this exercise is beneficial, you and your child can continue to repeat the exercise. With each lesson, your child learns more about his self-regulation.

LESSON: ONCE WAS ENOUGH

Setting up the lesson

Repeated behaviour—where a joke goes on too long, your child talks obsessively about one topic, or she campaigns for her way or nags her friends—becomes tiresome to her peers. Once Was Enough lessons help your child recognise the behaviours that impact her friendships.

Activity

1. Read this description of Once Was Enough behaviour.

   When your brain is activated and hyped up, sometimes it's hard to remember to manage your behaviour. Sometimes when you feel big emotions, you may tell a joke too many times or talk too long about a topic. Maybe your tone becomes sarcastic, or you laugh too long or make too many negative comments. I call this Once Was Enough behaviour. It may not be what we mean to do (our intention). It is hard sometimes not to get stuck. When we are stuck in Once Was Enough behaviour, then we are not making a good impression on friends. We are making a Social Wrong Turn.

2. Read the list of common Once Was Enough behaviours to your child.

Common Once Was Enough behaviour:

- Telling a joke over and over
- Laughing when everyone else stops
- Being too silly
- Asking questions over and over
- Campaigning to get your way
- Reminding people of something you want or need over and over

- Talking about a topic over and over
- Poking someone over and over

3. Ask your child to role-play: What does Once Was Enough behaviour look like? Ask her to describe a time when she saw or demonstrated Once Was Enough behaviour. Ask her what impression Once Was Enough behaviour creates. What do people feel about Once Was Enough behaviour? What are the consequences? During Once Was Enough behaviour, what does she feel in her body? How does she know when she is becoming too activated and too much?

Wrapping up

Create a subtle cue or code word for your child to remind her when she is beginning to push her agenda and engage in Once Was Enough behaviour.

LESSON: ONCE WAS ENOUGH SCENARIOS

Setting up the lesson

Helping your child improve his self-awareness is key to improving his self-regulation. If necessary, add to this lesson by using his real-life Once Was Enough behaviours as examples. Have a coaching discussion about it. The key is to focus on what others feel and the impact of his behaviour, and then how other people treat him as a result.

Activity

1. Read the scenario, then ask your child the questions in step 2.

Scenarios:

- Patrick plays rough and loses control. His friends seem to regain control quickly and they do not like how silly Patrick becomes. They say things like, "It's not that funny anymore." Patrick tends to think things are funny and repeats them, and then wears out his friends. When the subject changes and his friends are talking about something else, Patrick brings the joke back to what he thinks is funny. Patrick does not give anyone airtime to speak.

- Jenny rushes into a crowd. She hops around the room, and other children scamper out of her way. She doesn't just hold a pencil at the small group tables; she waves it like a weapon. At a school picnic, she throws herself onto a blanket and the other kids look visibly annoyed, moving away from her. At circle time, she lies across her chair and giggles. She pushes her face up close to her neighbour. The teacher reprimands her repeatedly. Jenny wiggles in her seat. She grows hot and flushed and annoyed with the look on another girl's face. She begins to stand up and shout at the girl for looking at her. Her teacher grows angry at Jenny and tells her she has two strikes. Jenny sees the looks exchanged by the other kids. She loses it and shouts in her classmate's face, "Stop looking at me!"

- Oscar is imitating people and doing different voices all through a summer BBQ. After a while, kids seem to tire of the joke, but he keeps going. When someone changes the subject, he changes it back and just keeps making the same joke.

2. After the scenario, ask your child: "What was the Once Was Enough behaviour in the scenario? What state of activation did you notice for the characters? How important is other people's reaction to the character's Once Was Enough behaviour? What actions can the character take to stop or change the Once Was Enough behaviour? How does a Once Was Enough behaviour affect this person's friendships?" Replay the characters in the scenario and ask your child to act out what the character needed to do to stop his Once Was Enough behaviour.

Wrapping up

Saying something to prove a point or get your way more than two times turns from making a point to campaigning and nagging. If your child is struggling with Once Was Enough behaviour like telling a joke too long, asking questions, campaigning, or obsessing, suggest he make an agreement that he can only ask for something, bring up a joke, or other Once Was Enough behaviour two times.

19

Never Let Them See You Sweat

Emotional Regulation

LESSON: FIGHT, FLIGHT, OR FREEZE AND YOUR INNER SABRE-TOOTHED TIGER

Setting up the lesson

To help your child learn to manage her emotions, it helps her to understand how the emotional management system in the brain works. The more your child becomes aware of when and how she becomes flooded with emotions, the more she can prevent that flooding and cope with stressors.

Activity

1. Introduce the concept that sometimes we all experience big emotions and have big emotional reactions to a person, a circumstance, or stress. If your child does not know what stress is, some examples are having too much homework, being left out, or worrying about a party or an event. Read the following introduction below for Fight, Flight, or Freeze and Your Inner Sabre-Toothed Tiger to your child and show her the visual.

   When something upsets you or when you have a big emotional reaction, then your brain may become flooded with emotions, meaning your brain is overrun with emotions and they swamp you—like a flood from a river running over the shore, making it hard to control your emotions. Your brain has an ancient alarm system it used in ancient times to protect you from sabre-toothed tigers and attacks when we were living in caves and hunting in the wild. When you experience big stress, your brain goes into fight, flight, or freeze mode, meaning you feel like you want to pick a fight, run away, or just shut down. Fight, flight, or freeze happens because our brain doesn't know we are living in modern times and that we are safe. No sabre-toothed tiger is coming to attack.

2. Refer to Things That Make Me Experience Big Emotions in Chapter 11. Ask her what kinds of stress, circumstances, or people might cause her to become flooded with emotions. What does it feel like to be flooded with emotions? If she is stumped, tell her being flooded with emotions can feel like your head is buzzing and your whole body is tingling and you are so angry or upset you can barely stay in one place and you are ready to run, or hit, or shout.

Wrapping up

Ask your child to watch out for big stressors and feelings and fight, flight, or freeze.

LESSON: REACTIVE ME AND THINKING ME

Setting up the lesson

Part of fight, flight, or freeze is that the child is experiencing emotional flooding and the limbic system and emotional reactivity in the brain is taking over, so he cannot access the key planning and analytical tools in his brain. This affects your child's behaviour and yet he may not be aware of how his emotional state changes his behaviour.

Activity

1. Read this description of Reactive Me* to your child.

   When you are flooded with emotions, you are experiencing the Reactive Me state. You are feeling anxious or sad or angry or irritated and you may feel out of control. You may feel like you can't stop. And you may do things you are not proud of, but at the time you feel like you are on a runaway train.

© 2016 Maguire

2. Read this description of Thinking Me.

   When you are calm and in control, you can puzzle things out and problem-solve—you are experiencing the Thinking Me state. You feel like you are able to remember information and ask for help and calmly approach any task.

---

* Adapted from Goldsmith, 2016; Goleman, 1995; LeDoux, 1998; Shanker, 2016; Smith and Weinfeld, 2017.

© 2016 Maguire

3. Ask your child when he has experienced his Reactive Me and Thinking Me state.

4. Read aloud the list of Reactive Me behaviours and the Thinking Me behaviours.

Reactive Me behaviours:

- Feeling I can't stop
- Arguing
- Hitting
- Yelling
- Picking verbal or physical fights
- Running
- Jumping
- Being irritable
- Feeling distracted
- Taking risks
- Feeling ready to jump out of my skin
- Feeling overwhelmed
- Having an out-of-body experience
- Exploding
- Using a snappy tone
- Feeling like I can't remember anything or learn new things
- Feeling like my whole brain is focused on my emotions and nothing else
- Being unable to notice social cues

Thinking Me behaviours:*

- Able to problem-solve
- Able to ask for help
- Able to remain calm and manage reactions
- Able to learn
- Remember information
- Make calm decisions
- Interpret social cues
- Think about other people's feelings
- Pay attention

5. After you read the Reactive Me and Thinking Me behaviours, ask your child to think of a time when he may have felt so flooded with emotions that he was in a Reactive Me state. What does Reactive Me behaviour look like? What does Thinking Me behaviour look like?

Wrapping up

The next time your child is experiencing big emotions, present the idea of collaborating with him to use the Calming Strategies found in the Starter Track in Chapter 11.

LESSON: SPY ON REACTIVE ME AND THINKING ME

Mission

Go to school or a large shop and spy on people. Try to notice who is experiencing Thinking Me behaviours and who is experiencing Reactive Me behaviours. Notice and spy on how they show that they are experiencing big emotions in their body, in their actions, and in what they say. Then report back your spy findings.

LESSON: BLUE SKY BREATHING

Setting up the lesson

When your child is able to stop and breathe, this allows her to restore the balance between the emotional and the reasonable or analytical

---

* Adapted from Goldsmith, 2016; Goleman, 1995; LeDoux, 1998.

parts of the brain. Deep breathing is the body's way of accessing key executive functions like critical thinking and decision-making that your child needs to manage her daily life.

Activity

1. Explain that taking deep breaths is a calming strategy that you can use anywhere, anytime. Read aloud these simple instructions for Blue Sky Breathing and ask your child to watch you breathe as you walk through the instructions: (1) Breathe in deeply through your nose for a belly breath, thinking "blue sky" with your in-breath. (2) Hold for a count of three. (3) Exhale out your mouth, thinking "grey sky" in your mind. (4) Repeat four times.

2. Present to your child the fact that when you take short, shallow breaths, you are not giving the brain and the body the oxygen it needs. Explain that Blue Sky Breathing can actually flood your body with positive chemicals that help you calm down and manage your emotions.

3. Ask your child if she can picture something that is bugging her. Ask her to do the Blue Sky Breathing and then check in with her to see how she feels.

Wrapping up

Discuss with your child that breathing deeply is a technique that slows down emotional reactions and helps her de-escalate, or calm, an emotional reaction.

LESSON: NAME IT TO TAME IT

Setting up the lesson

When your child is experiencing a fight, flight, or freeze moment, you can still move to a state of calm. Naming and identifying the feeling sends calming neurotransmitters or chemicals through your child's whole body and tells his inner sabre-toothed tiger to calm down, that there is no threat.

Activity

1. Read the following introduction of Name It to Tame It to your child.
    When you are flooded with emotion that takes over your brain, it may seem like there is nothing you can do. But actually, you can engage in a process that we call Name It to Tame It.

❑ You need to recognise that you are having big emotions and that they are taking over—you are in a Reactive Me state.

❑ You need to name or identify the feeling, because talking actually helps!

❑ Once you name the worry, you may want to use a calming strategy found in the Starter Track so you can work through what you are feeling and regain your Thinking Me behaviour!

❑ Picture a lift moving from the top floor down to the bottom. This helps you move from Reactive Me to Thinking Me again.

Wrapping up

Ask your child permission to practise this method over the next week in private. Create a plan with your child for common situations like school so he can Name It to Tame It.

LESSON: TRIGGERS

Setting up the lesson

A trigger is an event, person, situation, circumstance, or environment that causes an overly emotional reaction. This reaction can spark a chain of emotional reactions and can overwhelm the child's five senses and cause a meltdown. This exercise* is meant to help your child become aware of any specific triggers that create big emotional reactions.

Activity

1. Explain to your child that triggers cause the overly emotional reactions to an event, person, situation, circumstance, or environment. For example, a parent reminding you to do your homework or being left out can cause you to feel instantly upset and lose control. Discuss the concept that these triggers may make you feel like you are jumping out of your skin. They can gobble up your thoughts and make it hard to be social.

2. Share with your child the list of triggers. Ask your child to circle what triggers make it hard for her to manage her emotions. Ask your child what triggers make it hard for her to remember to read social cues or even be social. What was it about the trigger that made her

---

* Adapted from Febus, 2018; Goldsmith, 2016; Goleman, 1995; LeDoux, 1998; Smith and Weinfeld, 2017.

have a big emotional reaction? Talk through past situations where this event, person, or situation made her lose control.

Triggers

Physical triggers

- Being hungry
- Feeling tired
- Feeling you have too much energy
- Feeling you do not have enough energy
- Having a bad thought in your head
- Feeling unwell

Emotional triggers

- Feeling confused
- Feeling I do not fit in
- Feeling sad
- Feeling frustrated
- Feeling anxious
- Feeling bored
- Feeling like I do not have control over ___
- Feeling irritated
- Feeling annoyed
- Waiting
- Hearing loud noises
- Smelling something unpleasant
- Transitioning from activities
- Hearing certain words like *homework* or *time to go*
- Being called on in class
- Seeing clutter in a small room
- Being around too much commotion

Social triggers

- Having friendship problems
- Going to birthday parties
- Being bossed around
- Being the subject of gossip
- Feeling left out
- Confusing social situations
- Having to talk to people you don't know

- Making conversation
- Not knowing where to sit at lunch
- Being alone at break time

3. Present the scenarios where the character experiences a trigger. Then ask your child to explain what made the character have a big emotional reaction.

Scenarios:

- Cindy was criticised by a friend who said that she did not do well at a football match. Now every time Cindy enters football practice or sees the friend, Cindy has a big reaction. Cindy feels suddenly so angry. She begins to stew and churn in her head about the comment.
- Mena felt left out when she was at a birthday party. She felt like everyone ignored her and did not bother to talk to her. When her mum asked Mena how the birthday party went, Mena yelled at her mum and was suddenly so sad she began to cry.
- Owen struggles to get his homework done. He finds it boring. Owen's mother told Owen it was "time to start his homework," which made Owen angry and frustrated. He had an argument with his mum and became so angry that he could barely speak.

Wrapping up

Discuss with your child any triggers you have identified and how you feel in your body and the concept that triggers make you act differently.

LESSON: NEVER LET THEM SEE YOU SWEAT

Setting up the lesson

Your child needs to learn to process emotional reactions and to create coping techniques to help her manage her emotional reactions. When your child overreacts, it makes a negative impression and other children grow tired of her overreactions. Learning to understand that we have to process and manage emotions is a key social skill.

Activity

1. Read this introduction aloud to your child.

   Sometimes your worries and feelings grow so big that they take control. When other people see you out of control, things don't turn out very well. It helps to learn how to calm those feelings down because other people don't need to know your feelings are too big. It takes practice to be able to notice when your feelings are getting too big and then take care of yourself so that you only show on the outside what you want other people to see.

2. Discuss with your child the concept of having an overreaction where you show your big emotions on the outside. Explain how it can make a negative impression and other playmates may be surprised. Walk your child through the concept of showing emotion "big" on the inside and "small" on the outside. Have your child role-play and act out when she shows *too much* to the outside world. Ask her to show you what emotions being too much look like.

3. Ask your child, "When do you have an overreaction? What are your feelings? How can you express your feelings and name and tame them?" Role-play having a big emotion on the inside but taming it so you show it smaller on the outside. Discuss the exact steps your child can go through and what she can do to down-regulate and calm down.

Wrapping up

Identify specific calming strategies your child can use to help with emotional regulation. (See the Lists for Everyone! in Chapter 11 for calming exercises.) Ask your child what she could do differently next time and what her typical reaction is to the (insert trigger or reason for emotions).

LESSON: THE EMOTIONAL VOLCANO

Setting up the lesson

Emotional Volcano helps your child understand that emotional triggers flood his brain with emotions and that those emotions affect his actions, thoughts, decisions, and reactions. Often overreactions affect your child's social interactions. The more your child can learn to become aware of his inner emotional life and the triggers that set him off, the more he can learn to manage his emotions.

Activity

1. Show your child the visual of the Emotional Volcano and read the following introduction.

   A trigger is something that can make your emotions grow until you explode. When your brain goes into fight, flight, or freeze mode, it may be because a person, place, or situation has turned on a switch in your brain and you are quickly flooded with emotions.

Like a volcano, eruption does not occur instantly, but is a process. First, below the surface of the earth, the heat is so intense that the rocks melt, creating magma. As the heat continues to grow, pressure increases, and gases and magma begin to climb up the walls of the volcano. If the reaction continues to move forward, eventually the lava will flow over the top of the volcano.

Notice the emotional volcano in the picture. It shows your emotions growing until finally you explode.

© 2016 Maguire

Sometimes there are things that bug you, and bit by bit they just keep building until you explode. As the volcano eruption grows, just like your emotions grow, there is a point where you can pause and use strategies to Name It to Tame it.

2. Share the image of the volcano and the eruption with your child. Using the How Calm Am I? graphic, discuss how at each point in the 5-point scale your child's emotions are changing, just like the emotional volcano grows. The scale that follows can help your child identify what he feels like at each stage of his reaction, ranging from 1 to 5, until he loses control. Ask your child to describe how he feels at each point in the eruption process.

3. Role-play what he looks like and feels like using How Calm Am I? language such as feeling just right or about to lose control. Have him pause and become aware of his body signals. He can change the

course of his behaviour with strategies that help him manage his emotions rather than erupting in a meltdown.

4. Now pick one or two calming strategies from the Lists for Everyone! in the Starter Track. Act out being very upset and then moving down the self-regulation scale from a 3 or 4 to a 1 to 2 using those strategies. Ask your child to also role-play and act out that process.

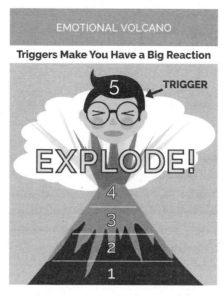

© 2016 Maguire

"How Calm Am I?" Five-Point Scale

1	2	3	4	5
CALM	HAPPY	GETTING GRUMPY	GETTING REALLY UPSET	OVER-THE-TOP UPSET
In control of my feelings	Feeling just right	Starting to feel my emotions getting to be too much	About to lose control	My emotions are too much

Wrapping up

Create a plan to use when your child experiences a big emotional reaction at school or at home.

LESSON: PINPOINTING HOW YOU FEEL AT EACH POINT IN THE DAY

Setting up the lesson

It is difficult at times to understand what event or situation resulted in your child's emotional state when you greet them at the door. The more your child learns to stop and think about what has occurred over the day and to pinpoint what upset her, the more she can succeed in naming the emotions and taming them.

Activity

1. Ask your child to rate* what she feels at each point in the day. Write down her responses. Explain to your child that you are trying to identify with her the times of the day and situations where she experiences triggers and where her emotional reactions might start to grow. Using the How Calm Am I? 5-point scale from the Emotional Volcano lesson, ask your child to rate what she feels at each point of the day.

2. As part of the conversation, ask your child what she feels in that particular situation. What is it about the teacher, people, or class that makes her experience big emotions? What does she feel when she enters the situation? Is there anything specific that happens in that situation that affects her?

| PINPOINTING HOW YOU FEEL AT EACH POINT IN THE DAY ||
How I Felt	Rating 1 to 5
Morning	
On the bus	
In maths	
In science	
In English	
In history	
In language	
In art	
In music	
In PE	

* Adapted from Kuypers, 2011; LeDoux, 1998.

How I Felt	Rating 1 to 5
Before break time	
After break time	
Lunchtime	
After school	
During homework	
At bedtime	
At night	

Wrapping up

Discuss any situations where your child felt she experienced a 5 and then brainstorm coping with those feelings using the calming strategies from the Starter Track.

LEVEL 2 LESSON

LESSON: HOW WORRIED SHOULD I REALLY BE?

Setting up the lesson

As we grow older, other people expect us to manage our emotions rather than letting our emotions manage us. When your child has high levels of anxiety or an overreaction to a situation, other children may grow frustrated. Children are not expected to repress their emotions, but they need to learn if they are overreacting. Help him understand how other people feel about this overreaction.

Activity

1. Ask your child to pick a time when he overreacted to a situation and he felt flooded with emotions. Ask him to act out and role-play what overreaction looks like. Some examples include running from the room, wailing, stomping, pushing, or screaming. If he cannot remember, you can say, "I am thinking about a time..." or give an example you have observed. Note to parents: it is important to stress to your child that you are trying

to examine what overreaction looks like and feels like for him; you are not trying to blame or revisit ancient history.

2. Present your child with the visual of How Worried Should I Be? and read aloud the following introduction.

When you feel a big worry, you may overreact because you feel your worry is as big as a huge lorry. Some worries feel as small as a bicycle. How our worries feel inside affects us and our reactions.

3. Pick a specific worry your child has experienced or refer to the list of Things That Make Me Experience Big Emotions from the Lists for Everyone! in the Starter Track. Ask your child, "When you overreact, what does your worry feel like? Is it as big as a dumper truck? Is it as small as a bike?" Using a 1- to 5-point scale with your child, ask him, "What would you need to help you carry this worry and feel okay? How much horsepower do you need to carry these worries and manage them?"

4. Since the worry feels like a (car, lorry, scooter, etc.), if he overreacts to the worry, ask him, "What do other people feel when we overreact?"

How Worried Should I Be?

What does this worry feel like?

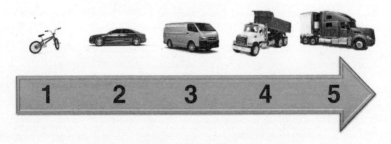

**How much horsepower do you need
to carry these worries and manage them?**

Wrapping up

Feel free to bring this visual with you, post it in the kitchen, or keep it in an easily accessible place. The next time your child experiences a worry, ask him, "What does your reaction feel like—as big as a car or as big as a huge lorry?"

PART IV

The *Play Better Plan*

To Playdates and Beyond

20

The Playdate Planner
How to Line Them Up and Plan Them Well

Playdates are the social playing field where your child can practise new skills, observe other kids, and learn from missteps, as well as success.

Playdates are the Holy Grail of childhood, the object of every child's social quest, and sometimes elusive no matter how hard your child—or you—tries to get them. You may not hear the yes you hope for at first. When invitations do come, your child may not be prepared to make the most of the moment. We're about to take a strategic approach to play-dates to help you create opportunities that dovetail with your child's skill-building goals in your home-coaching lessons and activities.

Think of these as practice playdates. That's their purpose in the *Play Better* coaching programme. As your child grows comfortable with the ideas and skills you're working on together in lessons, then the next step is to practise them in a real play situation, but one in which you're there on the sidelines, most of all to observe, so the two of you can compare notes later about the play-by-play.

For planning purposes, consider a playdate any play opportunity that includes (1) the expectation of social interaction, (2) a role for your child, (3) reasonable and predictable rules for behaviour in the setting, and (4) an identified time frame. A playdate might involve a child from school or could be just a casual get-together with young cousins or family friends. The point is for your child to practise new social skills in the "shallow water" and build confidence for diving into the deep end of the social pool when she's ready.

The Playdate Planning Cheat Sheet at the end of the chapter breaks the planning task into manageable pieces that make it easier for you to use what you know about your child to create the most supportive setting possible for practice. Use it as your worksheet to identify compatible playmates, and pick a setting, activity, and time that are optimal for your child at this early stage of learning new social behaviours. You wouldn't start a new diet by bringing a cake home to practise resisting temptation. More sensibly, you'd set yourself up for success by stocking the fridge with healthy foods to help make those choices a habit. So it goes for our children. Social interaction is already stressful for your child, so to start, plan practice playdates that avoid predictable stressors until the new behaviours are a habit. Common stressors include people, places, or conditions that are usually challenging for your child even on a good day. Hungry, tired, over-pressured kids crumble quickly. So plan for a time when your child is rested, fed, and has the energy for a playdate. If certain toys are hot buttons for conflict, leave them out for now; you can add them back later when your child is ready for the mission of sharing. A child who has been hard for your child to be around in the past is also best saved for another day, too.

The point of playdate planning isn't just to *get* playdates; it's to *use* playdates as an opportunity for your child to practise new and emerging social skills and behaviours. This means that in your coaching lesson times, together you'll identify the specific social-skills mission for the playdate. What is the new skill he is focused on most in coaching? Check the EFQ Lesson Track for your child's priority behaviours for change. Revisit *How Will You Know?* to see which skills he has made the most progress with and could be ready to practise in a playdate. Remember, the goal is to *practise* new skills. He won't have mastered them yet, but practice itself develops the executive functions of self-awareness, awareness of others, and attention to the task. Every small success is meaningful progress. That's how the brain develops, that's how brain-based social skills develop, and that's how your child's confidence will grow.

Your child's playdate planning task is to pick one or two jobs, or missions, for this playdate. You'll work on these in your coaching sessions, and you'll remind her of the mission just before the playdate. Be sure she knows what you are looking for in the new behaviour. For example, missions might include one or two from these common ones:

- Share the video game console.
- Meet people halfway.
- When you start to have big emotions, deep-breathe to calm yourself.

- Notice your body signals—when you start to get angry, use your strategy (which is...).
- Let your guest choose first.
- Only tell someone what you want twice. Then let it go for this playdate.

WHO, WHAT, WHERE, WHEN

Playmate compatibility is an important factor. If your child has difficulty with self-awareness or reading social cues, he may have an inaccurate picture of his relationships with other children. You may need to dissuade him from inviting certain friends, and help him choose children who are a better fit in temperament. For instance, a socially isolated pre-adolescent may wish to be friends with the most popular students at school. He may dismiss other potential friends in order to hold out for more popular friends, regardless of whether they have already rejected him. In this type of situation, you would need to encourage your child to give other playmates a chance.

Compatibility does not necessarily mean putting two like-minded children together. It means seeking children who complement one another. For example, two rambunctious, impulsive children would not make a wise fit for a playdate in which your child needs to practise new skills or behaviours. Try to find a playmate who shares common interests with your child, and whose temperament is patient, flexible, and non-judgemental, someone your child could emulate socially.

Teachers, coaches, the school guidance counsellor, or a psychologist can be helpful sources of suggestions for potential playmates for your child. Take a friend into your confidence who is in your community and is familiar with the temperament of potential playmates and is willing to listen and plan with you. Siblings can also be brought into the fold to share their observations.

For a playdate activity, be strategic. Consider options for what they'll do and where they'll play. There is no one-size-fits-all optimal activity and environment. Ask yourself:

- What is an activity my child enjoys?
- Will it be a structured or an unstructured environment?
- In what environment does my child do well? Where do I have the most success with her? At home? A park or playground?

- What environment will also make it possible for me to be present in some way to observe how it's going?
- Consider someplace special that your child loves and another child is likely to find appealing, too.
- Remove toys that cause conflict or make your child possessive.
- If a sibling is super-personable—a kid-magnet—then have them off on a playdate of their own so the child who needs to practise doesn't get ignored in favour of their popular sibling.
- Have good snacks.

Be sure your child helps choose the activity, and use that discussion to point out how different settings and activities are more stressful than others, or less so. The conversation about these choices is important far beyond this playdate. This is how, as your child's coach, you're guiding him through this process of making choices that work out well so he can learn to do it himself.

Avoid scenarios that you know tend to trigger a negative reaction from your child. In this programme, you're asking your child to work really hard, so choose a place that is familiar and comfortable, so she can put her best foot forward. Just hanging out with no plan is not the best plan. For example, Randy, age nine, is quite accomplished at his favourite video game. Unfortunately, he also hogs the controls, refuses to change when another kid suggests it, and won't play if he can't get his way. It may be that you're working together in coaching on those video game behaviours, and that's exactly what you want to do in a playdate so he can practise his sharing behaviours. In preparation for the playdate, in coaching you can ask: "What can you do to share like a friend? What can you do when your friend suggests a change? What can you do when you feel frustrated or disappointed and want to walk away?" Then plan to include some game time, but orchestrate it so that's not their main activity. Be specific and simple about the mission. Don't bog your child down with fifteen things to remember. One or two are ideal, three max.

Time of day and duration of play can be a setup for success— or a deal breaker. Remember that a playdate requires them to practise new skills that are hard for them. A playdate at the end of the day may not work well for them. Most children aren't at their best when they're tired or hungry.

How long should a playdate be? For a child working on these new and emerging skills, forty-five minutes to an hour can be plenty. Until your child can handle playdates solo, plan to be there for the duration. The time will come when you can drop your child for a playdate and leave to run some errands. But in the beginning, it's important to think of a playdate as your coaching observation time.

If everything else about the playdate plan looks good—the children are compatible, the time of day is good—then if a longer playdate seems possible, focus on ways to build in some break times, perhaps with a snack or transition to another play activity. You might also consider an activity that involves you to some degree, like baking or making slime. Or some art time that allows the children to work on something separately or together. A big roll of art paper, with markers, crayons, stickers, or other glue-on materials, can be a creative activity that allows both sharing and independent expression. They don't have to agree on everything!

How frequently should you schedule playdates? For this coaching programme to be successful, aim to schedule at least one playdate a week and one other social opportunity—something in a regular group setting, like a class or a Scout meeting, is fine. Kids with social difficulties typically have fewer reliable invites for opportunities to socialise, and they need this real-world practice. You may also find a ready resource in extended family and friends who want to support your child's efforts and are pleased to plan get-togethers with that in mind.

ROLE-PLAY AND REHEARSE

Before your child's playdate, role-play or rehearse new behaviours with her until she feels confident about taking them on as a mission for a playdate. These skill-building activities may need to be repeated several times before your child really understands what's being asked of her. Otherwise, the words that describe desired behaviour—*Be nice! Take turns!*—are just words. Role-play and rehearsal translate the words into specific action your child experiences. Role-playing also helps build confidence.

Caleb

Caleb was unsure what his mother meant by "fighting less" with his best friend, Tyrone. He was trying to be good on playdates, but he kept falling into old behaviours. "I just don't know how else to play," he told me.

Caleb and his mother discussed different role-playing scenarios. Together, they decided that Caleb's new behaviours would be to first take a deep breath and count to ten when he got upset. Second, try to use words to express his emotions instead of pushing, punching, or wrestling. Third, take a time-out in another room when he felt the urge to be physical. Caleb's mother rehearsed with Caleb frequently. This simulation allowed Caleb to experience *using* his strategies, not just trying to memorise them to remember later. (See Simulation Practice in Chapter 3.)

Here is an example of one of her coaching sessions with her son:

> MOTHER: Caleb, let's say Tyrone has just picked up your new Nerf gun and is shooting arrows at you. What would you do?
>
> CALEB: First, I'd take a deep breath.
>
> MOTHER: And?
>
> CALEB: Count to ten.
>
> MOTHER: And what would you do if he was still shooting arrows at you?
>
> CALEB: I'd use my words.
>
> MOTHER: How?
>
> CALEB: Um...I don't know.
>
> MOTHER: How about saying something like, "Tyrone, please stop shooting arrows at me. I don't like it."
>
> CALEB: Yes. That could work.
>
> MOTHER: What else could you say?
>
> CALEB: "Tyrone, that hurts. Can we shoot at my new targets?"
>
> MOTHER: That's great! Now, what would you do if you were so angry you couldn't calm down and use your words?
>
> CALEB (WITH EXCITEMENT): I'd go into the other room to calm down!

Caleb practised these types of scenarios with his mother five different times in the week before the playdate, and eventually, towards the end of a session, Caleb grew excited because he knew the right answers to his mother's questions. He knew what was expected of him. His growing confidence during rehearsals extended into his playdates, and he was able to use the skills effectively. Now, he and Tyrone no longer fight, and they remain best friends.

Sometimes, children forget to use new behaviours in the heat of the moment during playdates or at school. Supports include subtle cues or prompts, and strategies that help your child remember—and succeed.

Wilson

Wilson never joined in. In gymnastics, he lurked at the corner of the play mat—he just didn't know how to engage with the other children. When he had a playdate, he tended to avoid being in the driver's seat. He was so terrified that he didn't really show his personality. On weekends, he went to School of Rock, but he didn't speak up to self-advocate for the instrument or the place onstage he wanted. So, Wilson and his mother used rehearsal—a simulation activity—to give him an experience of advocating for himself socially by actively approaching other kids or initiating conversation. His mother role-played his friends to show Wilson how his friends' interests could help as he interacts with them. When he freezes in a real play situation, Wilson needs to have a plan—a go-to strategy. He decided that "Suggest we play outside" would be his go-to. If Wilson got physically uncomfortable, he'd suggest they something active, like play football. The physical activity helped him release some stress and self-regulate. He also memorised a few things to talk about—a popular movie and upcoming school event—and he worked on reading the other kids' interest, so if they were interested, he'd be able to build on the conversation, and if they weren't interested, he'd have a backup plan.

But ... What if my child is too old to have Mum arranging playdates?

Your role as playdate planner does depend on the age of your child. Parents usually schedule playdates for primary school children but take a less active role for older children. If your child is "aging out" of the time when mums and dads are doing the heavy lifting on playdate planning, you can help by role-playing how to approach peers, how to ask other children to hang out, and how to join new social networks. For more help for your older child, turn to Friendship Is a Two-Way Street in Chapter 11 for the lessons on mixing in and the tools on Build on It. You can also guide him through the *who, what, when,* and *where* and help him write the text or form a plan to ask someone to hang out.

But ... What if my child resists my efforts to plan a playdate?

Resistance happens, especially when we're asking a child to do something that's uncomfortable and difficult for her. First, explore the reasons for the resistance. Sometimes with a younger child, a simple solution is to use incentives. For older children who already are forming visions of what they "want to be" in their adult life, discuss how socialisation and these basic social skills are essential to get where they want to go. A habit of meltdown, blowups, or social conflict will get in their way. Whatever objections your kid brings up, you can coach around them. You can say, "What is your worry about (the issue)?" rather than dismissing it. Other responses that can continue the conversation and help get to the core of what's holding your child back include:

> What would you like to do on a playdate?
> Are there any playdates that you've had that you've enjoyed?

What's your objection to planning a playdate?
How often do you want to play with other kids?
What I hear you saying is...

Your point is to try to find out more about your child's objection and understand how the situation looks and feels to him, and what he'd like to see as a positive outcome. For more about overcoming resistance, refer to Chapter 23, "Troubleshooting."

But... What if it's hard to find anyone to set up a playdate with?

If you've run into problems or dead ends in your efforts to set up playdates, know that you aren't alone. Social skills development is a growing problem and you can be sure that it affects many children and families in your area. You may need to broaden your search for a new social network your child can join. You might enroll her in a new activity, go to a park in a different neighbourhood, or meet up with a social skills group. Even among kids who know your child's reputation, there may be second chances. Consider explaining to another parent that your child has struggled with friendship skills but that you've been coaching her. Ask if their child might give yours another chance. Other suggestions from parents who have been in that spot and found a way forwards include the following:

■ Ask a teacher or coach to suggest a potential playmate.
■ Practise skills and then join a new activity.
■ Ask siblings if they could help by suggesting possible playmates.
■ Tap cousins and close friends you can confide in.
■ Approach a parent whose child also struggles and suggest a playdate.
■ Consider younger and older kids.
■ Try small group activities such as Scouts, crafts clubs, indoor play space, or club and chaperone.

The Playdate Planning Cheat Sheet

■ Limit the duration of the playdate. Forty-five minutes is often ideal—it allows time to practise new social skills and sustain energy and attention.
■ Minimise unstructured downtime. It adds to the challenge of cooperative play.

- Create structure. Nothing rigid. Just enough to give children a sense of the playing field and social rules for the get-together.
- Anticipate problems that have occurred historically.
- If your child has trouble sharing a specific item or toy, take that toy out of the equation.
- Agree on cues or prompts to signal simple reminders.

YOU'VE GOT THIS!

It's easy to joke about planning as a futile exercise when you're dealing with kids. We all get it. But jokes aside, planning is at the heart of coaching because it's part of preparing to be successful on the playing field, no matter what comes your way. Your child is practising new skills and behaviours to bring to the field of play. It's your job as coach to plan playdates to minimise pitfalls and maximise opportunities for success.

Playdates

Coaching from the Sidelines

No need to run interference—your role as coach is to observe,
take notes, and use cues to guide when needed.

When you have a kid who swims, you spend a lot of time at the pool for team practice and events. One thing you notice is that swimming coaches don't jump in the pool. They watch closely as their swimmer does what she came to do, and occasionally they'll call out an encouraging word or quick comment. But mostly they watch and make mental notes they review with the swimmer when the heat is done. Around the world, from sports to music to championship chess, you see the same thing: come match time, the coach is on the sidelines.

When it's time for your child to put her practice to the test in a playdate, you shift to the sidelines, too. Your role as coach is no less important, but your direct involvement will be minimal. You'll be taking notes about your child's successes and missteps to discuss later in debriefing. You'll also look at other aspects of the setting, including playmates' personalities and the interactions and emotions that played out, so that you and your child can discuss these kinds of social details when you debrief about their experience and their own behaviour.

Your coaching from the sidelines is a unique step in your child's experience, too. As playdate coach, you want to encourage your child to manage his own social interactions or dilemmas. You'll intervene only when necessary, and (this is very important to remember) you may need to adjust your idea of "necessary." It's part of your child's task to self-monitor and recognise when he needs to do something differently than he has in the past, draw on a skill he's been practising, and give it a try. Whether that is entirely successful or not, your place as coach needs to be on the sidelines for the more detached view. You're there to offer a cue if it's needed, but mostly to observe and note the successes and slip-ups to discuss when you reconnoiter and debrief in your next coaching session.

In the natural social interaction and give-and-take of a playdate, your child needs to try to work things out with friends and practise friendship skills on her own as much as possible. You give her room to make mistakes because mistakes are a critical part of the learning process. Debriefing, which we'll turn to in the next chapter, helps your child look at those bumps in the road and reflect and learn from them like never before.

AS YOU START

Remember: This is a work in progress—and it *is* going to work! During playdates, children sometimes forget their mission or fumble with the skill they've practised. It's hard for kids to remember new skills when they're excited in the moment. But unlike past experiences, when you watched in horror as playdates disintegrated before your eyes, you and your child have created some support structures that give you a shared language to use when you discuss how things went after the fact.

You'll be practising a new skill, too: how to limit your involvement and use discreet cues to communicate. For example, what if your child becomes inflexible about going along with the group, reverting to some familiar unhelpful habits that she's trying to break? You will have rehearsed in advance and you'll specifically prep in these key areas that call for your child's new skill. In simulation and role-play exercises at home, you'll have agreed upon a few code words or cues that you can use if she needs a reminder.

If your child comes to you with problems rather than solving them for himself, you can turn the tables and pose problem-solving questions to him. By doing so, you don't get snared in a discussion about the problem. The conversation becomes about his ability to work on finding some solutions. (See the "Pocket Coach" section next for specifics.)

As you take notes, include any interactions you have with your child and the prompts that worked best for her. You'll see which questions connected with her and built her confidence to read the situation independently. That's important information for you both to have the next time.

POCKET COACH: COACHING FROM THE SIDELINES

If your child steps out of the play activity and comes to you with a complaint or a problem, you can ask:

- What's the problem?
- How come? What's going on?
- What are the signs you're picking up on?
- What can you do to keep play going?
- What was your mission for this playdate, and how can you get back on track?
- What does your friend want?
- What would it be like to go along with your friend? What might happen?
- We prepared for (this problem). What did we plan?

SEVEN WAYS TO ENCOURAGE INDEPENDENCE DURING PLAYDATES

Confidence comes from doing. If independence is a challenge for your child, then practising independence could be the mission for a playdate. Three common behaviours by kids are common hot buttons for parents to intervene in ways that, in effect, let their children off the hook for independent problem-solving.

Boomerang. Your child keeps coming back to you to complain, or ask for help, or just to duck out of playing with the other kids. You can say to your child that you want her to think about how she can handle the situation, and ask what is making her come back so often. Ask your child what her mission is. What can she do to have fun in the circumstances she's in?

Volcano. Meltdowns or blowups probably bring you running to intervene. Remind your child of his calm-down strategies and ask him what he can do to calm himself. Ask your child, "What is bothering you?" What can he do to work out any conflict or to change what is bothering him?

Disengaged. You see your child holding back, being reluctant, or refusing to participate, or perhaps she was forgotten or excluded by the other children, and you step in to fix it. Ask your child what's going on for her. What is making her disengage? Remind her of what you rehearsed. Ask what games would interest her. What can she do to ask her friends to play those games?

Your first parenting impulse may be to intervene, but remember: The goal is for your child to practise a new skill, get some experience, and learn from successes and failures alike. Your goal is to foster independence. Here's how to encourage independence, in home coaching and then during playdates:

1. Role-play to show your child what it looks like when you have a conflict, asking your friend what they want and letting things go, like you rehearsed in Flexible Me; or picking from a pre-planned list of things she has brainstormed with you, to try when she's not sure what to play.

2. Discuss ahead of time what to do if things start to go off the rails. "When you make a mistake, you stay calm and follow your plan for getting back on track. If you pause, then remember, your plan is to breathe slowly in and out when you start to get upset."

3. Simulate challenges at home or practise with family friends, so your child has practised independence with cousins, siblings, and in emotionally safe situations over and over.

4. Place a timer (a wind-up kitchen or office timer is fine) that even a small child can use in every play space so they get used to the idea of time passing, the time they have for a turn, and when it's time for someone else's turn. If your child struggles with independence, rehearse using the timer well ahead of the playdate. Use it to encourage a sense of time around ordinary things—dinner, computer time, homework—and with interactions as well.

5. If your child goes off on his own too much, or certain toys are likely to be the trigger for conflict, introduce a "close off and take away" policy. Talk through a plan in advance with your child and put those special toys away. Discuss that you want him to explain to his guest, if asked, that certain toys have been put away for another day.

6. "You have to try to solve the problem without me" can be the playdate policy. Role-play and ask your child to try to ask her friend if they can work out their differences. *What can we do to compromise?* is a phrase your child can use. Explain that you expect her to try that before coming to get you.

7. If your child seems especially needy, ask about any worries. You can say, "The problem seems unrelated," and then ask, "What is your worry about this?" Ultimately, your goal is to help your child generalize the new skills and behaviours—take them from the small stage of home practice to the larger one of a playdate. To do so, your child needs to learn to recognise and address what's getting in the way.

Q: How long is long enough? How long is too long?

This is the era of playdate drop-offs for extended periods while parents run errands or drive carpool duty for other kids. They may not be amenable to picking their child up after an hour or less. You'll need to weigh options and make decisions. Don't plan a playdate at a time or for a period of time that you know will tax your child's ability to stay engaged. The point is to practise his newly emerging skill—not test it to see how long he can hold out till he snaps. Shorter is better. Forty-five minutes to an hour and a half gives everyone time to warm up, engage in a game or free play, and wrap up, perhaps before anyone gets overtired, overstimulated, or overwhelmed in some other way.

But once a playdate is under way, the deal is your child must stick it out. If a change in plans means the playdate lasts longer than your child's energy for sustained socialising one-on-one, then have a Plan B in mind that shifts to an activity in which you are more present—not intervening but perhaps facilitating something such as crafts, cooking with you, or going somewhere where they will be better able to engage and where your child's skills for socialising aren't under as much pressure.

If it's difficult to find playmates whose parents can accommodate the shorter playdate, turn a closer eye to community opportunities for open play at the local park or recreation centre. Without oversharing about your child's specific social considerations, seek out other parents who may be more flexible and would welcome the opportunity for their child to enjoy forty-five minutes with a new friend. As your child's skills grow, so can the length of playdates.

But... It's Hard Not to Intervene!

Of course it is. But we have to be the grown-ups and control our impulse to intervene when the dustups are over everyday kid stuff: sharing, bickering, rules, rivalry, and all-purpose getting along. Here's why it's important to hold back:

- Your help is embarrassing for your child. By the time your child is out of preschool and old enough for independent playdates, other kids wonder, *Why is this kid's mum jumping in every two seconds?*

- Kids can be rude or thoughtless, your child included, but this is also how they learn about social communication and its consequences: what's funny, what isn't, what builds bridges to friendship and what burns them, what crosses a line, and what's needed for all to overcome bumps and keep play going on their own. This is how they begin to find their own voice and stand up for themselves or others.
- Most importantly, your intervention means that your child won't be learning how to self-advocate and problem-solve in social situations, and that's the goal of all this.

When you feel the impulse to intervene, purposefully shift to coach mode. Guide your child through problem-solving steps that have her use those brain-based skills to sort the matter out and decide what action to take. There will be moments in a playdate when you or another parent are likely involved in helping in some way. But if you are constantly instructing children on how to interact, you rob them of the chance to practise, fail, or succeed. You may worry from habit—your child has struggled in the past, and worry is a hard habit to break. When you know your triggers, you can be more mindful of your impulse to react and choose to give your child the practice she needs. To interrupt the impulse, ask yourself:

- What behaviours are triggering this?
- What would I like my reaction to be?
- What do I need to do to remain calm?

You've both got a playbook now. Your child will learn from this experience. You will, too.

Cues, Code Words, Prompts, and Questions

Avoid singling your child out in their peer group with intrusive cues or comments. Keep signals subtle. Some kids like a code word. The code word might represent *stop interrupting* or *think about others*. One child's code word was *clown*. His mother's previous habit of giving him the eye or the raised eyebrow to warn him about his behaviour had become invisible to him. When he was involved with other kids, he told her later, "I don't see that." Agree on a subtle code, whether it's a word or gesture. I've seen most success when the code word or cue is chosen by the child, so let them take the lead on deciding what works best for them.

A simple question is often the best and most direct cue. If your child's turn on a video game has gone on too long, you could bring by some juice boxes and offer a prompt: "Joe, what's your friend doing here? Are you guys both getting to do this?" That direct question also implies: *Wake up and pay attention to your friend's situation, unspoken cues, and how your behaviour might be making him feel.*

But...My Child Is Clingy—What Should I Do?

Being clingy is often a child's way of saying, "I don't know how to handle things." Ask your child, "Why do you feel you need to come to me about that?" Is it insecurity? Boredom? Feelings getting too big to handle? Conflict resolution? Ask, "What can you do instead, when you feel like coming to me?" If your child has some specific things they seem to be struggling with, use coaching sessions to work on role-playing and developing those skills. For instance, (1) he cannot self-advocate with friends and they always choose the game for him; (2) he gets choked up and cannot speak when he is upset; (3) he is bored easily and does not like what people are doing, so he leaves the game; (4) he gets upset when people break the rules; (5) he gets into conflict with one particular kid who rubs him the wrong way. Is your child clingy with other people? Ask him why or why not. Discuss any anxiety or lack of clarity your child has with managing the playdate on his own. Go back to the best question ever: What makes this hard?

WRITE IT DOWN!

For playdate coaching, bring a small notebook along and take notes on your child's behaviour to review later in the debriefing conversation. Watch for moments when your child responds in ways that are an improvement over past habits of interaction. When a child tells your child, "I don't like what you're doing," make a note of what you saw and review it in debriefing. Your child may remember it as "that boy was pushing back, being mean." You can share your observation through your notes, and ask, "Was this the moment when your friend said something to you and you did what you did? I'm wondering, how did that work out?"

Your child may forget most of the detail from a playdate, but your notes will serve as prompts for your debriefing session. It's important to give your child examples of behaviour and interactions you saw. You're the fly on the wall. You are not meant to be the fixer who jumps in constantly. Note-taking can also help you manage an impulse to intervene—when you're tempted to step in, stop and jot a note of it instead!

Q: When do I let them go to another child's house?

An away playdate is likely to be more successful if your child has shown progress you can gauge by *How Will You Know?* (see Chapter 8). For example, Griff was able to start going on away playdates when he began to show awareness that his past behaviour wasn't working for him, and he showed progress at home with his mission of not interrupting when someone was talking—one of his high-priority missions.

Whether the playdate is at your house or elsewhere, playdate planning remains important. Choice of playmate, activity and setting, and timing: set them up so your child has the best opportunity for success and small wins. Signs of readiness for away play are the following:

- Shows signs of self-awareness
- Demonstrates some of his high-priority desirable behaviours
- Compatible with playmate
- Some past success in the environment and activity

Evaluate where your child is in the EFQ Lesson Tracks. If you can do a couple months of hosting playdates as they start to catch and correct themselves more, then other parents tend to be more forgiving because they see your child trying.

YOU'VE GOT THIS!

Your child's performance won't be perfect. There are bound to be some small stumbles along with small successes. That's part of learning. The difference now is that these experiences aren't hit-or-miss. Your child is actively engaged in coaching and practice to develop skills and behaviours for social success. Every playdate becomes a learning experience.

22

How'd It Go?

Debriefing and the Post-Playdate Huddle

Constructive review, reflection, and encouragement build your child's executive function skills for self-awareness and social awareness.

After a playdate comes one of the most important steps in coaching: debriefing with your child to learn, from her point of view, how it went.

Debriefing gives you and your child a chance to reflect on a play activity while it's still fresh in his mind, to note what went well and what didn't go so well during the playdate. This is the time to celebrate every "win"— every time your child used the skill he's been practising—however small it may seem. Every small step is progress in building the bridge of social skills your child needs. The purpose of debriefing is to guide your child to practise self-awareness, self-evaluation, planning, and goal-setting. It also helps your child witness, in retrospect, what went on, and the mechanisms of this reciprocal relationship. These are all executive function skills that shape the social skills your child needs to play well with others.

I often get long emails from parents about a playdate disaster and then when I talk to the child, they barely have any memory of it because their self-awareness is very low. So, when you're trying to talk with them, remember that their memory of it is likely fuzzy. The more you talk about specific behaviours in a timely fashion, the more they can witness their own process and really look at the situation before it's been too long. Whether you debrief right away or have to make it later—perhaps during your regular *Play Better* session—debriefing within twenty-four hours is the goal.

AS YOU START

It's always helpful to start with praise for specific actions or behaviours your child displayed: "I noticed so-and-so showed you with only his body language that he wasn't into that game and you really picked up on it and changed the game. You can do that better now than two weeks ago. I can see the change." Start and stay casual and positive: *Ask, don't tell.* "How was the playdate? What did you think went well?"

As you move through the checklist, you'll discuss what went well and, after praising that, what needs improvement. Refer to your notes to ask about specific things you overheard or incidents you observed; keep a neutral tone. Your point isn't to chastise, or even to critique; it's to hit replay to hear more about the details from your child and discuss what she could have done and what could have happened instead.

In response to a particular dilemma, you might say, "What was the social guideline in that situation? What would make the best impression?"

The more your child thinks about his behaviour and is asked questions so that he hears himself describe his feelings and actions—witnessing his own thought process—the more he develops self-awareness and metacognition. This is a big piece of the coaching process. He becomes a "noticer"—someone who does not say, "Wow, this came out of the blue," but rather, "Okay, as I look at this, I see where this came from." Doing is learning. Review and reflection make learning stick. In the brain, this process of debriefing connects the dots—creates neural networks—so that your child can more readily call up the memory, the lessons learned, and generalise the insight to use another day.

In coach mode, your calm voice and demeanour, and your practice of listening rather than lecturing, are especially critical. You'll have your own observations and conclusions, but start by giving your child a chance to tell you her experiences. Guide her through the self-evaluation process, encouraging her to think about the choices she has made, reflect on how they worked for her or didn't, and how she could shift her behaviour to achieve better results in the future. As coach, your practice of positive predictability means that you bring an encouraging, constructive approach to the debriefing process, praising small wins and framing missteps in a positive light.

After you've heard your child's view of how the playdate went, you can put forward your perspective on the progress you observed. In this step, you discuss with your child what went well and what needs improvement. By hearing your observations, your child also learns to compare her perspective and ideas with yours. As she practises this perspective-taking—holding her own and yours in mind at the same time—she's strengthening one of the most important basic social skills.

The Debriefing Checklist below takes you—and your child—through the debriefing process step-by-step.

THE *PLAY BETTER* TOOL: DEBRIEFING CHECKLIST*

STEP 1: Praise behaviour

Pick one or two specific behaviours that went well and were in line with your child's mission.

    Identify aloud new positive skills demonstrated
    Some conversation starters:

I like how you...
I notice you...

STEP 2: What went well? How did you do with your missions?

Ask your child what went well and what was challenging in her mission. Then ask her to rate herself 1–10 on her effort during the playdate.

Tips

- Focus on the facts.
- Praise even small improvements.
- Praise specific actions the child displayed.
- Discuss the teachable moments.
- Make the child aware of the display of positive behaviour.
- Do not be a historian. Refer to the present, not the past.
- Refrain from lengthy lectures.
- Make messages clear and precise.
- Offer the child empathy and understanding.
- Remain calm.

---

* Some probes adapted from livesinthebalance.org by Dr. Ross Greene.

STEP 3: Present rewards

If your child has some kind of reward tied to the mission or behaviours he was meant to display right away, say, "Here, you get a sticker for these three things," or "You did this really well and you get tick marks!" We want them to realise that all this hard work pays off. It's good to link back to *How Will You Know?* here and focus on this growing awareness rather than expecting full-fledged change.

STEP 4: Discuss behaviour that you are working on

State the facts and remain neutral. You are looking to gather information and hear what the child's perspective is.

State one or two behaviours that were the most disruptive or that relate directly to the skills you are working on during your in-home coaching sessions.

Conversation starters:

I have noticed...
There was this one moment...
I wonder what (playmate's name) felt when you...
I am curious—tell me what happened when....
Tell me more about that....
Let's look at the situation—tell me more about what happened?
Let's maybe think about the conversation. What did you say and what did they say?
Do you suppose there was something else going on?—what would it be?

STEP 5: Evaluate all elements of the playdate

Playmate compatibility
Location of playdate
Structure or unstructured play
Environment
Activities during playdate
Duration
Time of day
Nutrition
Parent involvement needed
Child's energy
Child's participation with playmate

STEP 6: Discuss important lessons and teachable moments

There are key moments in a playdate, and you want to bring these forward in your discussion. Perhaps when your child made a choice that did not go well or when you noticed him struggle or when he was not sure what to do. Sometimes it's about the duration of the playdate, and when he started to struggle and had no idea what to do. That is where you might say, "I noticed that you did so well with cooperating until we took out the video game. What changed? What did that feel like? I am wondering what this was like for you?"

When your child is like a deer in the headlights, you can initiate your coach mode of reflective listening. Think of it as jump-starting your child's executive function.

Hmmm, can you say more about that?
What do you mean?
What was that like for you?

If your child says "I don't know" and does not know, it's okay to say, "All right, I am going to suggest some reasons why and you tell me if this is why. . . . Is that when you were feeling unsure of what to do or you did not want to do it?" Something like that will show they can use either/or answers.

Reflect and recap what you noticed: "I noticed a few times when you had a disagreement about rules—what was the disagreement about?"

Feel free to say things like, "Okay, I am trying to understand and get a picture of this." Then recap what you saw or think happened. If kids are unsure, you can begin to share your bird's-eye view.

STEP 7: Replay

Start by asking your child if there is a moment he would like to replay or suggest one yourself. You can ask:

What would you have wanted to do differently?
What could you do instead?
What do you think you could have done?
What was your social role?
What do you have to do to keep play going?

STEP 8: Identify the skills that need to be developed

Perhaps during the playdate you noticed that your child had trouble managing her feelings. Perhaps she was not sure how to compromise and either went too far, bending over backwards to please the other child, or gave up. Each situation is just a problem to be solved or a gap in skills that you're addressing bit by bit. You can use any of the lessons, tools, and activity sheets in the *Play Better Plan*. You do not have to do all the lessons in an executive function area if she did not need it according to the EFQ. Perhaps you find you need to problem-solve and figure out a replacement behaviour.

LET'S TALK ABOUT IT

Debriefing gives your child the chance to witness her behaviour and review and reflect on it.

Discuss what went well and, after praising that, what needs improvement.

- What needs improvement? Now we're talking about the replay and helping your child step into what he could have done and what could have happened instead. This is important because your child won't inherently imagine there was an alternative. They don't get it.
- They may tell you where it all went south, that they recognise when that happened, but they don't have the idea "If I had just done this or that, it would have gone differently." You can say, "Things were going pretty well up to (the moment in question). Here's what I'm seeing that you did. Okay, then what could you have done instead? Here's what I think you could do in this situation. What would you think of this? What were your options?"
- Sometimes it's a matter of self-regulation and they know it. They'll say "I was too annoyed, too unhappy, but I could have done (a different behaviour they think of) instead."
- If you ask and your child has no idea what she might have done differently, then you need to suggest other options and ask what she thinks about an idea.
- I often will say, "What was expected in that situation? What was the social norm?" That's such a useful question, because it has them

reflect on what they're learning in the coaching lessons and activities about expectations around social behaviour and their role in a group.

Part of the replay is you're replaying with this alternate scenario but also coming up with these strategies for coping with the factors that got in the way. Some kids are clear about expectations and they want things to work out, but then an emotional or sensory issue throws them off and they don't have the strategies in mind to self-regulate.

So often parents describe a rocky playdate only in terms of their child's missteps. When we carefully go over the events of the playdate, we find that it was too long or that other factors affected their child's behaviour. Factors that their child was not yet prepared to accommodate all at once. My goal with these checklists is to step back from whatever happened and take a deep breath and look at all the factors to see which ones can be tweaked for the next playdate. If the playmate was a child they had wanted to play with and you had had your reservations but agreed, now's your chance to discuss playmate compatibility and maybe choose someone different next time. This discussion helps your child practise recall, an executive function.

You have to look at the skills that your child needs to build. Beyond the EFQ or the tools menu of the activities, there may be something that came up during the playdate, and you, as a parent, want to use your questions to facilitate recall: "I'm curious—what about...(insert example)." For example, one child might be like a passive rider on the train of life. She's the kind of kid who lets the other kids run the playdate show and she's hosting but literally sitting on the sofa waiting for stuff to happen. Meanwhile, the other child is bored, and the host child is kind of anxious. Part of that is her personality. For her, it would be helpful for you to say, "When someone says x to you, what do you do? What is your role?" She might say, "Well, it's my house." This would suggest that she needs to build the repertoire skills for engaging, not retreating. Some kids don't get that if they want play to continue, then they have to show a certain level of energy and participation. Engagement is a nuanced thing that the parent has to pinpoint and coach for.

How many playdates do they need to have?

Once a week would be the reference but may not be possible.

But playdates aren't the only opportunity for social play. In activities such as Scouts, they can go into a group activity like that with a mission of their own.

You have to have five to six opportunities to practise a skill and reassess.

And there is such a thing as too much. Avoid overscheduling your child for activities that are heavily social. Sofa girl will need to debrief and then role-play, rehearse, have your sessions, maybe use the skill with some siblings or other places. She needs time to process the experience, absorb the lesson, and reflect in anticipation of the next time. It's better to have a few practice sessions before she's back into that action.

To wrap up, check in and make sure your child is clear about what you two have discussed and what she can take away from the debriefing session. You can say, "So, with all we've discussed, what will you do next time?"

Part of the big message is if you're not asking the child about *his* feelings or what the particular situation is about for him and you're jumping into assumptions, then you're jumping into solution mode. It's a mind-set. In almost any other setting, we don't do that. In business, if there's a problem, you wouldn't assume you know what's causing it until you went in and looked at every part, talking to everyone with a hand in it. With kids, we don't always ask them. We often just jump into problem-solving mode. If it helps to remember this way, remember the "co" in coaching. Coaching is a collaborative relationship. We don't problem-solve alone. We don't problem-solve *for* our child. We problem-solve *with* them, and we can't solve the problem until we know what it is—from our child's perspective.

The mother of a six-year-old boy with a history of impulse issues and school avoidance was frustrated because he was refusing to go to camp. He had gone before, and while he was not wildly happy about it, he did it. Now he refused. She began by trying to persuade him. I call it "so-and-so-ing": "Hey, so-and-so will be there today." All these tactics we try so often. She had places to go and things to do, and she thought if she just pressed him, he'd give in and go. He did not. She fussed and scolded and pleaded and cajoled to try to get him to go. The more he resisted, the more she began to fume. And then, something clicked and she remembered coach mode. She took a deep breath, let go of the tell-tell-tell, and simply (and calmly and sincerely) asked him why he didn't want to go to camp. Because she had never asked him.

When they were able to have that conversation, she learned that he didn't want to go to camp because he didn't like the crowds. They made him nervous and jumpy, and in addition to the social tension, he felt overwhelmed by his own impulsivity. Before that conversation, she had assumed that it was her long working hours that made him unhappy about having to go to camp. As a coach, you can't assume; you have to ask. It turned out that he had a bunch of things that stressed him out to a degree he wasn't able to manage: drop-off, the stimuli of the setting. He had significant anxiety and no coping skills. That had been overlooked while the adults were focused on other reasons they could imagine to explain his anti-camp behaviour.

And what if our life is chaotic enough and we want to avoid turning this into a fight? *You don't want to go to camp? You don't want to go to swimming lessons? Fine. Stay home.* Or give it your best shot and try to find some other way around the gridlock, and when that doesn't work, we just say fine. So my child isn't a camper. Not everybody needs to be into camping. My child likes to read books. That's true to a point, but if what's really happening is that anxiety is running the show, then that's what needs to be addressed.

COACHING IN ACTION/LISTEN IN

There are times in debriefing when you have to bring up hard things or something your child denies. To help him move forward, you hold up the figurative mirror, describing what you observed so he can see it and you two can talk about it. Sometimes we want to jump in, but paving the way opens up the conversation for your child to join in. Here are two examples you can use together. If the first statement is too direct, just begin with the second:

- "There is something we need to talk about, even if it's super uncomfortable."
- "I'm thinking about an incident during play when you told your friend to be the stormtrooper and you picked being Luke Sky-walker and he seemed to want a different role. Let's look at the situation—can you tell me more about what happened? Let's think about the conversation. What did you say and what did your friend say?"

Then your child has to fill in and give you the details and tell you what happened. (See Steps 4 and 5 in the Debriefing Checklist for how to approach debriefing on incidents.)

Playdates hit bumps or sometimes derail for different reasons, and, as parents, we sometimes just declare it a failure without really looking more closely to see what specifically was the trouble. Use this checklist to step back from a playdate, take a deep breath, and just look for ways to tweak the planning factors. If this playmate is someone your child wanted to play with and things didn't go so well, discuss how some settings work better with some playmates than others and consider that the next time.

Your child is more likely to be honest and tell you if she feels that something didn't go well if you show that you're there to listen and reflect with her—not criticise or judge. If your child does identify something she feels she didn't handle well, your job as coach is to put it in perspective by pointing out something positive. You can say, "Well, that's true, but here's what I saw that you did do really well."

When your child says, "I didn't do what I was supposed to," then you can say:

- "Yes, it was not exactly as we planned, but look at all the good parts."
- "I'm hearing you say or do so many things you did not do a month ago."
- "Wait, I want to focus on this big *aha* you had and the fact that you are working so hard to change this. I noticed that you started to interrupt or push to get your way, and then you stopped yourself."
- "Wow, you did such a great job noticing that it was time to pause and stop talking about your favourite topic."

If You See Something (Good), Say Something!

Parents sometimes worry about overpraising or "making a big deal about every little thing." I'd rather you adopt the habit of "If you see something, say something," and use it to point out your child's successes. Effective praise is specific and sincere. When you know that your child struggles with social behaviours, then you want him to know when his hard work is producing results. That's not empty praise. That's coaching. When you point out something positive that you know took effort, that's meaningful praise. Some examples:

You made such an effort today—I noticed you caught yourself and let your friend have a turn.

You really started to listen better after you problem-solved with your friend—that is such a big win!

You went along with the group's game choice even when it wasn't your first choice—mission accomplished!

I saw you try to play a new game—way to go!

I noticed you let your friend go first.

YOU'VE GOT THIS!

When you keep a food diary, it shows you your eating habits. When you debrief with your child after a playdate, you hold a mirror up to her social thought processes and behaviours so she can see them more clearly—and so you can celebrate her wins. If you're upset about your child's playdate behaviour, then pause before debriefing to process your own feelings. They don't belong in this coaching conversation. Your role is to help your child develop the critical executive function capacity to look at what she does, take a bird's-eye view, learn from her past behaviour, and actively choose what happens next time.

23

Troubleshooting

How to Make the Most of Snags, Setbacks, and Resistance

*Obstacles create the opportunity for fresh conversation that
deepens our understanding of our child's experience and keeps
communication open.*

Every coach runs into unexpected obstacles from time to time, and
some resistance and regression are natural as children grow. Social,
emotional, physical, and cognitive development is always uneven to
some extent, and resistance is like a leak in your roof—the source of
the leak may be twists and turns away from where the spot shows up
on your ceiling. If your child has had to deal with extra stress from
other sources—new academic pressures, illness, loss, or significant
family disruption or stress—those can drain the energy and attention
he has for what he may consider less pressing matters, like his social
situation.

Some kids push through the worst things to keep on coaching; others pull up short with a case of the sniffles. Holidays or other interrup-
tions may throw off momentum. Perhaps you're dismayed to discover
that your child isn't using her new skills outside your home coaching
and practice time. Your child may complain that she's bored or has had
some success and thinks that's enough. Maybe she has found a particular lesson especially tough and tiring. Motivation may dip. Out of their
comfort zone and feeling pressured, children may insist coaching just
isn't necessary—you're the one with the problem. There are countless
reasons that resistance can arise. None of them are a reason to quit.

Resistance can feel like a tug-of-war, but this doesn't have to be a battle of wills. In coach mode, you can choose to respond to resistance as a red flag for attention, a cue to engage, not disengage. To learn what's behind your child's resistance and respond effectively, you'll ground yourself in the same core *Play Better* coaching principles and communication techniques you started with: reflective listening, open inquiry, and praise and prompting. (See the Eight Elements of Highly Effective Social Skills Coaching in Chapter 5.)

This doesn't mean you're starting over, back to square one. Not at all. Your focus at this point is to understand your child's resistance, so you tailor your coaching inquiry to that.

Sometimes the sticking point is simply that a child doesn't know what he doesn't know. He isn't resisting change so much as he honestly doesn't realise why these unhappy interactions keep happening to him. You're not there at school to see it unfold with this familiar group of kids, but maybe it's at family gatherings with the cousin pack, or a weekend outing with family friends or some other group event that's got some unstructured social time when the kids hang out—or don't hang out with your child. Maybe your child accepts this fate, quietly forlorn, or perhaps boomerangs back to you, complaining about the others.

Whether the reasons seem clear to you or not, as coach you'll resist pointing out what seems obvious to you. Instead, use a troubleshooting conversation to help your child provide details about the situation. Your mission is to help your child see patterns without directly telling her yourself. Because the most powerful learning experience—the lesson that sticks—comes with the insight they reach for themselves, see for themselves, not the one we tell them again and again.

But how do you start that conversation? First, stay calm and detached; don't jump in to commiserate or fix. Second, stay centred in fact-finding mode, modelling this problem-solving skill for your child. I often start by walking through what's gone on, as they see it.

Finally, using open-ended questions and reflective listening, lead your child through the problem-solving steps involved, from fact-finding to reflection to interpretation.

Here are some opening lines to start that conversation:

What's going on?
What were they doing when you walked up to join them?

What were you doing or talking about when they behaved the way
    they did?
What happened the last time you played with them?

COACHING IN ACTION/LISTEN IN

You're going to encounter resistance at times—a slump in your child's
energy or commitment. But that doesn't mean you need to stop the
conversation. Just the opposite, in fact. There are degrees of resistance,
and different reasons for it. A simple shift or compromise in routine
may be all that's needed to effectively push the restart button. Or if
your child is discouraged because progress isn't instantaneous, then
it can be especially helpful to highlight the positive changes that have
begun—those are significant accomplishments for a child who struggles with social skills! But whatever lies behind resistance, the most
effective response is to keep the conversation going to learn more and
search for some common ground for compromise. A helpful approach
can be: "What would you change if we could work it out?" Here is an
example, based on the real-life conversation between a mother and
her ten-year-old son, who wanted to throw in the towel. The mother
acknowledged that it's hard sometimes to reach out for help when
we're stuck:

PARENT: Did I ever tell you how I got help with (name an example)?
CHILD: I may not want to do this....
PARENT: What do you mean?
CHILD: I think it sounds like it might cut into my free time, and I
    like to relax after school.
PARENT: I get it. What if we could find balance?
CHILD: No, we can't.
PARENT: Hmm, I feel like we can. I am wondering if there is any-
    thing else that makes you think you don't want to do this?
CHILD: Because it won't help.
PARENT: Hmm, what makes you say that?
CHILD: It's just the way it is.
PARENT: So, I am hearing that it's not just free time that worries you.
    It's that you wonder if things can change....
CHILD: Yeah, well, the free time is important too.

PARENT: OK, I hear you. I get that it is. So, what is important to you about that?

CHILD: I just like that—having free time. School is so hard.

PARENT: What if we could find a compromise? What if we tried this as an experiment—what would you like to change if you knew it could work out?

CHILD: I just don't see how it can.

(Child shrugs.)

PARENT: What are your worries?

CHILD: I guess that this will take time and then I can't make more friends.

PARENT: What if you and I worked out some rewards so you have some fun time *and* it helps you make friends?

(Child shrugs.)

PARENT: What if we did an experiment and just tried it? Let's talk about how that might look and how we might give it a try.

If we surrender the conversation, let them stonewall or scare us off, we're teaching them that they can choose not to engage in the harder processes of life. That's not what you want to teach your child. When we stay in the conversation with them, we're teaching them that that's how you tackle the tough stuff. You don't avoid it. However you and your child may adapt the conversation to fit the circumstances, you stay in it.

There are going to be times when your child seems pumped and times when this whole change thing is hard and progress slows. But the more you highlight where he has been and how far he has come, the more he'll be able to recognise his progress and eventually want to continue the journey!

POCKET COACH: TROUBLESHOOTING

Strategies to meet resistance

Look for meaning

Resistance may be a measure of your child's shifting commitment or buy-in to the work you're asking her to do. There are degrees of buy-in, and just because your child isn't as gung ho as you wish doesn't mean she's unwilling to go along with it. A shrug now doesn't mean they'll never buy in again, especially once they start to experience the positive change their efforts to date begin to deliver. Resistance may also be an expression of fear or anxiety—like a newbie swimmer who steps to the edge of the high diving board, sees where this is headed, and tries to back out.

Listen for the stories, myths, and little lies cropping up and be prepared

When your child hits a rough spot, variations on the story he tells himself often pop up again like a Whac-A-Mole challenge:

> This is too hard.
> There's no point anyway.
> I don't see why I should be the one who has to change.
> I made a friend. That's enough.
> Things are better now. We can stop.

Sometimes they really do see an improvement, but what they don't see is that it's based on a change in circumstances—the start of a new term, a move or change of school—and the improvement will be temporary unless your child's social skills continue to develop enough to initiate and sustain positive social interactions and friendships. If she genuinely has made some progress, then she may feel that means "mission accomplished." You know best what she still needs to work on, and how important it is to develop those brain-based social skills now instead of waiting and hoping for the best.

Check the basics

Take a fresh look to be sure you're giving each step the attention your child needs. If any steps come up short, look for ways to revitalise.

- Follow the lesson plans; don't skip steps for planning or activities.
- Your child likely hears negative comments amplified by the negative social experiences. Point out all small wins and positive changes anytime, but especially in debriefing.
- Social engagements to practise are essential. If you're having trouble lining them up, talk with your child's teacher, a family friend, or other community source who may have ideas regarding playmates or social activities for your child.
- Ask your child's teachers for any fresh observations or ideas to support your child's restart on efforts to change social behaviour and develop social skills.
- Enlist family members to renew their encouragement and make family time more social.

Ask your child:

- What most bothers you about the coaching plan right now?
- What could we do to make the plan work better for you?
- What would make the plan fun?
- If you could change anything, what would it be?

But... How can I talk with my child when he does a disappearing act?

When our kids want to avoid talking to us, they can do quite the Houdini act—slip free of any effort to rope them into a conversation. Here are some steps that can help reset the dynamic:

- Look at how your family time is structured or your child's school and after-school hours are scheduled, to find ways to change things up so that you have some one-on-one time together. Try drive times, snack or meal times, a craft or cooking project, a special activity that your child chooses, a walk, or a meal out together.
- If your child is not engaging with you routinely in the course of everyday life—if your eight-year-old buries herself in her bedroom with books or sits glued to the TV or computer, then have a conversation (see the Interactive Conversation Guide in Chapter 9) about expectations and opportunities for contact. What can you do, and what can your child do, to create more opportunities for simple social get-togethers?
- You can say, "I feel like you are spending a lot of time in the playroom or reading in your room. Let's talk about things you might choose to do to balance screen time with more active things."

But... My child asked, "Can't we just take a break?" What do I say?

We're all working on something, and when it comes to life skills, we don't just take breaks from something as fundamental as learning how to get along with others. But can you collaborate with your child to make something more tolerable? Absolutely. One ten-year-old girl told her mum, "I just don't want to do this on Sundays anymore. I want my weekends free." They talked it through, and her mum agreed she could trim that session from the weekly schedule, provided her daughter continued to demonstrate the skills she had developed thus far and stayed engaged in coaching to set new goals and make new gains. They struck the deal and it worked.

My experience is that if you take a collaborative approach and problem-solve with your child, you'll be able to reinvigorate the coaching partnership.

YOU'VE GOT THIS!

If your child has really dropped off or dug in his heels about continuing, or keeps boomeranging back with the same issues, then it only underscores the importance of your coaching work. Because problems like these don't just go away, the sooner we can tend to them, the sooner life's possibilities open up. Whatever you do, whatever it takes, however flexible you need to be, don't surrender the conversation.

24

You've Got This!

Storybook miracles tend to come with a certain fanfare. Hopes, dreams, prayers, all answered unequivocally. The trouble is that storybook miracles train us to expect the dramatic flash, while in real life, it is the quieter wins, the hard-hat miracles—the ones that you work for—that deliver the most profound transformations.

This book is all about those hard-earned miracles that children create as they work through the *Play Better Plan* to develop the brain-based social skills they need, with you as their coach. Now you've got the playbook in your hands to guide your child through the conversations, lessons, activities, and practice to build and strengthen executive functions that have been lagging. What I want to be sure you have as well, what is essential that you have, is the willingness and capacity to coach for and recognise the small wins, the small *ahas*, small moments, and step-by-step movement forwards. If you want to see the big change in your child's social behaviour, then, as Volkswagen once famously advised, "think small." Small wins add up to big gains.

You know this from personal experience. Whenever you are trying for big change, you end up having these incremental wins. You lose three pounds on the way to ten, your not-yet-toddler child pulls himself up, then scoots and then takes a step. They recognise a letter of the alphabet, then learn to trace it and then eventually to write it. Every child I've ever coached, and every parent who has used the *Play Better Plan*, has seen this pattern of small gains happen for their child to some demonstrable degree.

One of the most common comments I hear from parents is that one of the most significant changes they have seen through the *Play Better Plan* process has been *their own*. They've learned how to see the chain of behaviours their child must address, and so have been able to help their child see the connections. That awareness has given them traction in coaching, and given their children the needed traction to tackle the tasks and the work, and make those small, necessary wins. Kids and parents alike tell me about their experiences, their *aha* moments, and the success they have found in the years that followed their *Play Better* experience. From children in pre-school, primary school, and secondary school, to those on their way to university, and from their parents, I hear how they've taken their new skills and mind-set into new and challenging social settings.

In these new circumstances, they discover that the skills they learned for reading the room, listening and responding to others, interpreting social cues, and self-regulating—their *people skills*—help them meet the moment, adapt, and carry on. Not that it's always easy. But then, it's not always easy for any of us. Nonetheless, the skills they developed in the programme, and their continued growth through every new experience, give them the confidence to stay in the game socially. They are able to socialise more comfortably, get along with others more effectively, and problem-solve their way through social situations that would once have seemed insurmountable. The difference always comes back to this shift, their awareness of the small steps in behaviour, and the skill building that helps them make the larger strides. The details look different for every child, but let me tell you about Annie.

Annie was in year five when her mother brought her to see me. She had spent the first month of school lunch breaks as she had spent lunch breaks for the past five years: eating by herself, unable to bring herself to go to the lunchroom with her classmates. Her shyness, her overwhelm, her conviction that everything she said was not cool enough, made entering that lunchroom impossible for her. She gave her parents the impression she was going to lunch, told them it was great, but in fact she was spending her lunch breaks hiding out in the library, computer lab, or elsewhere to avoid her peers.

Annie's epiphany came about because, through the coaching process, she had held up a mirror to her behaviour and realised it wasn't enough to want friends; to have friends she had to make changes. Our *aha, yay!* moment with her was the day she actually did go to lunch. Period. Not that she carried on a fluid conversation or sat with the best people. She went. "I went to lunch this week." *Yay!* Without this small win, she could not move forward, so this was a step on the bridge she needed to cross from where she was to where she wanted to be. Her realisation that she did want it, and wanted it enough to work for it—that this was not her mother pushing, but herself wanting this for herself—was a huge step.

As you might imagine, her mother had told her that on more than a few occasions over the years before they began the *Play Better Plan*. The old tell-tell-tell approach hadn't worked. The coaching conversations, lessons, and practice changed everything. Annie had been practising her skills in Build on That and had been doing so well in her home coaching that eventually she had the confidence to give it a try in a new setting. That's what we see time and again. With Annie, we rehearsed so long for her to be able to join a conversation and build on it, that once she began using these techniques, she saw for herself: *Yes, I can do it!* But first, it was getting her to try, and coaching makes that possible.

Part of our responsibility as parents, and especially as coaches, is to help our children see the big picture—that brain-based metacognitive task!—and keep it in mind. To be able to recognise failure as a temporary setback, to pick ourselves up and problem-solve, not allow it to hold us back anymore, is a monumental task for any of us. But it becomes instrumental in the coaching process—the teachable moment: adapt and carry on. Together with our child, we're moving the ball forward towards this vision of a person who can go out into the world with the skills everyone needs to be socially successful: to manage their emotions, read the room, meet people halfway and see things through their eyes, understand social cues, and be prepared to adapt and stay flexible. With that goal in mind, then the outcome of every playdate doesn't matter as much because your child is working towards the goal. Practice makes progress. It's not about every bump; it's about the journey.

At the end of the day, wherever your child is on the *Bridge to Betterment*, if he understands that he needs to adapt, if he understands that everybody impacts everybody else, if he can stop being the Rule Police or filter more, his life would be immeasurably changed. So, the fact that your child is more aware is a huge step forward and the other little steps will come.

My inspiration in developing the *Play Better Plan* so that children could learn these brain-based social skills at an early age came from adults I've known and others I've coached, whose personal lives and careers have been so constrained by these lagging skills. They talk about being unable to leave a job, switch colleges, or change almost anything, no matter how unsatisfying or even soul-crushing it is, all because they don't make friends easily, don't adapt or get the lie of the land in a new setting. Whatever the story they tell to rationalise their unhappy circumstances, the truth is that if they had these skills, they would have more opportunity to shape the life they want.

What do you want for your child? What is their best self and what do you want your relationship to be with them as they grow into their adult life? Where do you want them to be? Helping them develop these skills is not micromanaging them or trying to engineer them. The question is: *What do you wish for them?*

Some years ago, a father brought his eleven-year-old son to me for executive function coaching when his academic struggles had become overwhelming. The boy had a pushy, prickly presence, and clearly struggled with the kinds of executive function social skills you know well by now. In the follow-up meeting alone with his dad after that first session, we talked about his son's situation. The dad had been all about the school marks in our earlier conversations, but as I explained the social skills component of executive function, his expression softened. He took a deep breath and was quiet for a moment, then confided what he said was actually his "worst fear."

Marks had been the impetus for the initial consultation, but this deeper fear he had for his son was something he could barely put into words.

"I just want to know that he's going to be *okay*. That he's going to grow up to be a guy who can find work he wants to do and keep a job. That he'll have some friends who really care about him and who he cares about. And he can find someone to make a life with and just be, well, happy in the ordinary ways that make your life matter." At that moment, he couldn't envision that future for his son.

I think about this father and his son. I think about the mother who cried every time she drove past the penitentiary on the way to my office, fearing that's where her son would end up if he couldn't break out of the socially isolated life he was trapped in at the time. Those parents, and so many others I've known through my work with their children, faced their fears and decided to take action. They got help for their kids and eventually became partners with their children, successfully coaching them in these skills, using the *Play Better* techniques.

Today while I was cleaning the garage, a client that I coached when she was ten years old, a young woman now twenty-two, stopped by on her bike. Cass and her mum were out taking a jaunt along the scenic route and saw me by the road and stopped to tell me all about her life. She is becoming a veterinarian now and is doing so well. Out of college and so full of zest. Right away Cass told me that the reason she is doing so well is that she continues to problem-solve when she meets challenges, and she continues coaching conversations with her mother when she needs a little more peeling-the-onion-focused reflection than their usual freewheeling conversations provide. Just last week she was having trouble sorting out a dilemma and she'd called her mum for that particular kind of coaching conversation, which they'd honed in the decade since taking those first steps with the *Play Better* techniques. They had a conversation—her mother listening, not telling, holding the mirror up for Cass as they deconstructed the situation and possibilities—and Cass used her problem-solving skills to figure everything out. A young adult now, she continues to draw on the biggest *aha* that she got, and all children get from this programme: that each of us has to adapt and change—the world will not change for us.

Social skills aren't just about chitchat and manners. They define your life because they are the foundation for connection with other people, understanding your role in a bigger picture, and being able to contribute to—and benefit from—a life among others. That's a consistent must-have skill set, whether we're talking about your interactions within your family, on the playground, in the classroom, in college or in your community or on the job. Coaching gives our children a lasting legacy because it teaches them to continually try to evolve, to be a person who works on things. After all, we are all working on something. Now, with the benefit of your coaching, your child will know how.

ACKNOWLEDGEMENTS

Friendship is so important. And I have long known what it is like to want to be part of something and to wonder why you are not. My first real friendships involved reading *Nancy Drew* under the bedcovers with a torch and playing outdoors until the streetlights came on. Those memories stay with me just as the moments of bullying and pain have left an imprint. The journey to bring this book to millions of children has been long, and I have continued to strive because of the children and families who have reminded me that they need this book.

Children are the best thing society has to offer. And yet so often they are lonely or feel trapped in their childhood and yearn to grow up. To the many children, teenagers, and adults I have worked with: I always knew you could do it. You have made me laugh so hard that the babysitter asked me what was going on in my office. You surprise and inspire me.

Throughout this journey there were times when I wondered if I should continue and in each moment the universe sent me a resounding yes. Each parent who rode the lift up and down to keep talking to me, who wrote me impassioned, four-page emails about their child, or who reminded me of the importance of this book have been like bright green lights pushing me to go forward on this mission.

I am so grateful for my husband, Craig della Penna, for supporting me all along and for being my best friend who is there for me, no matter what. I truly know that this book would not have come to fruition without your support. And I know that hearing someone constantly say it's D-day and being with a whirling dervish can be exhausting. As you know, I believe everything that has happened was meant to be. And your part in that bit of destiny is prodigious. Throughout this journey you reminded me to find balance, since our children are our greatest legacy.

To my daughter, Lucy, and to my son, Finn, who are my greatest joy and always full of fun and play. Your curiosity lights me up inside every day. Lucy, you will likely never forget this process. I know sometimes you have had to go with the flow so this book could get done and into the hands of many families. Your maturity and understanding show the kind of young woman you will become. You are brave and kind, and I learn constantly from you with your gift of seeing the big picture and the details all at once, and with such compassion.

Finn, you are a constant reminder why play and creativity are so important—watching you perform your skits, playing with you, and witnessing you work so hard to learn and grow are magical. I know you will be too young to read this right now, but I want you to know you have been an inspiration for this book, and your spark reminds me of what childhood should feel like for everyone.

To my parents, Kaethe and Edward Maguire: as I grow older and now am a mother I realise how incredibly supportive my parents were. They truly put me first and advocated for me tirelessly. Mum, you said you used to listen until you could not listen anymore. In the 1980s, your belief that I could do anything was rare. Kids with learning challenges like I had were more often sidelined without the basic supports for learning that they needed to make the most of their potential. Somehow you tuned out the noise of friends and community and took the road less travelled with me. You had the vision to see that children can do anything with support.

I want to thank my friend and greatest champion, David Giwerc. You have left me countless voicemails cheering me on, supporting me, and reminding me of my strengths. You have a true gift to inspire people and help them. I am a grateful beneficiary. Marla Giwerc and Barbara Luther, thank you so much for your hard work to launch the Fundamentals of ADHD Coaching for Families. I know that often I am swamped and your patience and support has meant so much to me!

To my friend Dr. Ned Hallowell, for having the vision and understanding to see that social skills and friendship need to be talked about more and for seeing the value in this book years ago—and for supporting me all these years! Your help and belief in me have been invaluable. And to Ellen D'Ambrosia at the Hallowell Centre, who helped me time and again since we met in 2005 with her loving spirit and sparkling smile, always there to help me collaborate with Ned and always believing that this day would come.

My collaboration with Teresa Barker was magical. She supported me as a mother as much as she supported me as an author, understanding when my son burst in my office to hunt for Buzz Lightyear or when I had to balance being the mother of two young children with my beloved book. Teresa's husband, Steve Weiner, helped me and lent a hand in editing the many lessons in order to make this momentous curriculum come to fruition. My talks with Teresa are part of why this book provides so much to parents. She was able to capture my best self, the person who loves to talk about this topic and to teach others.

To my literary agents and friends, Dado Derviskadic and Steve Troha, I am forever grateful for your dedication to this book. Writing the book proposal took years and was both a cathartic process and a joy. To this day, you make me laugh with your funny texts and you continue to help me through every stage of this journey. As a new author, this process is mystifying and daunting but you have both helped me and made all of this possible! To Grand Central and our tireless team there: Leah Miller, Emily Rosman, Amanda Pritzker, Staci Burt, Ben Sevier, and Barbara Teszler. And to Julie Maguire, whose brilliant graphic designs light the pages of this book.

Dana Maher, I continue to be amazed by the support you give me. As a child, I wished for the kind of deep friendship we now share. And your support has been one reason this book came to be. As an Asperger's syndrome expert, you generously welcomed my calls at all hours. As my friend and confidante, you have always given me the emotional support I needed to live far outside my comfort zone. As a tireless advocate for all of our children, you have always exemplified why parents are the best people to help their child, and this book now carries that hopeful message to others.

There are people who believe in you and see your potential and help you even when it does not benefit them, and Duane Gordon, you are just that person. And so is my friend and colleague Jille Bartolome. I so appreciate both your friendships and your encouragement to "be a lighthouse shining bright"—also reminding me to be the lighthouse and not get mired in the waves.

To Becky Winkler, who helped me connect to my literary agents and who helped me get the original book proposal moving. Without this stroke of luck, this book might not have found a home at such a wonderful publisher.

To my cousin Conor Maguire, who has helped me network and promote this programme, and to his beloved wife and my cousin by marriage, Julie Maguire, whom I thanked above for her creative design genius.

My thanks to Jeff Copper of Attention Talk Radio, who allowed me to guest-host for so long and with whom I had so many happy debates about self-regulation and conversations about other aspects of executive function that helped me reshape my thinking about so many topics. Jeff is a thought leader in the ADHD space but also someone who saw the vision and reach of this book from our first interview and helped me with social media and other baffling new frontiers. To Dr. Ari Tuckman, thank you for reading my original master's thesis and for connecting me to people over the years. You were the first person who really suggested that this idea was worth pursuing!

A shout-out to my old friends Kendra and Darren Perry, who always believe in me and for your persistent texts to make sure I continue to connect to friends. To Gretchen Lanka Allen, who left her dinner in a dude ranch restaurant to take my call and raise my spirits and energy to continue the work.

To the late Ms. Shelley Tyre, my seventh-grade teacher, who helped me through that year so I could feel good about myself and could see that life would get better.

To Kat and Geoff Hollywood and Jen and Mike Hollywood, thank you for making me laugh and for being my Disney Cruise companions. Your friendships are truly my rock and I am so glad I have you in my life.

I am forever indebted to Andi Goldlust, Stephanie Carroll, Evelyn Green, Leigh Bintliff, Debbie Taylor, Roger DeWitt, Wendy Mozingo, Barbara Luther, Jan and Billy Maguire, Dr. Catherine Steiner-Adair, Adrienne Rubin, Rachael O'Keefe, Mira Weinfeld, Paula Duggins, Dr. Linda Forsyth, Julie Trelstad, Dr. Melinda Kulish, Angie Sousa, Dr. Roberto Olivardia, Lisa Pearl, Stacey Dalpe, Cheryl Almstrom, Lynn Worthen, Megan Petrola, Dr. Russ Ramsay, Theresa Garvin, Diane Mclean, Melanie Florsheim, Cydney Hubbard, Deanna Hyslop, Patty Blinderman, and Michelle Frank. To all the ADD Coach Academy students who have helped me along the way—thank you for your help spreading the word about this book.

I must give credit to my amazing study team at Lesley University: Marion Nesbit and Mary Mindess, who picked the memorable title for this book from my early brainstorm and supported the work on this book in so many ways.

Teresa adds:

In the world of book collaborations, stars align and some matches seem made in heaven, but the deft hand in the cosmos behind this one and so many others has been my literary agent, Madeleine Morel. I am indebted and grateful for her wisdom, humour, sharp eye, and warm heart. My deep gratitude to Michael Thompson, Catherine Steiner-Adair, and Stuart Shanker for teaching me so much in our work together, and to Sherry Laten, whose life and tireless child and family counselling career has inspired and informed my work. To my loving and supportive family, most notably my husband, Steve Weiner; my children and my grandchildren; and my beloved Dolly, whose home and company have been a cherished retreat in my writing life; my sister Holly, whose generosity with her insights from decades of experience as a primary schoolteacher has been invaluable; and of course to Caroline, who made all this possible, and to her family. Each of them has a special place in my heart now, too.

APPENDIX

PLAYDATE OBSERVATION LOG*

Mission for playdate:

	What Worked	What to Change Next Time
Setting		
Environment		
Parental Presence		
Playmate		
Time of Day		
Nutrition		
Length of Playdate		
Signs of Progress: Note things you hear and see		
Struggles to role-play		
Noteworthy comments made by playmate		
What went well (wins to celebrate)		
Progress with mission		
Use of strengths		
Any lessons to incorporate in *Play Better* in-home coaching		
Notes:		

---

* Adapted from Borgmeier, 2010; Dawson & Guare, 2009; Frost et al., 2008; Hemmeter et al., 2001; Santrock, 2009.

PLAYDATE PLANNING CHECKLIST

Below is a checklist of factors to consider for playdates. Track those elements that work best.

Settings	Environmental Characteristics	Parental Presence	Playmates	Time of Day	Nutrition	Length of Playdate

Settings	Environmental Characteristics	Parental Presence	Playmates	Time of Day	Nutrition	Length of Playdate
Home	Stimuli	Present	Mixed age	Early morning	Snack before	Short (~30 min.)
Playmate's home	Noise	Nearby	Same age	Midday	Snack during	Medium (~60 min.)
Off-site play space	Sensory	At a distance	Single gender	Midday on half-days from school	Snack after	Long with breaks (~2+ hr)
Outdoor play space	Tactile	Not present	Mixed gender	Right after nap		Longer with time to warm up (~2+ hr)
Indoor play space				End of day		
Playground				Right after school		
Pool or beach						

* Adapted from Borgmeier, 2010; Dawson & Guare, 2009; Frost et al., 2008; Hemmeter et al., 2001; Illes, 2004; Santrock, 2009.

REWARD CHART

Name: _____   Week of:_____

Activity	Monday	Tuesday	Wednesday	Thursday	Friday	Saturday	Sunday

If I earn _____ points for the week, then my reward is _____.

SOCIAL SPY BADGE

© 2016 Maguire

THE *PLAY BETTER* POCKET COACH

Coaches use non-judgemental, open-ended questions that begin with *what, how, who,* and *where.* These question starters invite conversation instead of yes/no responses. They often bring out the curiosity in kids, which leads to self-discovery and clarity about the social world. These questions ask, rather than tell.

Questions to help your child learn to walk in someone else's shoes

- What did (person) feel about your behaviour?
- How did they react to you?
- What did the other person's facial expression tell you about their feelings?
- What was the behaviour that would give other people reason to feel positive about you?
- What was the appropriate behaviour in the situation?
- What do you think I felt when you did (behaviour) to me?
- How will (person) feel about your email/action?
- What do you know about them? Based on that, what do you think you should do or say?

- What message are you sending? What message do you think they are getting?
- What does your tone of voice tell (person)?
- What did you intend to do?

Questions about friends and playmates

- How do you think other people feel when you don't show interest in (insert name or action)?
- What were the circumstances and how did you adjust?
- How were most other people behaving there?
- What did you notice about the other person?
- What could you do when you are bored?
- What happens if your tone is dismissive?
- What do you think your peers think when you are bored and abruptly stop talking?
- What was your experience like?
- What are some different ways you might respond?

Questions about actions

- How did your actions affect their thoughts about you?
- How did your actions affect how they view you?
- Was that what you meant to do?

Basic questions to learn more

- Tell me more about that?
- Can I share some information with you?
- What is the problem with that?
- What would it feel like?
- What does that look like?
- What was that like for you?
- What is hard about that for you?
- What choices do you have?
- What have you tried?
- What are the possibilities here?
- Where did this happen?

On-the-go coaching

- Hmm, I am curious.
- Tell me more about that...

- What does it feel like?
- What is important about that?
- What do other people feel when you (fill in behaviour)?
- What is hard about that?
- I have noticed (insert behaviour). Can you explain more?
- What patterns do you see here?
- What does (insert behaviour) mean to you?
- What is the price of staying the same?
- Let's brainstorm—what are your options?
- What does (fill in behaviour) look like?
- What do you like about (fill in behaviour)?
- What makes this (difficult, hard, important, overwhelming) right now?

WHO IS YOUR AUDIENCE?

© 2016 Maguire

REFERENCES

Abdelal, A. (2010). *Role of executive functions in pragmatic performance: Implications for intervention.* Presentation at ASHA Annual National Convention, Philadelphia, PA [PowerPoint slides].

Alaimo, K., Olson, C.M., & Frongillo, E.A. (2001). Food insufficiency and American school-aged children's cognitive, academic, and psychosocial development. *Pediatrics* 108(1), 44–53.

Alduncin, N., Huffman, L., Feldman, H., & Loe, I. (2014). Executive function is associated with social competence in preschool-aged children born preterm or full term. *Early Human Development* 90(6), 299–306.

Al-Yagon, M., Forte, D., & Avrahami, L. (September 2017). Executive functions and attachment relationships in children with ADHD: Links to externalizing/internalizing problems, social skills, and negative mood regulation. *Journal of Attention Disorders* 1–16.

Amen, D. (1999). *Change your brain, change your life: The breakthrough program for conquering anxiety, depression, obsessiveness, anger, and impulsiveness.* New York, NY: Three Rivers Press.

———. (2005). *Making a good brain great.* New York, NY: Three Rivers Press.

American School Board Journal. (2006). Lack of time for play hurts children: Report. *American School Board Journal* 193, 10.

Baggerly, J., & Parker, M. (2005). Child-centered group play therapy with African American boys at the elementary school level. *Journal of Counseling and Development* 83, 387.

Baker, J.E. (2003). *Social skills training for children and adolescents with Asperger syndrome and social communication problems.* Shawnee Mission, KS: Autism Asperger Publishing Company.

Bandura, A. (1977). *Social learning theory.* Englewood Cliffs, NJ: Prentice Hall.

Bandura, A., & Huston, A.C. (1961). Identification as a process of incidental learning. *Journal of Abnormal and Social Psychology* 63, 311–318.

Bandura, A., Ross, D., & Ross, S.A. (1961). Transmission of aggression through imitation of aggressive models. *Journal of Abnormal and Social Psychology* 63, 575–582.

Barkley, R.A. (1997). Behavioral inhibition, sustained attention, and executive functions: Constructing a unifying theory of ADHD. *Psychological Bulletin* 121(1), 65–94.

Barkley, R.A. (ed.) (2015). *Attention deficit hyperactivity disorder: A handbook for diagnosis and treatment* (4th ed.). New York, NY: Guilford Press.

Bauer, H., Burno, C., & Millstone, T. (2009). Increasing constructive behavior of intermediate grade students through the use of the response cost strategy (Undergraduate research paper). Saint Xavier University, Illinois.

Baumrind, D. (1966). Effects of authoritative parental control on child behavior. *Child Development* 37, 887–907.

———. (1967). Child care practices anteceding three patterns of preschool behavior. *Genetic Psychology Monographs* 75, 43–88.

Bedard, A.C., Nichols, S., Barbosa, J.A., Schachar, R., Logan, G.D., & Tannock, R. (2002). The development of selective inhibitory control across the life span. *Developmental Neuropsychology* 21, 93–111.

Belkin, L. (2009, May). The way we live now: Let the kid be. *New York Times.* Retrieved from https://www.nytimes.com/2009/05/31/magazine/31wwln-lede-t.html.

Berg, J., & Clark, M. (1986). Differences in social exchange between intimate and other relationships: Gradually evolving or quickly apparent? In V.J. Delega et al. (Eds.). *Friendship and Social Interaction.* New York, NY: Springer-Verlag, 101–128.

Berkun, S. (2010). *The myths of innovation.* Sebastopol, CA: O'Reilly Media.

Bertin, M. (2016, Fall). Executive function: What it is, why it matters. *Beacon Newsletter.* The Windward School, 2–3.

Besevegis, E., & Lore, R. (1983). Effects of an adult's presence on the social behavior of preschool children. *Aggressive Behavior* 9, 243–252.

Bibok, M.B., Carpendale, J.M., & Muller, U. (2009). Parental scaffolding and the development of executive function. *New Directions for Child and Adolescent Development* 123, 17–34.

Blain-Briere, B., Bouchard, C., & Bigras, N. (2014). The role of executive functions in the pragmatic skills of children age 4–5. *Frontiers in Psychology* 5(240), 1–14.

Blatt, S. J., & Homann, E. (1992). Parent-child interaction in the etiology of dependent and self-critical depression. *Clinical Psychology Review* 12, 47–91.

Bogels, S., & Mansell, W. (2004). Attention processes in maintenance and treatment of social phobia: Hypervigilance, avoidance and self-focused attention. *Clinical Psychology Review* 24, 827–856.

Borgmeier, C. (2010). Functional behavioral assessment and function-based support: Developing a behavior support plan based on the function of behavior (working paper). Retrieved from http://www.web.pdx.edu/~cborgmei/.

Bradberry, T., & Greaves, J. (2009). *Emotional intelligence 2.0.* San Diego, CA: Talent Smart.

Bright, M., & Stockdale, D. (1984). Mothers', fathers', and preschool children's inter-active behaviors in a play setting. *Journal of Genetic Psychology* 144, 219–232.

Brody, G.H., & Stoneman, Z. (1981). Selective imitation of same-age, older, and younger peer models. *Child Development* 52, 717–720.

Bromfield, R. (2008). Discipline dos: Creating limits for ADHD children. *ADDitudeMag-azine.* Retrieved from https://www.additudemag.com/adhd-discipline-advice -for-parents/.

Bronson, P., & Merryman, A. (2009). *NurtureShock: New thinking about children.* New York, NY: Twelve Hachette Book Group.

———. (July 2010). Creativity in America: The science of innovation and how to reignite our imaginations. *Newsweek* 44–50.

Brown, P., Roediger III, H., & McDaniel, M. (2014). *Make it stick: The science of successful learning.* Cambridge, MA: Bellenap Press of Harvard University Press.

Brown, T. (2006). Executive functions and attention deficit hyperactivity disor-der: Implications of two conflicting views. *International Journal of Disability, Development and Education* 53(1), 35–46.

———. (2013). *A new understanding of ADHD in children and adults: Executive function impairments.* New York, NY: Routledge.

Brown, T.E. (2005). *Attention deficit disorder: The unfocused mind in children and adults.* New Haven, CT: Yale University Press.

Buckingham, M., & Clifton, D. (2001). *Now discover your strengths: The revolution-ary program that shows you how to develop your unique talents and strengths and those of the people you manage.* New York, NY: The Free Press.

Buggey, T. (2009). *Seeing is believing: Video self-modeling for people with Autism and other developmental disabilities.* Bethesda, MD: Woodbine House.

Bukatko, D., & Daehler, M.W. (1995). *Child development: A thematic approach* (2nd ed.). Boston, MA: Houghton Mifflin Company.

Buron, K.D. (2007). *A "5" could make me lose control! An activity-based method for evaluating and supporting highly anxious students.* Lenexa, KS: AAPC Publishing.

Buron, K.D., & Curtis, M. (2012). *The incredible 5-point scale: Assisting students in understanding social interactions and controlling their emotional responses.* Lenexa, KS: AAPC Publishing.

Chang, L., Schwartz, D., Dodge, K.A., & McBride-Chang, C. (2003). Harsh parent-ing in relation to child emotion regulation and aggression. *Journal of Family Psychology* 17(4), 598–606.

Chase, M.A., & Dummer, G.M. (1992). The role of sports as a social status deter-minant for children. *Research Quarterly for Exercise and Sport* 63, 418–424.

Cherry, K. (2005). Why parenting styles matter when raising children. Verywell mind.com. Retrieved January 26, 2011 from http://psychology.about.com/od/ developmentalpsychology/a/parenting-style.htm.

Child Mind Institute. (2016). 2016 Children's Mental Health Report. Retrieved from https://childmind.org/report/2016-childrens-mental-health-report/.

Chodorow, N. (1999). *The reproduction of mothering: Psychoanalysis and the sociology of gender* (Rev. ed.). Berkeley, CA: University of California Press.

Choi, H., & Heckenlaible-Gotto, M.J. (1998). Classroom-based social skills training: Impact on peer acceptance of first-grade students. *Journal of Educational Research* 91, 209–214.

Clark, C., Prior, M., & Kinsella, G. (2002). The relationship between executive function abilities, adaptive behavior, and academic achievement in children with externalizing behavior problems. *Journal of Child Psychology and Psychiatry* 43(6), 785–796.

Cohen, C. (2010, April). Raise your child's social IQ—How to help when ADHD impacts people skills. *Attention Magazine.* Retrieved from https://chadd .org/attention-article/raise-your-childs-social-iq-how-to-help-when-adhd -impacts-people-skills/.

Cole, P.M., Dennis, T.A., Smith-Simon, K.E., & Cohen, L.H. (2009). Preschoolers' emotion regulation strategy understanding: Relations with emotion socialization and child self-regulation. *Social Development* 18(2), 324–346.

Cole, P.M., Zahn-Waxler, C., & Smith, K.D. (1994). Expressive control during a disappointment: Variations related to preschoolers' behavior problems. *Developmental Psychology* 30(6), 835–846.

Corcoran, J. (2017). Parents' experience of raising a child with attention deficit disorder. *ADHD Report* 25(4), 6–9.

Corey, R.E., & Elliot, S.N. (2006). Social adjustment and academic achievement: A predictive model for students with diverse academic and behavior competencies. *School Psychology Review* 35(3), 493–501.

Coulson, M., Oskis, A., & Gould, R. (2017). Avoidance of the real and anxiety about the unreal: Attachment style and video-gaming. *Contemporary Issues in Early Childhood* 18(2), 240–249.

Coutinho, T., Santos Reis, S., da Silva, A., Miranda, D., & Malloy-Diniz, L. (2018). Deficits in response inhibitions in patients with attention-deficit/hyperactivity disorder: The impaired self-protection system hypothesis. *Frontiers in Psychiatry* 8(299), 1–11.

Covey, S.R. (2004). *The 7 habits of highly effective people: Restoring the character ethic* (Rev. ed.). New York, NY: Free Press.

Cowen, E.L., Pryor-Brown, L., & Lotyczewski, B.S. (1989). Young children's views of stressful life events. *Journal of Community Psychology* 17, 369–375.

Crain, W. (2003). *Reclaiming childhood: Letting children be children in our achievement-oriented society.* New York, NY: Henry Holt and Company.

Cueto, S. (2001). Breakfast and performance. *Public Health Nutrition* 4(6A), 1429–1431.

Darling, N., & Steinberg, L. (1993). Parenting style as context: An integrative model. *Psychological Bulletin* 113(3), 487–496.

Dawson, A., Sacchetti, G., Egan, T., & Wymbs, B. (2017). Considering the family as a system when assessing the interpersonal relations of parents and children with ADHD. *ADHD Report* 25(4), 1–4.

Dawson, P., & Guare, R. (2004). *Executive skills in children and adolescents: A practical guide to assessment and intervention (Guildford Practical Intervention in the Schools).* New York, NY: Guilford Press.

Dawson, P., & Guare, R. (2009). *Smart but scattered.* New York, NY: Guilford Press.

Delahooke, M. (2019). *Beyond behaviors: Using brain science and compassion to solve children's behavioral problems.* Eau Claire, WI: PESI Publishing.

Dettmer, P. (2006). New blooms in established fields: Four domains of learning and doing. *Roeper Review* 28(2), 70–78.

Deur, J.L., & Parke, R.D. (1970). Effects of inconsistent punishment on aggression in children. *Developmental Psychology* 2, 403–411.

Diamond, A., Barnett, W.S., Thomas, J., & Munro, S. (2007). Preschool program improves cognitive control. *Science* 30, 1387–1388.

Dixon, W.E. (2003). *Twenty studies that revolutionized child psychology.* Saddle River, NJ: Prentice Hall.

Doyle, A.B., Doehring, P., Tessier, O., de Lorimier, S., & Shapiro, S. (1992). Transitions in children's play: A sequential analysis of states preceding and following social pretense. *Developmental Psychology* 28, 137–144.

Duckworth, A. (2016). *Grit: The power of passion and perseverance.* New York, NY: Scribner.

Duhigg, C. (2014). *The power of habit: Why we do what we do in life and business.* New York, NY: Random House.

Dweck, C.S. (2008). *Mindset: The new psychology of success.* New York, NY: Ballantine Books.

Eisenberg, A., Murkoff, H., & Hathaway, S. (2008). *What to expect: The toddler years.* New York, NY: Workman Publishing.

Elkind, D. (1976). *Child development and education: A Piagetian perspective.* New York, NY: Oxford University Press.

———. (1981). *The hurried child: Growing up too fast too soon.* Reading, MA: Addison-Wesley Publishing Company.

———. (January 2003). The overbooked child: Are we pushing our kids too hard?

More and more children, like adults, are involved in far too many activities. *Psychology Today.* Retrieved from https://www.psychologytoday.com/us/articles/200301/the-overbooked-child.

Ellis, M., Weiss, B., & Lochman, J. (2009). Executive functions in children: Associations with aggressive behavior and appraisal processing. *Journal of Abnormal Child Psychology* 37, 945–956.

Espelage, D., & Swearer, S. (2003). Research on school bullying and victimization: What have we learned and where do we go from here? *School Psychology Review* 32(3), 365–384.

Faber, A., & Mazlish, E. (2012). *How to talk so kids will listen and listen so kids will talk*. New York, NY: Scribner.

FACE Team. (2008–2009). *FACE Team talk listening activity. Communication: Effective listening skills: The bug activity*. Retrieved from https://vdocuments. site/active-listening-skills-the-bug-activity-08-09.html.

Feinburg, S.G., & Mindess, M. (1994). *Eliciting children's full potential: Designing and evaluating developmentally based programs for young children*. Pacific Grove, CA: Brooks/Cole Publishing Company.

Finder, A. (2008, April). Elite colleges reporting record lows in admission. *New York Times*. Retrieved from https://www.nytimes.com/2008/04/01/education/01admission.html.

Finnie, V., & Russell, A. (1988). Preschool children's social status and their mothers' behavior and knowledge in the supervisory role. *Developmental Psychology* 24, 789–801.

Flavell, J. (1979). Metacognition and cognitive monitoring: A new area of cognitive-developmental inquiry. *American Psychologist* 34(10), 906–911.

Fletcher, A.C., Darling, N.E., Steinberg, L., & Dornbush, S.M. (1995). The company they keep: Relation of adolescents' adjustment and behavior to their friends' perceptions of authoritative parenting in the social network. *Developmental Psychology* 31(2), 300–310.

Frost, J. (2005). *Supernanny: How to get the best from your children*. New York, NY: Hyperion Books.

Frost, J.L., Wortham, S.C., & Reifel, S. (2007). *Play and child development* (3rd ed.). Upper Saddle River, NJ: Merrill/Prentice-Hall.

Gable, R.A., Quinn, M.M., Rutherford, R.B., & Howell, K. (1998). Addressing problem behaviors in schools: Use of functional assessments and behavior intervention plans. *Preventing School Failure* 42(3), 106–119.

Galinsky, E., Bond, J.T., Kim, S.S., Backon, L., Brownfield, E., & Sakai, K. (2005). *Overwork in America: When the way we work becomes too much*. New York, NY: Families and Work Institute.

Gardner, H. (1993). *Frames of mind: The theory of multiple intelligences*. New York, NY: Basic Books.

———. *The unschooled mind: How children think and how schools should teach* (10th ed.). New York, NY: Basic Books.

Garland, M. (2007). The Reinforcement Matrix (RMX): A behavior management and change strategy for children, young people and adults caring for them. *Aotearoa New Zealand Social Work Review* 19(2), 22–30.

Gibbs, N. (2009, November). The growing backlash against overparenting. *Time*. Retrieved from http://content.time.com/time/magazine/article/0,9171,1940697,00.html.

Gibson, D. (n.d.). *Tower Building Activity for Team Building* [lecture notes]. Exercise available from the author at dgibson01@manhattan.edu.

Ginsburg, K.R. (2006). The importance of play in promoting healthy child development and maintaining strong parent-child bonds. *American Academy of Pediatrics* 119, 182–191.

Goldsmith, M. (2015). *Triggers: Creating Behavior That Lasts—Becoming the Person You Want to Be*. New York: Crown Business.

Goleman, D. (1995). *Emotional intelligence*. New York, NY: Bantam.

Goodenough, F.L., & Brian, C.L. (1929). Certain factors underlying the acquisition of motor skill by pre-school children. *Journal of Experimental Psychology* 12(2), 127–155.

Grandin, T., & Barron, S. (2016). *Unwritten rules of social relationships: Decoding social mysteries through autism's unique perspectives*. Arlington, TX: Future Horizons.

Greene, R. (June 2010). Parenting "difficult" children: A chat with Ross Greene. *Attention* 10–12. Retrieved from https://chadd.org/wp-content/uploads/2018/06/ATTN_6_10_ATE_Greene_Difficult_Children.pdf.

Greene, R.W. (2001). *The explosive child: A new approach for understanding and parenting easily frustrated, chronically inflexible children* (2nd ed.). New York, NY: HarperCollins.

Gutstein, S.E., & Sheely, R.K. (2002). *Relationship development intervention with young children: Social and emotional development activities for Asperger syndrome, autism, PDD and NLD*. London, UK: Jessica Kingsley Publishers.

Hahn-Markowitz, J., Berger, I., Manor, I., & Maeir, A. (2017). Impact of the cognitive-functional (Cog-Fun) intervention on executive functions and participation among children with attention deficit hyperactivity disorder: A randomized controlled trial. *American Journal of Occupational Therapy* 71(5), 1–10.

Hallowell, E.M. (2002). *The childhood roots of adult happiness: Five steps to help kids create and sustain lifelong joy*. New York, NY: Ballantine Books.

———. *Crazy busy: Overstretched, overbooked and about to snap! Strategies for coping in a world gone ADD*. New York, NY: Ballantine Books.

Hallowell, E.M., & Ratey, J.J. (1995). *Driven to distraction: Recognizing and coping with attention deficit disorder from childhood through adulthood*. New York, NY: Touchstone.

Harris, P. (2000). *The work of the imagination*. Oxford, UK: Blackwell Publishing.

Hartup, W.W. (1992). Having friends, making friends, and keeping friends: Relationships as educational contexts. *ERIC Digest*. Ill: ERIC Clearinghouse on Elementary and Early Childhood Education. Retrieved from https://www.ericdigests.org/1992-3/friends.htm.

Heininger, J.E., & Weiss, S.K. (2001). *From chaos to calm: Effective parenting of challenging children with ADHD and other behavioral problems.* New York, NY: Perigee Books.

Hemmeter, M.L., Maxwell, K.L., Ault, M.J., & Schuster, J.W. (2001). *Assessment of practices in early elementary classrooms (APEEC).* New York, NY: Teachers College Press.

Henrich, C.C., Kuperminc, G.P., Sack, A., Blatt, S.J., & Leadbeater, B.J. (2000). Characteristics and homogeneity of early adolescent friendship groups: A comparison of male and female clique and non-clique members. *Applied Developmental Science* 4(1), 15–26.

Hodges, K.M. (2009). *Processes and outcomes in prevention-focused preadolescent all female interpersonal groups.* Unpublished Doctoral dissertation. Antioch New England Graduate School.

Holmes, S. (November 1998). Children study longer and play less, a report says. *New York Times.* Retrieved from https://www.nytimes.com/1998/11/11/us/children -study-longer-and-play-less-a-report-says.html.

Homel, R., Burns, A., & Goodnow, J. (1987). Parental social networks and child development. *Journal of Social and Personal Relations* 4(2), 159–178.

Hood, B.M. (2011). Knowing me, knowing you: How social intuition goes awry in autism. *Scientific American Mind* 22(1), 16–17.

Horner, R.H., Sugai, G., Todd, A.W., & Lewis-Palmer, T. (2000). Elements of behavior support plans: A technical brief. *Exceptionality* 8(3), 205–215.

Howlin, P., Baron-Cohen, S., & Hadwin, J. (1999). *Teaching children with autism to mind-read: A practical guide for teachers and parents.* West Sussex, UK: John Wiley & Sons Press.

Hoza, B. (2007). Peer functioning in children with ADHD. *Ambulatory Pediatrics* 7(1), 101–106.

Hughes, C. (2002). Executive functions and development: Why the interest? *Infant and Child Development* 11, 69–72.

Hughes, C., & Ensor, R. (2006). Behavioral problems in 2-year-olds: Links with individual differences in theory of mind, executive function and harsh parenting. *Journal of Child Psychology and Psychiatry* 47(5), 488–497.

———. Executive function and theory of mind: Predictive relations from ages 2 to 4 years. *Developmental Psychology* 43, 1447–1459.

Hughes, C., & Graham, A. (2002). Measuring executive functions in childhood: Problems & solutions? *Child and Adolescent Mental Health* 7, 131–142.

Hughes, J.N., & Hall, R.J. (1987). Proposed model for the assessment of children's social competence. *Professional School Psychology* 2(4), 247–260.

Hurley, M.K. (ed.). (2004). *Course materials from parent to parent program: A perspective on the importance and difficulty of behavior modification with challenging children.* Landover, MD: CHADD.

Illes, T. (ed.). (2004a). *Course materials from parent to parent program: Behavioral management of AD/HD: Part One.* Landover, MD: CHADD.

———. (2004b). *Course materials from parent to parent program: Home management of the child with ADHD-supplement.* Landover, MD: CHADD.

———. (December 2007). Preventing problem behaviors: Six proactive strategies. *Attention.* Retrieved from https://chadd.org/wp-content/uploads/2018/06/ATTN_12 _07_Preventing_Problem_Behaviors_12_07.pdf.

Isley, S.L., O'Neil, R., Clatfelter, D., & Parke, R.D. (1999). Parent and child expressed affect and children's social competence: Modeling direct and indirect pathways. *Developmental Psychology* 35, 547–560.

Isquith, P., Gioia, G., & Andrews Espy, K. (2004). Executive function in preschool children: Examination through everyday behavior. *Developmental Neuropsychology* 26(1), 403–422.

Jabr, F. (2011). Blissfully unaware: Kids may lack self-consciousness because key network in their brain is not yet synchronized. *Scientific American Mind* 22(1), 14.

Jackman, M., & Stagnitti, K. (2007). Fine motor difficulties: The need for advocating for the role of occupational therapy in schools. *Australian Occupational Therapy Journal* 54(3), 168–173.

Jackson, Y., & Frick, P.J. (1998). Negative life events and the adjustment of school-age children: Testing protective models. *Journal of Clinical Child & Adolescent Psychology* 27, 370–380.

Jacobs, P.J. (1999). Play for the right reasons. *International Journal of Children's Rights* 7, 277–281.

Jenkins, L., Demaray, M., & Tennant, J. (2017). Social, emotional, and cognitive factors associated with bullying. *School Psychology Review* 46(1), 42–64.

Johns, B.H., Crowley, E.P., & Guetzloe, E. (2005). The central role of teaching social skills. *Focus on Exceptional Children* 37, 1–9.

Kamza, A., Putko, A., & Złotogórska, A. (2016). Maternal parenting attitudes and preschoolers' hot and cool executive functions. *Polish Psychological Bulletin* 47(2), 236–246.

Kavale, K.A., & Forness, S.R. (1996). Learning disability grows up: Rehabilitation issues for individuals with learning disabilities. *Journal of Rehabilitation* 62(1), 34–42.

Kezar, A. (2001). Theory of multiple intelligences: Implications for higher education. *Innovative Higher Education* 26(2), 141–154.

Khan, K., & Cangemi, J. (2001). Social learning theory: The role of imitation and modeling in learning socially desirable behavior. *Education* 100, 41–46.

Kiley-Brabeck, K., & Sobin, C. (2006). Social skills and executive function deficits in children with the 22q11 deletion syndrome. *Applied Neuropsychology* 3, 258–268.

Kiuru, N., Aunola, K., Vuori, J., & Nurmi, J. (2007). The role of peer groups in adolescents' educational expectations and adjustment. *Journal of Youth and Adolescence* 36(8), 995–1009.

Klingberg, T., Forssberg, H., Westerberg, H., & Hirvikoski, T. (2002). Training of working memory in children with ADHD. *Journal of Clinical & Experimental Neuropsychology* 24, 781–791.

Koyuncu, A., Alkin, T., & Tukel, R. (2016, July). The relationship between social anxiety disorder and ADHD. *Child & Adolescent Psychopharmacology News* 21(4), 1–6. Retrieved from https://guilfordjournals.com/doi/pdf/10.1521/capn .2016.21.4.1.

Krathwohl, D.R. (2002). A revision of Bloom's taxonomy: An overview. *Theory into Practice* 41(4), 212–219.

Kreider, R.M. (2008, February). Living arrangements of children: 2004. Current Population Reports, 70-114. U.S. Census Bureau, Washington, DC. Retrieved from https://www.census.gov/prod/2008pubs/p70-114.pdf.

Kuypers, L. (2008). *A curriculum designed to foster self-regulation in students with neurobiological impairments.* Unpublished Master's thesis, Hamline University, St. Paul, Minnesota.

———. (2011). *The zones of regulation: A curriculum designed to foster self-regulation and emotional control.* San Jose, CA: Think Social Publishing.

Ladd, G.W., & Golter, B.S. (1988). Parents' management of preschooler's peer relations: Is it related to children's social competence? *Developmental Psychology* 24(1), 109–117.

———. (1992). Creating informal play opportunities: Are parents' and preschoolers' initiations related to children's competence with peers? *Developmental Psychology* 28, 1179–1187.

Lai, E. (2011). *Metacognition: A literature review. Research Report.* Pearson, 1–41. Retrievedfromhttp://images.pearsonassessments.com/images/tmrs/Metacogni tion_Literature_Review_Final.pdf.

Landry, S.H., Miller-Loncar, C.L., Smith, K.W., & Swank, P.R. (2002). The role of early parenting in children's development of executive processes. *Developmental Neuropsychology* 21(1), 15–41.

Lane, K.L., Menzies, H.M., Barton-Atwood, S.M., Doukas, G.L., & Munton, S. (2005). Designing, implementing, and evaluating social skills interventions for elementary students: Step-by-step procedures based on actual school-based investigations. *Preventing School Failure* 49(2), 18–26.

Laugeson, E.A., Frankel, F., Mogil, C., & Dillon, A.R. (2009). Parent-assisted social skills training to improve friendships for teens with autism spectrum disorders. *Journal Autism and Development Disorder* 39(4), 596–606.

Lecce, S., Caputi, M., Pagnin, A., & Banerjee, R. (2017). Theory of mind and school achievement: The mediating role of social competence. *Cognitive Development* 44, 85–97.

LeDoux, J. (1998). *The emotional brain: The mysterious underpinnings of emotional life.* New York, NY: Simon and Schuster.

———. (2012). Rethinking the emotional brain. *Neuron* 73(4), 653–676.

———. (2015). Feelings: What are they & how does the brain make them? *American Academy of Arts & Sciences* 144(1), 96–110.

Lehrer, J. (2009, May). Don't! The secret of self-control. *New Yorker.* Retrieved from http://www.newyorker.com/reporting/2009/05/18/090518fa_fact_lehrer.

Leong, D.J., & Bodrova, E. (2006). Developing self-regulation: The Vygotskian view. *Academic Exchange Quarterly* 10(4), 33–38.

Letiecq, B.L. (2007). African American fathering in violent neighborhoods: What role does spirituality play? *Fathering* 5, 111–128.

Levine, M. (2001). *Jarvis clutch—Social spy.* Cambridge, MA: Educators Publishing Service.

Lin, H., Hsieh, H., Lee, P., Hong, F., Chang, W., & Liu, K. (2017). Auditory and visual attention performance in children with ADHD: The attentional deficiency of ADHD is modality specific. *Journal of Attention Disorders* 21(10), 856–864.

Linsey, E.W., & Colwell, M.J. (2003). Preschoolers' emotional competence: Links to pretend and physical play. *Child Study Journal* 33, 39–52.

Locke, E.A., & Latham, G.P. (2002). Building a practically useful theory of goal setting and task motivation: A 35-year odyssey. *American Psychologist* 57(9), 705–717.

Loukusa, S., Leinonen, E., Kuusikko, S., Jussila, K., Mattila, M., Ryder, N., Moilanen, I. (2007). Use of context in pragmatic language comprehension by children with Asperger syndrome or high-functioning autism. *Journal of Autism and Developmental Disorders* 37(6), 1049–1059.

MacKenzie, R.J. (2001). *Setting limits with your strong-willed child: Eliminating conflict by establishing clear, firm, and respectful boundaries.* New York, NY: Three Rivers Press.

Madan-Swain, A., & Zentall, S.S. (1990). Behavioral comparisons of liked and disliked hyperactive children in play contexts and the behavioral accommodations by their classmates. *Journal of Consulting and Clinical Psychology* 58, 197–209.

Maoz, H., Gvirts, H., Sheffer, M., & Bloch, Y. (2017). Theory of mind and empathy in children with ADHD. *Journal of Attention Disorders* 21(7), 1–8.

Marlowe, W.B. (2000). An intervention for children with disorders of executive functions. *Developmental Neuropsychology* 18, 445–454.

Marsh, J. (2017). The internet of toys: A posthuman and multimodal analysis of connected play. *Teachers College Record* 119, 1–32.

Marshall, S., Parker, P., Ciarrochi, J., & Heaven, P. (2014). Is self-esteem a cause or consequence of social support? A 4-year longitudinal study. *Child Development* 85(3), 1275–1291.

Mather, N., & Goldstein, S. (2001). Behavior modification in the classroom. *LD Online*, 10, 17–18. Retrieved from http://www.ldonline.org/article/6030.

Matjasko, J., & Feldman, A. (2006). Bringing work home: The emotional experience of mothers and fathers. *Journal of Family Psychology* 20(1), 47–55.

McAfee, J., & Attwood, T. (2013). *Navigating the social world: A curriculum for individuals with Asperger's syndrome, high functioning autism and related disorders.* Arlington, TX: Future Horizons.

McCandless, B.R., Bilous, C.B., & Bennett, H.L. (1961). Peer popularity and dependence on adults in preschool-age socialization. *Child Development* 32, 511–518.

McGlamery, M., Ball, S., Henley, T., & Besozzi, M. (2007). Theory of mind, attention, and executive function in kindergarten boys. *Emotional and Behavioral Difficulties* 12(1), 29–47.

McIntosh, K., Borgmeier, C., & Anderson, C.M. (2008). Technical adequacy of the functional assessment checklist: Teachers and staff (FACTS) FBA interview measure. *Journal of Positive Behavior Interventions* 10(1), 33–45.

Medeiros, W., Torro-Alves, N., Malloy-Diniz, L., & Minervino, C. (2016). Executive functions in children who experience bullying situations. *Frontiers in Psychology* 7(1197), 1–9.

Meltzer, L. (2007). *Executive function in education: From theory to practice.* New York, NY: Guilford Press.

Michaelian, K., Klein, S., & Szpunar, K. (Eds.). (2016). *Seeing the future: Theoretical perspectives on future oriented mental time travel.* London, UK: Oxford University Press.

Miers, A., Blote, A., Heyne, D., & Westenberg, P. (2014). Developmental pathways of social avoidance across adolescence: The role of social anxiety and negative cognition. *Journal of Anxiety Disorders* 28, 787–794.

Mikami, A.Y. (2010). Social context influences on children's peer relationships. *Psychological Science Agenda.* Retrieved from http://www.apa.org/science/about/psa/2010/09/social-context.aspx.

———. (2011, February). How you can be a friendship coach for your child with ADHD. *Attention* 16–19. Retrieved from http://adhdanswers.blogspot.com/2011/02/how-you-can-be-friendship-coach-for.html.

Miller, P., & Votruba-Drzal, E. (2017). The role of family income dynamics in predicting trajectories of internalizing and externalizing problems. *Journal of Abnormal Child Psychology* 45, 543–556.

Miller, S. (2007). Partners in play. *Scholastic Parent & Child* 1, 86.

Milyavskaya, M., Berkman, E., & De Ridder, D. (2018). The many faces of self-control: Tacit assumptions and recommendations to deal with them. American Psychological Association, Motivation Science, 1–7. Retrieved from http://dx.doi.org/10.1037/mot0000108.

Mischel, W., & Ayduk, O. (2002). Self-regulation in a cognitive-affective personality system: Attentional control in the service of the self. *Self and Identity* 1, 113–120.

Mischel, W., Shoda, Y., & Rodriguez, M.L. (1989). Delay of gratification in children. *Science* 244, 933–938.

Moore, T.C., Robertson, R.E., Maggin, D.M., Oliver, R.M., & Wehby, J.H. (2010). Using teacher praise and opportunities to respond to promote appropriate student behavior. *Preventing School Failure* 54(3), 172–178.

Mrug, S., Molina, B., Hoza, B., Gerdes, A., Hinshaw, S., Hechtman, L., & Arnold, L. (2012). Peer rejection and friendships in children with attention-deficit/hyperactivity disorder: Contributions to long-term outcomes. *Journal of Abnormal Child Psychology* 40(6), 1013–1026.

Murata, N.M., & Maede, J.K. (2002). Structured play for preschoolers with developmental delays. *Early Childhood Education Journal* 29, 237–240.

Murkoff, H., & Rader, L. (2001). *What to expect at a play date.* New York, NY: HarperCollins.

Murray, J., Theakston, A., & Wells, A. (2016). Can the attention training technique turn one marshmallow into two? Improving children's ability to delay gratification. *Behaviour Research and Therapy* 77, 34–39.

National Scientific Council on the Developing Child. (2004a). *Young children develop in an environment of relationships (Working Paper No. 1).* Retrieved from https://46y5eh11fhgw3ve3ytpwxt9r-wpengine.netdna-ssl.com/wp-content/uploads/2004/04/Young-Children-Develop-in-an-Environment-of-Relationships.pdf.

———. (2004b). *Children's emotional development is built into the architecture of their brains (Working Paper No. 2).* https://developingchild.harvard.edu/resources/childrens-emotional-development-is-built-into-the-architecture-of-their-brains/.

———. (2005). *Excessive stress disrupts the architecture of the developing brain (Working Paper No. 3).* Retrieved from http://edn.ne.gov/cms/sites/default/files/u1/pdf/se05SE2%20Stress%20Disrupts%20Architecture%20Dev%20Brain%203.pdf.

———. (2008). *Mental health problems in early childhood can impair learning and behavior for life (Working Paper No. 6).* Retrieved from http://research.policyarchive.org/20620.pdf.

Nauert, R. (2009, November). Helicopter parenting wrong for all cultures. *Association for Psychological Science.* Retrieved from https://psychcentral.com/news/2009/11/06/helicopter-parenting-wrong-for-all-cultures/9385.html.

Neuenschwander, R., & Blair, C. (2017). Zooming in on children's behavior during delay of gratification: Disentangling impulsigenic and volitional processes underlying self-regulation. *Journal of Experimental Child Psychology* 154, 46–63.

Novotni, M., & Peterson, R. (1999). *What does everybody else know that I don't?: Social skills help for adults with attention deficit/hyperactivity disorder.* Specialty Press/A.D.D. Warehouse.

Oeri, N., Voelke, A., & Roebers, C. (2018). Inhibition and behavioral self-regulation: An inextricably linked couple in preschool years. *Cognitive Development* 47, 1–7.

Outley, C.W., & Floyd, M.F. (2002). The home they live in: Inner city children's views on the influence of parenting strategies on their leisure behavior. *Leisure Sciences* 24(2), 161–179.

Panadero, E. (2017). A review of self-regulated learning: Six models and four directions for research. *Frontiers in Psychology* 4(422), 1–27.

Parker, J., Saklofske, D., & Keefer, K. (2017). Giftedness and academic success in college and university: Why emotional intelligence matters. *Gifted Education International* 33(2), 183–194.

Patterson, C.J., Kupersmidt, J.B., & Griesler, P.C. (1990). Children's perceptions of self and of relationships with others as a function of socio-metric status. *Child Development* 61, 1335–1349.

Paul, A.M. (2011, January 31). The truth about tiger moms: Is tough parenting really the answer? *Time*. Retrieved from http://content.time.com/time/magazine/article/0,9171,2043477,00.html.

Pellegrini, A.D. (1988). Elementary-school children's rough-and-tumble play and social competence. *Developmental Psychology* 24, 802–806.

Phelan, T.W., & Lewis, T.M. (2008). *1-2-3 Magic for kids: Helping your children understand the new rules*. Glen Ellyn, IL: Parent Magic.

Phillips, H. (2008). Resist. *New Scientist* 199(2673), 40–43. Retrieved from https://www.sciencedirect.com/science/article/pii/S0262407908623167.

Piek, J.P., Baynam, G.B., & Barrett, N.C. (2006). The relationship between fine and gross motor ability, self-perceptions and self-worth in children and adolescents. *Human Movement Science* 25(1), 65–75.

Poulou, M. (2003). The prevention of emotional and behavioral difficulties in schools: Teachers' suggestions. *Education Psychology in Practice* 21, 37–52.

Prochaska, J., & DiClemente, C. (1982). Transtheoretical therapy: Toward a more integrative model of change. *Psychotherapy: Theory, Research and Practice* 19(3), 276–288.

Prochaska, J., Velicer, W., DiClemente, C., & Fava, J. (1988). Measuring processes of change: Application to the cessation of smoking. *Journal of Consulting and Clinical Psychology* 36(4), 520–528.

Putallaz, M., & Wasserman, A. (1989). Children's naturalistic entry behavior and sociometric status: A development perspective. *Developmental Psychology* 25, 297–305.

Ratey, J.J. (2013). *Spark: The revolutionary new science of exercise and the brain*. New York, NY: Little, Brown and Company.

Reckmeyer, M. (2016). *Strengths based parenting: Developing your children's innate talent*. New York, NY: Gallup Press.

Riggs, N., Jahromi, L., Razza, R., Dillworth-Bart, J., & Mueller, U. (2006). Executive function and the promotion of social-emotional competence. *Journal of Applied Developmental Psychology* 27, 300–309.

Rosenfeld, A. (2004). Harvard, soccer & over-scheduled families. *Youth Studies Australia* 23(1), 15–18.

Rosenfeld, A., & Wise, N. (2000). *The overscheduled child: Avoiding the hyper parenting trap*. New York, NY: St. Martin's Griffin.

Rullo, G., & Musatti, T. (2005). Mothering young children: Child care, stress and social life. *European Journal of Psychology of Education* 20, 107–119.

Ryan, L. (January 2017). When Is a 'Performance Problem' Really a Personality Conflict? *Forbes*. Retrieved from https://www.forbes.com/sites/lizryan/2017/01/13/when-a-performance-problem-is-really-a-personality-conflict/#12ede1b26c28.

Safren, S.A., Otto, M.W., Sprich, S., Winett, C.L., Wilens, T.E., & Biederman, J. (2005). Cognitive-behavioral therapy for ADHD in medication-treated adults with continued symptoms. *Behavioral Research and Therapy* 43, 831–842.

Sammer, G., Reuter, I., Hullmann, K., Kaps, M., & Vaitl, D. (2006). Training of executive functions in Parkinson's disease. *Journal of Neurological Sciences* 248, 115–119.

Samuelson, L. (2011). Building biases: Word learning as a developmental cascade. *Psychological Science Agenda* 25(2). Retrieved from http://www.apa.org/science/about/psa/2011/02/building-biases.aspx.

Sandberg, J.F., & Hofferth, S.L. (2001). Family life changes in American children's time, 1981–1997. *Advances in Life Course Research* 6, 193–229.

———. (2005). Changes in children's time with parents: A correction. *Demography* 42(2), 391–395.

Santrock, J.W. (2009). *Life-span development*. New York, NY: McGraw Hill.

Schaefer, S. (2013, October 16). Coached through college: Professional academic coaches = decrease dropout rates. [Blog post]. Retrieved from https://academiccoachingassociates.com/coached-through-college-professional-academic-coaches-decrease-dropout-rates/.

Segrin, C. (2019). Indirect effects of social skills on health through stress and loneliness, *Health Communication*, 34:1, 118–124, DOI: 10.1080/10410236.2017.1384434.

Shanker, S. (2016). *Self-reg: How to help your child (and you) break the stress cycle and successfully engage with life*. New York, NY: Penguin Press.

Shiller, V.M. (2003). *Rewards for kids! Ready to use charts & activities for positive parenting*. Washington, DC: American Psychological Association.

Shillingsburg, A., Bowen, C., & Shapiro, S. (2014). Increasing social approach and decreasing social avoidance in children with autism spectrum disorder during discrete trial training. *Research in Autism Spectrum Disorders* 8, 1443–1453.

Shimoni, E., Asbe, M., Eyal, T., & Berger, A. (2016). Too proud to regulate: The differential effect of pride versus joy on children's ability to delay gratification. *Journal of Experimental Child Psychology* 141, 275–282.

Shure, M.B. (2000). *Raising a thinking pre-teen: The "I can problem solve" program for 8- to-12-year-olds*. New York, NY: Henry Holt and Company.

Siegel, D., & Bryson, T. (2012). *The whole-brain child: 12 revolutionary strategies to nurture your child's developing mind.* New York, NY: Bantam Books.

Smith, J. (2015, October). The 20 people skills you need to succeed at work. *The Hired Group.* Retrieved from https://hiredgroup.com/20-people-skills-need-succeed-work/.

Smith, J., & Meyerson, D. (2015). *Strategic play: The creative facilitator's guide, Volume #1: Activities that engage.* London, UK: Wordzworth Publishing.

Solanto, M.V., Marks, D.J., Mitchell, K.J., Wasserstein, J., & Kofman, M.D. (2008). Development of a new psychosocial treatment for adult ADHD. *Journal of Attention Disorders* 11, 728–736.

Spence, S.H. (2003). Social skills training with children and young people: Theory, evidence and practice. *Child and Adolescent Mental Health* 8, 84–96.

Spera, C. (2005). A review of the relationship among parenting practices, parenting styles and adolescent school achievement. *Educational Psychology Review* 17(2), 125–146.

Spruijt, A., Dekker, M., Ziermans, T., & Swaab, H. (2018). Attentional control and executive functioning in school-aged children: Linking self-regulation and parenting strategies. *Journal of Experimental Child Psychology* 166, 340–359.

Sroufe, L.A., Fox, N.E., & Pancake, V.R. (1983). Attachment and dependency in developmental perspective. *Child Development* 54, 1615–1627.

Steiner-Adair, C.S. (2013). *The big disconnect: Protecting childhood and family relationships in the digital age.* New York, NY: Harper.

Stevenson, C.S., Whitmont, S., Bornholt, L., Livesey, D., & Stevenson, R.J. (2002). A cognitive remediation program for adults with attention deficit hyperactivity disorder. *Australian and New Zealand Journal of Psychiatry* 36, 610–616.

Stewart, K. (2002). *Helping a child with nonverbal learning disorder or Asperger's syndrome: A parent's guide.* Oakland, CA: New Harbinger Publications.

Strain, P.S., & Schwartz, I. (2001). ABA and the development of meaningful social relations for young children with autism. *Focus on Autism and Other Developmental Disabilities* 16, 120–128.

Strichart, S.S., & Mangrum, C.T. (2002). *Teaching learning strategies and study skills to students with learning disabilities, attention deficit disorders, or special needs* (3rd ed.). Boston, MA: Allyn & Bacon.

Strohmeier, C., Rosenfield, B., DiTomasso, R., & Ramsay, J. (2016). Assessment of the relationship between self-reported cognitive distortions and adult ADHD, anxiety, depression, and hopelessness. *Psychiatry Research* 238, 153–158.

Sugai, G., Horner, R., Dunlap, G., Hieneman, M., Lewis, T., Nelson, M., Ruef, M. (2000). Applying positive behavior support and functional behavioral assessments in schools. *Journal of Positive Behavior Interventions* 2(3), 131–143.

Sunwolf, & Leets, L. (2004). Being left out: Rejecting outsiders and communicating group boundaries in childhood and adolescent peer groups. *Journal of Applied Communication Research* 32(3), 195–223.

Tarrant, M. (2002). Adolescent peer groups and social identity. *Social Development* 11, 100–123.

Thomas, J.R. (2000). Children's control, learning and performance of motor skills. *Research Quarterly for Exercise and Sport* 71, 1–13.

Thompson, M.G. (2004). *The pressured child: helping your child find success in school and life*. New York, NY: Ballantine Books.

Turecki, S. (2000). *The difficult child*. New York, NY: Bantam Press.

Ucar, H., Eray, S., Vural, A., & Kocael, O. (2017). Perceived family climate and self-esteem in adolescents with ADHD: A study with a control group. *Journal of Attention Disorders*, 1–9. Retrieved from https://doi.org/10.1177/1087054717696772.

US Council of Economic Advisers on the Changing American Family. (2000). Annual report 2000. *Population and Development Review* 26(3), 617–628.

Valcour, M. (2007). Work-based resources as moderators of the relationship between work hours and satisfaction with work-family balance. *Journal of Applied Psychology* 92(6), 1512–1523.

Wahlstedt, C., Thorell, L.B., & Bohlin, G. (2008). ADHD symptoms and executive function impairment: Early predictors of later behavioral problems. *Developmental Neuropsychology* 33(2), 160–178.

Waite, M. (2013). *Executive functions and social interactions: Developing social scenarios*. Unpublished master's thesis. Western Michigan University, Kalamazoo, MI.

Ward, S., & Jacobsen, K. (2014). A clinical model for developing executive function skills. *Perspectives on Language Learning and Education* 21(2), 72–84. Retrieved from https://pubs.asha.org/doi/10.1044/lle21.2.72.

Waters, L. (2017). *The strength switch: How the new science of strength-based parenting can help your child and your teen to flourish*. New York, NY: Avery-Penguin Books.

Welles, B., Rousse, T., Merrill, N., & Contractor, N. (2015). Virtually friends: An exploration of friendship claims and expectations in immersive virtual worlds. *Virtual Worlds Research* 7(2), 1–15.

Wentzel, K.R., Barry, C.M., & Caldwell, K.A. (2004). Friendships in middle school: Influences on motivation and school adjustment. *Journal of Educational Psychology* 96, 195–203.

Wilgoren, J., & Steinberg, J. (2000, July). Under pressure: A special report; even for sixth graders, college looms. *New York Times*. Retrieved from https://www.nytimes.com/2000/07/03/us/under-pressure-a-special-report-even-for-sixth-graders-college-looms.html.

Williamson, F., Johnston, C., Noyes, A., Stewart, K., & Weiss, M. (2017). Attention-deficit/hyperactivity disorder symptoms in mothers and fathers: Family level interactions in relation to parenting. *Journal of Abnormal Child Psychology* 45, 485–500.

Willis, J. (2007). *What you should know about your brain*. Retrieved from http://www.radteach.com/page1/page8/page45/page45.html.

Winner, M.G. (2005). *Think sheets for teaching social thinking and related skills.* San Jose, CA: Social Thinking Publishing.

———. (2007). *Thinking about you, thinking about me: Teaching perspective taking and social thinking to persons with social cognitive learning challenges.* San Jose, CA: Social Thinking Publishing.

Winner, M.G., & Crooke, P. (2011a). *Social fortune or social fate.* San Jose, CA: Social Thinking Publishing.

———. (2011b). *Socially curious and curiously social: A social thinking guidebook for bright teens and young adults.* San Jose, CA: Social Thinking Publishing.

Wood, J.J., Cowan, P.A., & Baker, B.L. (2002). Behavioral problems and peer rejection in preschool boys and girls. *Journal of Genetic Psychology* 163(1), 72–88.

Work, W.C., Parker, G.R., & Cowen, E.L. (1990). The impact of life stressors on childhood adjustment: Multiple perspectives. *Journal of Community Psychology* 18, 73–78.

Zeigler Dendy, C.A. (1995). *Teenagers with ADD: A parents' guide.* Bethesda, MD: Woodbine House.

———. (2000). *Teaching teens with ADD and ADHD: A quick reference guide for teachers and parents.* Bethesda, MD: Woodbine House.

Zeigler Dendy, C.A. (ed.). (1996). *Course materials from parent to parent program: Teenagers with ADD/ADHD.* Landover, MD: CHADD.

———. (2010). *Course materials from parent to parent program: Behavioral techniques for helping children.* Landover, MD: CHADD.

Zelazo, P.D. (2006). Executive function part six: Training executive function. The Hospital for Sick Children, Toronto.

Zelazo, P.D., Blair, C., & Willoughby, M. (2016). Executive function: Implications for education. Report of the Institute of Education Sciences, 1–148. Retrieved from https://ies.ed.gov/ncer/pubs/20172000/pdf/20172000.pdf.

Zelazo, P.D., Muller, U., Frye, D., & Marcovitch, S. (2003). The development of executive function in early childhood. *Monographs of the Society for Research in Child Development* 68(3), 1–89.

Zingoni, M. (2015). Performance effects of thinking you're more (or less) socially skilled than others think you are. *Basic and Applied Social Psychology* 77, 44–55.

Zulkiply, N. (2006). Metacognition and its relationship with students' academic performance. 1–8. Retrieved from http://eprints.utm.my/id/eprint/565/1/Norehan Zulkiply2006_Metacognitionanditsrelationshipwith.pdf.

INDEX

ABOUT THE AUTHORS

Caroline Maguire, ACCG, PCC, M.Ed., is a personal coach who works with children who struggle socially and the families who support them. She is the founder of a new training curriculum at the ADD Coaching Academy, the only Coach Training programme accredited by the International Coach Federation (ICF). She is a former coach for the Hallowell Centre in Sudbury, Massachusetts. While with the Hallowell Centre, Maguire was the main coach for children and teenagers.

Her revolutionary coaching programme and methodology helps teach executive function skills to children, teenagers, and young adults. Maguire co-leads social skills groups and consults with individuals, organisations, and schools internationally.

Maguire received a master of education from Lesley University. Maguire lives with her husband, two children, and their giant poodle, Winston, in Concord, Massachusetts. You can find her at www.carolinemaguireauthor.com.

Teresa Barker, a journalist and book collaborator, has co-written more than a dozen published titles in the fields of parenting and child development, education, creativity and ageing, personal growth, and healing. Collaborations include the *New York Times* bestseller *Raising Cain: Protecting the Emotional Life of Boys* and *It's a Boy! Understanding Your Son's Development from Birth through Age 18* and *The Pressured Child* with Michael G. Thompson, PhD. Other collaborations include *SELF-REG: How to Help Your Child (and You) Break the Stress Cycle and Successfully Engage with Life* with Stuart Shanker, PhD, *The Big Disconnect: Protecting Childhood and Family Relationships in the Digital Age* with Catherine Steiner-Adair, EdD, and *The Spiritual Child: The New Science on Parenting for Health and Lifelong Thriving* with Lisa Miller, PhD.